ALSO BY PAUL GOLDBERGER

BALLPARK

A baseball match
at Elysian Fields.
Hoboken,
New Jersey, 1859

BALLPARK

BASEBALL IN THE AMERICAN CITY

Paul Goldberger

ALFRED A. KNOPF | NEW YORK | 2019

For Susan

and for all the baseball fans in my family—past, present, and future

THIS IS A BORZOI BOOK
PUBLISHED BY ALFRED A. KNOPF

www.aaknopf.com

Knopf, Borzoi Books, and the colophon
are registered trademarks of Penguin Random House LLC.

Library of Congress Cataloging-in-Publication Data
Names: Goldberger, Paul, author.
Title: Ballpark : baseball in the American city / Paul Goldberger.
Description: First edition. | New York : Alfred A. Knopf, 2019. | Includes
bibliographical references.
Identifiers: LCCN 2018046223 (print) | LCCN 2018046867 (ebook) |
ISBN 9780307701541 (hardcover) | ISBN 9780525656241 (ebook)
Subjects: LCSH: Baseball fields—United States—History. | Baseball
fields—United States—Design and construction—History. | Baseball
fields—Social aspects—United States. | Baseball—United States—History.
| BISAC: SPORTS & RECREATION / Baseball / History. | ARCHITECTURE /
Buildings / Landmarks & Monuments. | ARCHITECTURE / Buildings / Public,
Commercial & Industrial.
Classification: LCC GV879.5 (ebook) | LCC GV879.5 .G65 2019 (print) |
DDC 796.3570973—dc23
LC record available at https://lccn.loc.gov/2018046223

Jacket photograph by Joe Robbins/Getty Images; (sky) Shutterstock
Jacket design by John Vorhees

Manufactured in the United States of America

Published May 17, 2019
Second Printing Before Publication

CONTENTS

PROLOGUE

*Whether in a real city or not, when we enter that simulacrum
of a city . . . the ballpark . . . and we have successfully, usually in
a crowd, negotiated the thoroughfares of this special, set-aside city,
past the portals, guarded by those who check our fitness and take
the special token of admission, past the sellers of food, and vendors
of programs, who make their markets and cry their news, and
after we ascend the ramp or go through the tunnel and enter the
inner core of the little city, we often are struck, at least I am, by
the suddenness and fullness of the vision there presented: a green
expanse, complete and coherent, shimmering, carefully tended,
a garden . . .*

A. BARTLETT GIAMATTI,
Take Time for Paradise

THE GAME OF BASEBALL may not truly be the ultimate American
metaphor—the attempts to make it so tend to be exaggerated, sentimental, and mawkish—but the baseball park, the expanse of green that begins
beside city streets and appears to extend forever, is. It is not only that it
is a "simulacrum of a city," as A. Bartlett Giamatti, the scholar of literature and baseball who served as both president of the National League
and commissioner of baseball, wrote. It is also that it contains a garden
at its heart, and as such it evokes the tension between the rural and the
urban that has existed throughout American history. In the ballpark, the

two sides of the American character—the Jeffersonian impulse toward open space and rural expanse, and the Hamiltonian belief in the city and in industrial infrastructure—are joined, and cannot be torn apart. They no longer represent two alternative visions of the world, as they so often do. In the baseball park, they each need the other. They must coexist. The exquisite garden of the baseball field without the structure around it would be just a rural meadow, bereft not only of the spectators themselves but of the transformative energy they bring. And the stands without the diamond and the outfield would be a pointless construction.

In the baseball park we can see how this country expressed a concept of community, and how we imbued the public realm with shared meaning. The baseball park was always a special kind of place, usually privately built and privately owned but able to instill people with a greater sense that it belonged to them than most places that had been built by their government: this garden in the center of the city, this piece of *rus in urbe,* was spiritually public if legally private, and in almost every city it formed a defining element of the civic realm. As much as the town square, the street, the park, and the plaza, the baseball park is a key part of American public space.

We can see through baseball parks how Americans went from viewing their cities as central to the idea of community in the first decades of the twentieth century to wanting to run away from them in the decades after World War II, and then how we have tried in our own time to use baseball parks to get our cities back. The first generation of ballparks, places like Union Grounds and Washington Park in Brooklyn and South End Grounds in Boston and Sportsman's Park in St. Louis, as well as the ornate and marvelously named Palace of the Fans in Cincinnati and the still larger Ebbets Field and Fenway Park and Wrigley Field that followed not far behind, grew out of neighborhoods, took their eccentric forms from the pattern of city streets, and were inextricably tied to their surroundings. The story of Ebbets Field is the story of Brooklyn, as the story of Tiger Stadium is the story of downtown Detroit.

The second generation of ballparks, places like Shea Stadium, is a different story: concrete bunkers, often circular, shaped not by the grid of urban streets but by a backward glance to the ancient Colosseum, an amphitheater built for gladiators, not pitching duels. (Not by accident, perhaps, were many of them designed to do double duty as football stadiums.) Set in a sea of parking, these ballparks were generally built during the years after World War II to escape the city, or at least to minimize any connection to it, and they were invariably suburban in concept if not in geography. They reveal how far Americans had come in the postwar years from thinking of urban neighborhoods as desirable turf. The most famous of the postwar structures built for baseball, the Astrodome, had a roof that rendered the entire ball field interior space, removing even the fig leaf of *rus* in the *urbe*. And the Astrodome was far from the only ballpark whose builders thought baseball would be better off played on artificial turf under a huge dome than on grass under the sky.

And the story changes again with the ballparks of the third generation. Beginning in 1992 with Oriole Park at Camden Yards in Baltimore, new ballparks in cities across the country brought baseball back to its downtown origins, often, as at Camden Yards, quite literally integrated into older urban neighborhoods, and returning to the field of grass under the open sky. (A few recent ballparks have had retractable roofs, very different from permanent domes; they use technology as a means of avoiding rain postponements, not of cutting all play off from nature.) But what is most important about the ballparks of the third generation is that most of them were designed in the hope of weaving together an urban fabric that had been broken, aspiring to use baseball to heal the city rather than to run away from it.

Today, more than a quarter century after Camden Yards opened to great acclaim, it still represents our most encouraging model. But the commitment to a vibrant and open urbanism that it aspired to is threatened by the very latest development in ballparks, the movement away from connecting to the real city in favor of envisioning the ballpark as more like the centerpiece of a developer-built theme park. This trend is exemplified by SunTrust Park in Atlanta, which opened in 2017 in the Atlanta suburbs as part of the Battery, a quasi-urban, instant neighborhood of restaurants, condos, bars, and hotels in which everything, even the streets, is part of a private development project, largely controlled by the Atlanta Braves. Atlanta is the most fully realized project of this type, but the idea it represents—the extension of the private space of the ballpark into the surrounding streets and neighborhood—is playing out around older ballparks such as Wrigley Field in Chicago and Busch Stadium in St. Louis, as these teams try to remake much of their surroundings. And it is the blueprint for future new ballparks, like Globe Life Field, which the Texas Rangers are building in Arlington, Texas, to replace Globe Life Park, which opened only twenty-five years ago, and the new ballpark the Oakland Athletics plan for the Howard Terminal section of the Oakland waterfront.

Until these recent developments, it looked as if you could summarize the saga of the ballpark as one of city to suburb and back again. But now, a generation after Baltimore reconnected baseball to the energy of the city, ballparks have begun to move in yet another direction, blurring the distinction between the real city and the artifice of the ballpark. The private realm of the ballpark has pushed its way into the public realm of the surrounding city, competing with it in places like St. Louis's Ballpark Village adjacent to Busch Stadium; in Atlanta, it has obliterated all traces of the real city in favor of the artificial neighborhood of the Battery, which is, for all intents and purposes, a theme park version of a city. Whether this phenomenon becomes a true fourth generation in the evolution of the ballpark remains to be seen. But these recent developments underscore what has been true of the baseball park throughout its life of more than a century and a half: that it has been an indicator not only of our architectural taste, but also of our attitudes toward cities and community, our notions of public space, and our changing views about the nature of place. The ballpark is one of the greatest of all American building types, and it reveals as much about how we treat our cities today as it ever has in the past.

The baseball field is much more than a random piece of landscape; it is a magnificently conceived piece of geometry, a diamond whose dimensions are precisely and brilliantly configured to connect to a marvelous moment of human possibility: whether it will take more time or less time for a player to run ninety feet to a base than it will take a ball hit by his bat to be retrieved and thrown to that same base. A baseball diamond is like no other field of play, since opposing teams occupy the same space at alternate times, and every player seeks to reach the same goal, which is to return home.

Giamatti has explored this eloquently: "*Home* is an English word virtually impossible to translate into other tongues . . . *Home* is a concept, not a place; it is a state of mind where self-definition starts." He has noted that "home plate also has a peculiar significance for it is the goal of both teams, the single place that in territorially based games—games about conquering—must be symbolized by two goals or goal lines or nets or baskets. In baseball, everyone wants to arrive at the same place, which is where they start. In baseball, even opponents gather at the same curious, unique place called home plate. . . . The tense family clusters at home, facing the world together, each with separate responsibilities and tasks and perspectives, each with different obligations and instruments."

But the geometry of the ball field is more complex, and more subtle, than the precisely measured diamond itself. The infield sweeps above the grass diamond in a great arc of dirt, reaching from above third base across second to first, a clearing that marks the transition from infield to outfield and that makes the green diamond look, from above, almost like the base of a mocha-colored ice cream cone. If the arc marks the bottom of the outfield, its sides are defined by a pair of perpendicular lines that run straight out from third base and from first base, continuing the base paths and extending, at least theoretically, into infinity. These lines mark the distinction between fair and foul balls, and while they usually come to an end where they meet grandstands or bleachers set far out in the field, there is no rule specifying where these grandstands or bleachers can be, or whether they need to exist at all, other than a requirement that they can be set no closer than 325 feet from home plate in right and left fields, and no closer than 400 feet from home plate in center field.

The leeway given here, in total contrast to the absolute precision of dimensions in the infield, is critical to understanding the nature of baseball itself, and of baseball parks. The outfield is expected to vary from place to place, making the field of play different from one ballpark to another. Often, the dimensions of an outfield were determined by the nature of the surrounding streets of an urban ballpark's site. It was only in 1958, during the height of the postwar period of concrete doughnuts, that the minimum distances were set, a reflection of that era's preference for standardization and its indifference to the particularities, not to say eccentricities, of distinct urban sites. But even the setting of minimum distances did not make all outfields the same; it just invalidated the most extreme variations from the norm.

But the most important thing about the absence of a firm definition of the outfield lies in its potential to be infinite. It could go on forever, just as a baseball game with a tied score lasts until a team scores a winning run, and there is no formal limit to the number of innings. Games do not truly last forever since something always intervenes—whether it be darkness or rain or an umpire's decision—and the outfield does not truly go on forever because practical needs to have seating somewhere close enough to see the action, as well as to have an enclosure to separate out paying customers from those outside, mandate a fence someplace. But these are all circumstantial things, dictated by the specifics of time and place; they are not rules. So far as the rules of baseball are concerned, the game could go on forever, and so can the outfield. All other American team sports are played against the clock, and limited in time, and played on clearly defined spaces like basketball courts or football fields or soccer pitches. Only baseball has no clock, and no limits in space.

That absence of limits in time or space, as much as anything else about the game, reflects the rural yearnings that are critical to its nature. As the countryside appears to go on forever, so does the baseball outfield. The connections between baseball and the American sense of open country run deep. They are behind the location of the Baseball Hall of Fame in Cooperstown, New York, a rural town whose role in the development of the sport has been proven to be largely mythological. They were underscored by one of the most beloved of all baseball movies, the 1989 *Field of Dreams,* in which an Iowa farmer constructs a ball field in the middle of his cornfield, far from anything remotely urban. The field attracts ghosts of celebrated players who appear in fulfillment of the film's mantra, "If you build it, they will come."

But the true history of the ballpark has nothing to do with imaginary diamonds in Iowa cornfields. If there is something about baseball that bespeaks a nostalgia for the country, the reality of the game is far more connected to the city. This is a book about how the histories of baseball and the American city have been intertwined for more than a century and a half, and about how the architecture of the baseball park expresses their interdependence. The tie between baseball and the city goes beyond the fact that the true fields of dreams were in Brooklyn and Boston and

St. Louis and Chicago rather than in cornfields in Iowa. Baseball was indeed a city game.

But there is also something inherent in the design of the baseball park itself that spans the tension between rural and urban, the two realms of American culture that so often coexist uncomfortably. The baseball park is a metaphor for the joining together of rural and urban. It can be thought of as a place in which the field represents the Jeffersonian ideal of the rural landscape stretching out indefinitely while the structure of grandstands and clubhouses that surrounds and encloses it represents the Hamiltonian vision of American industry and urban vitality. In the baseball park, the two need each other: the structure of the grandstand exists to allow people to watch what is happening on the field, while the field exists to give the grandstand its purpose.

And we might also say that the two parts of the field, the infield and the outfield, replicate the same dichotomy. The infield is the urban world of straight lines, rigid dimensions, and frequent action; the outfield is the rural world of open, easy, sprawling land, quiet but for the occasional moment of activity. For the game to succeed, the two worlds have to work in harmony. In the ballpark, the urban and the rural worlds become one.

A WORD TO THE READER

THERE ARE HUNDREDS of baseball parks in the United States, and many more around the world. This is not a history of all of them, which would be an encyclopedia, not a narrative. I want to tell the story of an extraordinary building type, and what it has meant both for the sport of baseball and for the architecture of the American city. That has meant leaving out many ballparks that are appealing, and emphasizing those ballparks that have meant the most to the evolution of the baseball park and its role in American urbanism. I have focused almost entirely on major league ballparks, a choice I made only to keep the story within manageable bounds; that is why only a handful of minor league and Negro League ballparks make appearances in these pages, even though the full story of minor league and Negro League ballparks is a compelling saga in itself. By the same token, no college and university ballparks or ballparks outside of North America are included at all. And while this book does tell the story of many of the greatest ballparks that are now gone—Ebbets Field most tragically among them, followed closely by Tiger Stadium—I know that many of the fine ballparks that we have lost are not in this book. But like the ballparks of the Negro League and the minor leagues, the ballparks of the Caribbean and the ballparks of Asia, they matter no less for this. They are just a different part of the story.

BALLPARK

1

Brooklyn Beginnings

THE FIRST BASEBALL GAMES were played in open fields, but the first baseball park—the first place constructed specifically for the game, with places for paying spectators and surrounded by walls to keep non-payers out—was constructed in Brooklyn, New York, by a politically well-connected entrepreneur named William Cammeyer, who built it on land he owned, called Union Grounds, on Rutledge Street in the southern portion of Williamsburg. The year was 1862, a year after the start of the Civil War and more than half a century before another politically well-connected entrepreneur, Charles Ebbets, would open a far more famous baseball park in Brooklyn. Ebbets Field would last for forty-seven years and become the stuff of legend; Union Grounds survived for barely more than two decades, but its short life belied its influence: from Cammeyer's enclosure the baseball park was born. Union Grounds marked the beginning of the idea that baseball, the game of infinite space, should be played in an urban structure of very finite space, fitted and sometimes contorted into the urban grid. Union Grounds, constructed on a site bordered by Marcy and Harrison Avenues and Rutland and Lynch Streets, was a green field of play, a thing apart from the city and at the same time intimately connected to it.

Cammeyer, whose resources came from a family-owned leather company, did not build his baseball park out of a love of the sport. He was a businessman, and known to travel in the social circle of William Magear Tweed, the notorious boss of Tammany Hall. Like Tweed he endeavored to present a respectable face to the world even as he was trying as hard as he could to fill his pockets. Cammeyer preferred to use Union Grounds for the more genteel activities of horseback riding in the summer and ice skating in the winter—the problem was that those activities weren't making him enough money, and he could not afford to maintain Union Grounds as a losing investment. Williamsburg, a prosperous and tranquil enclave early in the nineteenth century, was, like many parts of Brooklyn and New York, already giving way to the dense, gritty city of the industrial age, and its population was increasingly made up of immigrants whose notions of summer recreation did not include horses. Cammeyer saw that baseball, which in the middle of the nineteenth century was a game played mainly by a collection of clubs that operated more like fraternal associations than professional teams, was becoming increasingly popular as a source of working-class entertainment, and was beginning to be an economic entity as well as a recreational one. It was moving toward professionalism in awkward fits and starts that included, among other things, players paid under the table and, in the case of a team that Tweed sponsored, players who were given no-show jobs on the city payroll. When the Fashion Race Course, a racetrack on Long Island, sponsored an all-star game in 1858 pitting players from various Brooklyn teams against their counterparts from New York, then a separate city, the track owners charged an admission fee of ten cents, probably the first time people were required to pay for the privilege of watching other people play baseball.* There was potential in this, Cammeyer realized, especially if the game could be played in a place designed specifically for it rather than on a racetrack taken over for the occasion. Instead of charging the teams rent for the use of his field, he would charge the spectators.

Cammeyer caught the wave of baseball's steady progress toward professionalism, and pushed it forward. In the years before the Civil War, the game, which had been played in various forms in the United States for several generations, was codified into something roughly like modern

* The eminent baseball historian John Thorn, in *Baseball in the Garden of Eden*, cites an admission fee of ten cents. In Michael Gershman's *Diamonds*, the fee is listed as fifty cents, which would have been an unusually high charge for 1858.

baseball, as differing sets of rules gave way to relatively consistent practices. For all that some historians of the game would embrace a mythology of its rural origins, baseball's ultimate form would be established more on the streets of New York than in the meadows of New England. It was in the metropolitan sprawl of New York and neighboring Brooklyn that the greatest number of teams was located—according to historians Mike Wallace and Edwin G. Burrows, there were nearly one hundred of them by 1858—and it was through their mutual negotiations that the rules were established. The sport was largely self-governing. In the spring of 1854 the New York Knickerbockers, one of the earliest and most established teams—it was set up with a constitution, bylaws, and a set of playing rules in 1845—convened a meeting at Smith's Hotel on Howard Street with the two other best-known teams in the city, the Gothams and the Eagles, to try and sort out inconsistencies in the manner of play, most particularly the standard distance between the bases. The meeting at Smith's set the distance between the bases as "forty-two paces," and from home to the pitcher as "not less than fifteen paces," according to John Thorn, the baseball historian. The first team to score twenty-one "aces"—*runs* in today's parlance—was the winner.

Three years later, the Knickerbockers organized another gathering at Smith's, which by then had moved to new quarters on Broome Street. At this second meeting the teams agreed to dispense with the rule of twenty-one aces and instead limit games to nine innings, with each team having three outs per inning. More relevant to the form of the ballpark, the teams agreed to establish the idea of foul territory, demarcating a line that extended from first base toward right field and third base toward left field to determine precisely where a batted ball had to go to remain in play.*

New York had players, it had a clear set of rules, and it had fans. (It also had the major national sports journals, which by giving extensive coverage to the city's baseball teams further institutionalized New York's version of baseball's rules as the standard.) What New York lacked was wide-open playing fields, since the years of baseball's development coincided with the city's own explosive growth, as blocks of tenements and

---

* This decision would come to have great implications for the variances in play from ballpark to ballpark, when tall poles were added in the outfield to mark the foul lines and help the umpire to determine whether fly balls hit over the fence were in fair territory, and thus qualified as home runs, or were foul balls.

brownstones and factories, not to mention railroad tracks, spread out over the grid of streets. They made most of New York a city in which the man-made all but squeezed out any presence of nature. It was not just Williamsburg that was changing; New Yorkers from all neighborhoods who wanted to play baseball had trouble finding flat, open space large enough to accommodate the game. Early games were often played in Madison Square, but games were technically illegal in city-owned open space, and while that law may have been enforced only sporadically, the pressures of urbanization, including the presence of nearby streetcars, brought an end to active baseball play at Madison Square by the mid-1840s. The favored locale of many of the region's baseball teams, including Alexander Cartwright's Knickerbockers, shifted to the other side of the Hudson River to one of the area's most popular pleasure grounds, the Elysian Fields in Hoboken. Its owner, John Cox Stevens, began hosting organized baseball games in the 1840s, attracting New Yorkers not only with the allure of his pastoral setting but with the claim that Hoboken was free of the yellow fever that afflicted New York.

Stevens's site was definitely free of the encroachments of the industrializing city. And, as A. Bartlett Giamatti would observe many years later, the very name Elysian Fields evoked classical aspirations to paradise, a metaphor that Giamatti would use frequently to describe baseball.* Hoboken would have a decent run as the baseball capital. But it would not remain pastoral for long. Stevens, scion of an aristocratic family with a riverfront estate in Hoboken and a mansion in Manhattan, owned the ferries that transported visitors across the Hudson, and he wanted a larger crowd than baseball could provide. He positioned the Elysian Fields as an amusement park offering people of every stripe an escape from the pressures of the hectic city, and he gave them a merry-go-round, a race-track, a bowling alley, and events staged by P. T. Barnum. Bars and hotels were built near the ball grounds, and Stevens was so convinced that he was providing New York with a necessary public amenity that he asked

---

* Giamatti's comment, in an interview with Nick Johnson of the *Transcript-Telegram* of Holyoke, Massachusetts, was in response to a question about what Dante would have made of the appointment of Giamatti, a scholar of Renaissance literature, as president of the National League. "I think Dante would have been delighted. I think Dante knew very well what the nature of paradise was and what preceded it," Giamatti said. "He would have approved of any sport whose first game in 1845 was played on something called the Elysian Fields in Hoboken, New Jersey."

the city for a subsidy, even though Hoboken was outside the borders of New York City and, indeed, of New York State. With Stevens's success at turning Elysian Fields into a proto–Coney Island, whatever wholesome appeal Hoboken's natural setting might have had soon evaporated. It was a place that attracted the less respectable crowds, not to mention respectable folk hoping to pursue less respectable activities. George Templeton Strong, the lawyer and diarist, visited Hoboken from his home in Gramercy Park and reported, "I saw scarce anyone there but snobs and their strumpets." It was, Strong observed in his diary, a "pity it's haunted by such a gang as frequent it."

Baseball was hardly the sport of the elite, but neither did the players nor their growing base of fans want to see the game played in the shadow of a raffish amusement park. With more and more teams in Brooklyn, Cammeyer saw that he could provide at Union Grounds a field both closer to home and free of competition from other forms of amusement. Brooklyn by the end of the 1850s had so many teams that "games [were] being played on every available plot within a ten-mile radius of the city," according to *Porter's Spirit of the Times,* which called

A Currier & Ives lithograph of a "grand match for the championship at the Elysian Fields"

Brooklyn "the city of base ball clubs." Many of the clubs were intimately connected to neighborhoods, sometimes even taking their names from local streets like Putnam Avenue and Atlantic Avenue, or local businesses like the Eckford and Webb shipyard. Brooklyn's rapidly growing, heavily immigrant population—the borough had gone from a population of twenty-five thousand in 1835 to two hundred thousand in 1855, nearly half of whom were immigrants—sorted itself naturally into localized fan groups for each team. "More than any other American game, baseball was built on a geographical and psychological sense of localism—if we take localism to be simultaneously an attachment to one place and fear, antipathy or competitiveness toward other places," Warren Goldstein has written. And Cammeyer realized that however bitter their neighborhood rivalries might be, the loyalists who rooted for the various clubs had one thing in common besides Brooklyn addresses: they could all become his customers.

The six-and-a-half-foot-high wooden fence that Cammeyer erected around Union Grounds was intended to keep non-paying customers out, not to create a dividing line between fly balls that could be caught and those that were out of play, the critical role that ballpark fences would come to play soon thereafter. Cammeyer saw his fence—which was more than five hundred feet away from home plate at the far point of center field, a distance no batted ball could reach—as a matter of capitalism, not ground rules. His motivations for presenting baseball inside a fenced enclosure were to attract a large crowd, make money, and yet retain some degree of decorum. The Union Grounds had a covered viewing section set aside for women and their gentlemen companions, a further statement of gentility intended to encourage the attendance of women, whose presence was thought to dampen the raucousness of men. "Wherever [the ladies'] presence enlivens the scene, there gentlemanly conduct will follow. Indecorous proceedings will cause the offenders to be instantly expelled from the grounds," reported the *Brooklyn Eagle*, in praise of Cammeyer's decision to market the Union Grounds as a place of modesty and good manners, "where ladies can witness the game without being annoyed by the indecorous behavior of the rowdies who attend some of the first-class matches."

Cammeyer knew better than to make the entire place into a demonstration of Victorian gentility. He saw, as Warren Goldstein wrote, that "the game appealed simultaneously to the culture of urban streets . . . and to the respectable and newly vigorous culture of middle class Victorian men." And so there was another viewing section, distinctly separate from the one for ladies and couples, that was set aside for gambling. There, men could smoke, drink, and make bets on the game. Cammeyer had given them the equivalent of a saloon in the open air.* He was prescient enough to realize that to market baseball to a broad audience he needed some degree of propriety, but not too much. He sought to position the Union Grounds as a place of mass entertainment, more respectable than the honky-tonk of Hoboken and yet lively enough to assure that no one would mistake it for a church. Not only was gambling encouraged, Cammeyer had a band playing throughout the ball game, keeping the crowds entertained.

When Cammeyer drained the skating pond and filled it in to create the playing field, he left intact a small, peaked-roof structure, something like a pagoda, that had stood at the far end of the pond. It was in what became the outfield, somewhat to the right of center field, about 350 feet from home plate, very much within the field of play. The outfield pagoda gave the Union Grounds the beginning of an architectural identity, and its very quirkiness, and the way in which its intrusive form made playing baseball on Cammeyer's field different from playing anywhere else, established another pattern for early baseball parks: they were designed, as often as not, around obstacles, which made for certain eccentricities. There was no expectation that any field would look like any other, and if that meant that play was slightly different from one ballpark to another, that was all considered part of the nature of the game.

Cammeyer's other innovations included the provision of a clubhouse large enough to accommodate three teams at a time when most ball fields did not have indoor facilities for any. He provided wooden stands with seating for roughly 1,500 spectators, and there was plenty of standing room around the field. On opening day, May 15, 1862, somewhere between two and three thousand people showed up at the Union Grounds, according

* *Ballparks Yesterday and Today* states that Cammeyer included an actual saloon on the property as well, although no other sources confirm this. It is clear that he wanted to be sure that the park allowed for male camaraderie, however much he tried to accommodate female spectators as well.

to the *Brooklyn Eagle*. Admission was free on opening day; Cammeyer charged ten cents a head thereafter, raising it to twenty-five cents for major games and changing it permanently to twenty-five cents when the players began to demand a cut of the proceeds. Cammeyer signed up three Brooklyn teams as regular tenants for the field, the Eckford, Putnam, and Constellation clubs, and for opening day he staged his own version of an all-star game with two sides made up of members of all three teams, called, presumably for their captains, "Manolt's Side" and "McKinstry's Side." The game began at 3:00 p.m. after the band played "The Star-Spangled Banner," another tradition that reportedly originated at Union Grounds.* Manolt's team won, 17–15.

Harper's illustration of William Cammeyer's first attempt to make money off his land in Brooklyn: turning it into a public skating rink

* The song did not become the national anthem until 1931, and there are varying reports of when it began to be commonly sung at baseball games. In *A History of the Star-Spangled Banner,* Mark Ferris states that the tradition began as a patriotic gesture in 1918, during World War I, when the Boston Red Sox played the Chicago Cubs in the World Series. There are reports of the song being played at the Polo Grounds in New York before certain games in the 1890s. *SI.com* reports that it was not until World War II that it became standard practice to play the anthem before every game, not just on special occasions or for championship games.

It is not clear why Boss Tweed, who for several years had sponsored a team called the New York Mutuals, did not immediately move his team to his friend's new field. The Mutuals were unusual among ball clubs in that Tweed provided many of its players with political patronage jobs, allowing the New York City treasury, in effect, to subsidize baseball, or at least Tweed's portion of it, by paying its players. The Mutuals were one of the New York teams that regularly played at Elysian Fields in Hoboken, where they remained until 1867, the year that John Cox Stevens's heirs, upset by a betting scandal in 1865, decided to ban further championship games. But the decision may have masked other objectives, since by then Elysian Fields was on the verge of giving way to Hoboken's own increasing urbanization. George Templeton Strong had noted back in 1844 that Hoboken was already becoming "built up," and by 1893, a local writer would observe that "all of the old Elysian Fields have been swept away in the demand for building lots." (Eventually, Elysian Fields would become the site of a huge Maxwell House coffee plant.)

The Mutuals made the inevitable move to Union Grounds in time for the seventh season at Cammeyer's ballpark. Numerous other teams came and went as tenants—the day when teams would build and control their own ballparks was still far off—and the field played host to major games, including many that did not involve its regular teams. Other entrepre-

When the skating rink failed, Cammeyer turned to baseball and made his Union Grounds the first enclosed baseball park.

neurs, impressed by Cammeyer's success and equally eager to take over the position of Elysian Fields as baseball's dominant locale, followed his lead. Reuben S. Decker did so literally, since like Cammeyer he converted a skating pond into a baseball park. Decker's Capitoline Grounds in Bedford-Stuyvesant, which replaced his Capitoline Skating Pond, was first used for baseball in 1865. Decker's ballpark was the site of the first stolen base, by a player named Eddie Cuthbert, who ran uncontested to second base during a game in 1865, provoking laughter at what was thought to be no more than a stunt. The umpires declared that Cuthbert had violated no rule and that he was entitled to remain where he was. The stolen base had been invented.

Capitoline Grounds was also the site of one of the greatest games in early Brooklyn baseball history. On June 4, 1870, the Brooklyn Atlantics defeated the mightiest out-of-town team, the Cincinnati Red Stockings, whose record was an astonishing 89-0.* The Atlantics won by a single run, with the 8–7 score bringing to an end the longest victory streak in baseball history. That may be the greatest legacy of the Capitoline

*The Mutuals of
New York*

* Sources do not agree on the duration of the Cincinnati streak, which is sometimes put at a more modest eighty-one games.

Grounds, although Decker did devise a pleasing ground rule: he gave a bottle of champagne to any batter who succeeded in hitting a home run over the top of a small, cone-shaped structure in right center field. More important to the history of ballparks, however, were the four successive structures known as Washington Park, the first of which was opened in 1883 in the Gowanus section of Brooklyn, not far from the Gowanus Canal, with wooden stands that had a seating capacity of three thousand. Its prime tenant was a team with the wonderful designation of the Brooklyn Bridegrooms, so named because several of its members chose to marry shortly after the team was formed. The first Washington Park burned down after only six years, and was replaced by a new Washington Park on the same site that was constructed to allow room for eight thousand spectators. By 1898 the demand for seats necessitated yet another expansion, and this time Washington Park was rebuilt on an adjacent

Studio portrait of the Brooklyn Bridegrooms baseball team in 1889

site with eighteen thousand seats. It was an oddly proportioned field, since the new site left a historic stone building, Gowanus House, which George Washington had used as his headquarters during the Battle of Long Island, in place in right center field. The fences jogged around it, yielding a very short right field, while center field and left center field were exceptionally deep, stretching five hundred feet from home plate. A 1908 renovation added center field bleachers, taking fifty-six feet off the center field corner distance.

The third Washington Park didn't last much longer than its predecessors. Possibly to correct the awkwardness of its layout, an architect, Zachary Taylor Davis, was brought in—one of the first times a ballpark is listed as having been designed by an architect. For the 1914 season the orientation of the diamond was changed and new grandstands were built, with seating capacity upped slightly to 18,800. In its fourth incarnation Washington Park still had an ample degree of eccentricity, particularly in the design of its scoreboard, which stood on legs in center field, requiring the center fielder to run beneath the scoreboard to field a ball that was still considered in play. (Eventually the space below the board was covered in netting, giving it the air of a soccer goal.)

Washington Park, Brooklyn, during a game between Brooklyn and St. Louis in 1887

But to speak of the idiosyncrasies of the fourth Washington Park is to get ahead of the story, since by 1914 Ebbets Field had been built a little more than two miles away. By then, baseball parks had become fully and completely creatures of a sprawling, urbanized, and industrialized nation, public gathering places twenty times the size of Cammeyer's original field. They were part and parcel not just of New York and Brooklyn, but also of Boston, Chicago, Milwaukee, Cincinnati, Philadelphia, St. Louis, and other cities, as much an expression of dynamic urban growth as of the quest for an escape into rural pleasures that brought people to the Elysian Fields and then to Union Grounds. They were buildings of the city, through and through. But it was out of the search for a rural ideal that the ballpark came to be.

Indeed, the very use of the term *ballpark* is revealing. As George Vecsey observed in his *Baseball,* the place where the game is played is "not the stadium, not the arena, but the ballpark, a homey title claimed only by baseball." And what, in the end, is a park except an exercise of *rus in urbe,* an illusion of the countryside within the city? It is no exaggeration to say that the very idea of baseball is itself an example of *rus in urbe,* a way in which city folk might briefly break away from the grit and noise

Players from the Buffalo Buffeds and the Brooklyn Tip Tops hold a large American flag in Washington Park, Brooklyn, 1914. A message to the fans on the stadium wall in the background reads, in part: "Base Ball Players are all human and therefore lo[. . .] If you want a winning team—root for them—spe[. . .] your friends; and while we are here, let u[. . .] so that the ladies may find it pleasant[. . .]."

and pressures of the harsh city and indulge in the delight of rusticity. It was not so much a game of the countryside as a device by which the city might sustain an illusion of rural pleasures.

Baseball is more closely connected to place than any other major American sport, and for most of the game's history, for all the attempts to tie it to rural America, it has been a game of the city. But there is a paradox at its heart, for it yearns to bring the country to the city in a way that no other sport does. There is something urban about the fixed and limited dimensions of the basketball court or the football gridiron, their even lines bespeaking the pattern of an urban grid, and their borders absolute, like those of an ancient, walled city. The baseball outfield, once you get beyond the fixed dimensions of the diamond, is infinite, like the open land of the country. It goes on forever, or at least it wants you to think that it could. But that openness is contained within the ballpark. It bespeaks infinity, yet it is finite and enclosed. At every moment you are conscious of the contradiction in terms: cities are set within the larger surrounding countryside, but in the baseball park, it is the country that is set within the city. When it comes to baseball, the urban contains the rural.

The desire to bring the country into the city grew strong in the nineteenth century, as American cities became large and industrialized, and as their tenements filled with immigrant workers who had no opportunity for relief from what was, for many of them, an oppressive and crushing environment. Urban life may have held forth the promise of economic benefit, but it was hardly easy or attractive for most people. It is no accident that the rise of baseball in the early decades of the century came at the same time as two major movements in the history of American planning, the urban park movement and the cemetery movement, both of which were motivated by a desire to improve the city by bringing nature within its borders. Parks offered nature in the form of open space for relaxation and recreation, an obvious counterpoint to the city streets. Less apparent was the connection of cemeteries to city life, but it may have been even more important historically, since the first expansive, landscaped cemeteries were in the 1830s, and they prefigured the urban park movement. Places like Mount Auburn Cemetery outside of Boston were envisioned not only for burial of the dead but as "pleasure grounds," carefully cultivated compositions of rolling land with ponds and clusters of trees at the outskirts of settled cities, with carriage drives along curving roads to enhance their appeal as leisure destinations. Baseball, parks, and cemeteries were above all forms of psychic escape from the harshness of the city, ways of establishing a connection to nature without physically leaving the city.

The relentless growth of the city sparked all three movements. Until the early part of the nineteenth century, the dead were buried in church-yards or in small cemetery parcels in the center of villages, but church-yards were filling up, and rapid urbanization made it impossible, not to mention undesirable, to expand them. When General Henry A. S. Dearborn designed Mount Auburn Cemetery on seventy-two acres on the edge of Cambridge, Massachusetts, in 1830, its picturesque design, inspired by Père Lachaise Cemetery at the edge of Paris, was so admired that it was quickly followed by picturesque burial landscapes in Phila-delphia, Brooklyn, Cincinnati, Baltimore, and Pittsburgh, among other cities. As with baseball parks, Brooklyn produced one of the earliest and finest examples. Its rural cemetery, Green-Wood, which opened in 1838, filled 478 acres, a landscape nearly seven times as large as Mount Auburn's. To Brooklynites accustomed to seeing only dense streets and dirty, dusty vacant lots when they went outdoors, Green-Wood must have seemed like a revelation, a lush, meandering landscape that could make the city disappear. It quickly became a major tourist attraction. By the early 1860s, when Cammeyer opened Union Grounds, Green-Wood was attracting half a million visitors a year, second only to Niagara Falls.

They came for carriage rides and for family outings as well as to bury their dead and to visit the monuments that were built at the more lavish gravesites. What they did not come for, of course, was recreation, since the concept of the cemetery as pleasure ground did not extend to active sports, particularly not to those involving team play. It is not surprising that the appeal of the rural cemetery led directly to a desire to bring some of its amenities closer to the city center, both to make it more accessible to a greater number of residents—Green-Wood and the other picturesque cemeteries were by design located away from urban centers, making them difficult for some people to reach—and to allow for more active recreation.

The problem was particularly acute in New York City, since Manhat-tan Island was tightly bound by rivers. In 1811 a city commission laid out its numbered grid of streets, plotted from Lower Manhattan up to 155th Street, and while New York's population was not yet remotely in need of that much land, the very possibility that the city might one day fill Manhattan Island set off waves of real estate speculation, and made real estate, in effect, a commodity. Would there be any relief from block after block of building lots? The commissioners took the position that the city's ample riverfronts would be sufficient, and made few additional provisions for public open space. Within a generation, however, shipping, industry, and freight had come to command much of the waterfront, and with every inch of dry land potentially available for houses, offices, and factories, there appeared to be little opportunity to bring nature into the city. John Randel, the surveyor who laid out the grid, which became known as the Commissioners' Plan, did allow for a few open spaces for public use, but as the city grew, many of them were cut back or eliminated altogether to make way for more developable parcels. The rich had their country houses, where they spent much of the year, and may well have been untroubled by the meanness of public space in the growing city; the less fortunate were tethered to the city, and their lives alternated between overcrowded and dank tenements and difficult workplaces, with the animated environment of the street as their only escape.

For all the vibrancy of the New York City street, it is not surprising that many of the nineteenth century's most thoughtful observers doubted that it was sufficient as a public realm. The appeal of Green-Wood Cemetery only deepened the belief that more open space and a greater connection to nature were needed if the city's residents were to have an environment conducive to healthy life. But to truly have an impact on the daily life of the city, a park had to be easily accessible, which Green-Wood was not, and available to all for active recreation, which Green-Wood also was not. It was clear by the 1850s that the city was growing faster than even the pro-growth Commissioners' Plan had foreseen. Development was galloping northward so rapidly that it had already gobbled up much of the space Randel had imagined as the city's "Parade Ground" between Twenty-third and Thirty-third Streets, the largest open space he had provided. (A small portion of it would remain as Madison Square, where it would become the site of early baseball games.) If New York were ever to have a large public space in a central location it needed to be set aside quickly before it, too, was developed.

The poet William Cullen Bryant, who was editor of the *New York*

Evening Post, and the architect Andrew Jackson Downing were the most prominent public advocates of a large public park. "Five hundred acres is the smallest area that should be reserved for the future wants of such a city, now, while it may be obtained," Downing wrote in *The Horticulturist* in August 1851, arguing that this would provide "space enough to have broad reaches of park and pleasure grounds, with a real feeling of the breadth and beauty of green fields, the perfume and freshness of nature. . . . In such a park, the citizens who would take excursions in carriages, or on horseback, could have the substantial delights of country roads and country scenery, and forget for a time the rattle of the pavements and the glare of brick walls." In 1853, the state legislature authorized the city to purchase all of the land between Fifth and Eighth Avenues and between 59th and 106th Streets, a total of 624 acres. The site was expanded in 1859 to 110th Street, bringing the total to 843 acres, but not until an attempt by the city council to eliminate the portion of the park below 72nd Street had been beaten back, an early sign of the politics that would bedevil Central Park for much of its existence.

The story of Central Park has been well told: designed by Frederick Law Olmsted and Calvert Vaux, it is a brilliant, artificially created landscape, weaving multiple rural experiences into a coherent and masterly composition. More relevant to this story is Olmsted's determination to make the park the property of no single group or class of New York's citizens, but a place in which all of them could mingle with an ease that they were unlikely to experience on the city's streets, and were certain not to find behind most of its doors. The park, in other words, was intended to be a democratizing force in urban life.

What did that mean for sports and recreation? It was not long before it became clear that the city's commitment to making Central Park a place for everyone did not mean that all activities would be allowed to take place within its borders. Organized team sports were not what Olmsted and the park commissioners favored, and while they recognized that "the amusements and the routine of the daily life of the Sicilian and Scotsman are dissimilar . . . and it would be difficult to prescribe rules that would satisfy these dissimilar tastes and habits . . . the most that can be attained at the Park is to afford an opportunity for those recreations or entertainments that are generally acceptable, and to exclude such as will, though perhaps acceptable to a considerable number, in practice impair the attractions of a common place of recreation to much larger numbers."

Thus, the commissioners of the park concluded, there was to be no baseball playing. When ball clubs requested permission to play on the park's open meadow, the commissioners rejected it with vehemence, declaring that organized activities such as baseball would be damaging to the carefully wrought landscape. "It seems difficult for [the ballplayers] to realize that the large open surface of turf that to the cultivated taste is among the most attractive features of the Park can have any other use than of a playground," the commissioners complained. "Nothing is more certain than that the beauty of these lawns would soon be lost, and that they would be rendered disagreeable objects, if these games were to be constantly played upon them. If the play of one club is allowed, others will demand the same privilege; and these clubs are so numerous, that if space were provided for the ordinary practice of their games, it would tend to depreciate the attractions of the Park to the far greater number who visit it for the refined pleasures that its landscape affords to those who are sensitive to natural beauties." Olmsted, the philosopher-king of American landscape architecture, saw recreation not as active sport but as the process of rejuvenation through exposure to nature. His commitment to the democratic spirit of the park was deep and sincere, but so was his belief that large crowds at organized events were antithetical to the landscape he and Vaux had worked so hard to create. In time, of course, baseball would make incursions into the park, and ball fields would be established at multiple points. Olmsted and Vaux's hope that natural beauty alone would be sufficient attraction was naïve at best. But their determination that the park be treated primarily as a natural landscape nevertheless prevailed over time, and it assured that Central Park would never be used for the kind of sporting events that attracted large crowds.* The needs of baseball would have to be fulfilled elsewhere.

Baseball and Central Park had one critical element in common, the quest for *rus in urbe*. It was fundamental to the allure of both. Baseball

---

* The ball fields that were later added to the park often hosted organized games, but they did not provide bleachers, clubhouses, or dugouts, and so their incursion into the landscape was relatively limited. A proposal to build a large sports stadium in the park in 1919 was denied approval, as were many other projects over the years that would have placed amphitheaters and other buildings in park structures that were not part of Olmsted and Vaux's plan and would have detracted from the primacy of their landscape.

players and their fans, like park goers, were urbanites who sought the opportunity to look at grass instead of streets. But it would not be Olmsted and Vaux who would shape baseball's place in the city, any more than it would be the designers of Green-Wood Cemetery. It would be William Cammeyer, Reuben Decker, and the builders of the multitude of baseball parks in other cities who followed them, who took the yearning to have a piece of the country inside the city that had inspired the new cemeteries and the new parks, and combined it with the showmanship of sport to create a new and entirely American kind of place.

2

Amusement Versus Virtue

BASEBALL GREW STEADILY through the 1860s and into the early 1870s, as the sport that made its field of play a replication of the rural landscape tightened its hold on the nation's growing cities. While the pressures of development squeezed baseball in its earliest years out of central areas like Madison Square in Manhattan, as the game became more popular and baseball parks grew in size, they seemed, paradoxically, to fit better into the urban environment. Larger structures brought more protection from the surrounding cityscape, and a greater sense of enclosure made the grass of the field seem not like a continuation of the surrounding landscape, as it had been at Elysian Fields in Hoboken, but more an occasion for surprise, a delightful burst of perfect green nature that revealed itself inside an urban construction.

But practical factors were even more important. Baseball, which once had no purpose other than to please its players, was becoming increasingly a game for spectators and, with them, bettors. The city was where the fans were; it was where baseball could flourish as a business, both legitimately and as a venue for gambling. Increasingly, the chief constraint of the urban environment, density, was becoming an advantage. And the baseball park could offer the chance to satisfy the desire for *rus in urbe* in a different way from the rural cemetery and the Olmstedian park: it allowed visitors to be rambunctious, to be celebratory, to shout and jump and scream. Olmsted's vision, however democratic it may have been, was genteel. The public space created around baseball was democratic and exuberant. If the cemetery and the park were reflective, the baseball park was participatory.

The emotional impact of the cemetery and the park depended to a large extent on how well they could make any sense of the city disappear. The baseball park was different. However joyful the glimpse of green grass at the moment of arrival may have been, the overall experience of being in a ballpark was nothing like an Olmsted park. It was never intended to blot out the city and create even a momentary illusion of nature. Most ballparks acknowledged, even celebrated, their role as a part of the urban scene, and indeed, at most ballparks the harshest aspect of the city, its industrial underside, was rarely far from view. Land in the choicest urban neighborhoods was unlikely to be made available for ballpark construction, which often took place in outlying, rapidly developing neighborhoods. Factories were often close by, and so was an equally potent reminder of urban life: trains and streetcars.

While the intrusive presence of trains and streetcars in the very earliest years of baseball had helped to drive the sport out of Madison Square in Manhattan, that had less to do with the noise, soot, and destruction of the illusion of rural escape that the trains brought than it did with staying one step ahead of the march of real estate development. A baseball park was rarely going to compete with the most profitable uses of land, and especially not in the earliest years of the sport, when baseball grounds were smaller and existed more for players than spectators. The early baseball grounds near Madison Square were there mainly for sport, not moneymaking.

But soon enough ballparks were business ventures. By the 1870s, the explosive growth of cities had become the friend, not the enemy, of baseball, which learned quickly to coexist with and even profit from the industrial world of urban expansion. As ballparks got bigger, they were less likely to fit into existing urban cores, and the story of Madison Square repeated itself: since it was usually more profitable to divide land into small lots suitable for housing and commercial uses, ballparks, like factories and other enterprises that needed large parcels, migrated toward the urban edge. That, in turn, meant that many spectators needed a way to reach the ballpark, which led to a natural alliance between streetcar companies and baseball.

"Proximity to streetcar lines partially fixed the location of the ballparks," the historian Bruce Kuklick has written. Streetcars brought paying spectators to the ballparks, and teams became so dependent on them that several owners of baseball teams invested in trolley companies, and vice versa. "It was natural for transportation moguls to own ball clubs," Michael Gershman wrote in *Diamonds*. The two businesses, streetcars and baseball, were mutually reinforcing. In an age before the automobile, the streetcar was the only way that large crowds of people could move easily across a city, a necessity as teams were increasingly identified with entire cities and not with individual neighborhoods, and as ballparks became correspondingly bigger. The trolley was needed to deliver these bigger crowds to the ballpark, which in turn gave the streetcar companies a guaranteed source of revenue. The second Washington Park in Brooklyn, built in 1898 between Third and Fourth Avenues and First and Third Streets, was just one of many parks that would be financed in part by streetcar companies.

Intercity trains were another matter entirely. They delivered not fans but the teams themselves, enabling teams in distant cities to play each other and, for all intents and purposes, creating the leagues that allowed baseball to become a national network of interconnected play and not simply a series of disparate local teams. For most of the 1870s, the Brooklyn Atlantics could play Boss Tweed's New York Mutuals by traveling just a short distance within New York or Brooklyn. But by 1878 the National League, formed in 1876, had teams in six cities—Milwaukee, Indianapolis, Providence, Cincinnati, Chicago, and Boston—playing a sixty-game season. Without the train there was no way the Boston Red Caps could have played in Cincinnati and returned home to South End Grounds to play the Red Stockings two days later, as they did in July 1878.

Railroads and baseball, then, grew up together. While their sagas are hardly the same—baseball could not have developed into a national sport without the railway system, but the railroad would have been just as powerful if baseball had never existed—their histories parallel each other's, and they are noticeably intertwined. Both baseball and railroads were products of the growing industrialization of the United States in the second half of the nineteenth century, trains literally so, baseball because watching the game and rooting for a local team became a central pastime of factory workers in urban neighborhoods. Neither baseball nor the train constituted a major presence in the national consciousness in 1850, but twenty years later, both of them mattered a great deal to the culture and, to an increasing degree, to the economy.

Without trains, baseball would not have become a national game. The first two "major leagues," which were founded in 1871 and 1876, would not have developed as associations of teams in different cities seeking a system of common rules and organized intercity play, since before the explosive growth of intercity railroads in the 1870s, there was no way to travel between cities other than by stagecoach or boat, both of which were far too slow to support a regular schedule of games. By 1876, according to Paul Dickson, writing for the National Pastime Museum, a baseball history website, intercity train travel by baseball teams had become so common that "game times were being coordinated to coincide with train schedules." Teams traveled by Pullman car if they could afford it, by regular passenger car if they could not, and sometimes games were called if they had not ended when the departure time of the visiting team's train approached.

By 1882 the National League had expanded to eight cities, and the tracks stretching from Boston to Chicago provided the shortest route to the other six National League cities between them. There was simply no alternative if time was of the essence. When the competing American Association formed that year, the two professional leagues culminated the season in a set of interleague, intercity games that were the precursor of the World Series. In 1885 the Chicago White Stockings and the St. Louis Browns—the franchises that would become the Cubs and Cardinals and had already formed a fierce rivalry—played a controversial seven-game series over the course of ten days, a schedule that only train travel made possible. The railroads not only enabled a true "national" league to form, but in a very real sense laid the foundation for the intercity rivalries that remain to this day.

The economic might of the railroads was growing so rapidly in the early years of baseball that they controlled significant amounts of land in major cities for their train yards and terminals, and sometimes these holdings affected baseball directly. In Chicago, Lakefront Park was adjacent to the tracks and switching yards of the Illinois Central, between

This woodcut taken from an 1885 photograph shows the grandstand of the National League Boston Red Stockings' field, at South End Grounds in Boston.

Michigan Avenue and Lake Michigan. In Boston, the property of South End Grounds was leased directly from the New York, New Haven and Hartford Railroad, whose tracks ran adjacent to the field—so close, in fact, that the baseball historian Bill Felber was moved to observe that "passing trains could be counted on to periodically rain smoke and cinders down on the third base patrons and on the field itself. If the wind was right and the [train] traffic heavy, games were halted in order to allow the haze generated by the trains to clear."

It was not just the railroad's tracks that passed beside South End Grounds. A roundhouse and a coal shed stood just to the north of the field, which was tucked awkwardly into an exceptionally long and narrow plot of land between the tracks and Columbus Avenue, a further reminder of how South End Grounds, like so many early ballparks, was a product of urban happenstance as much as conscious design. After the ballpark was built, the Waitt & Bond company chose to erect a cigar factory just beyond right field, and right field itself had a slight incline. The site of South End Grounds, which opened in 1871, was rectangular, but long, and it yielded a disproportionate outfield, with a shallow left field that was just 250 feet deep and a right field only five feet deeper, while

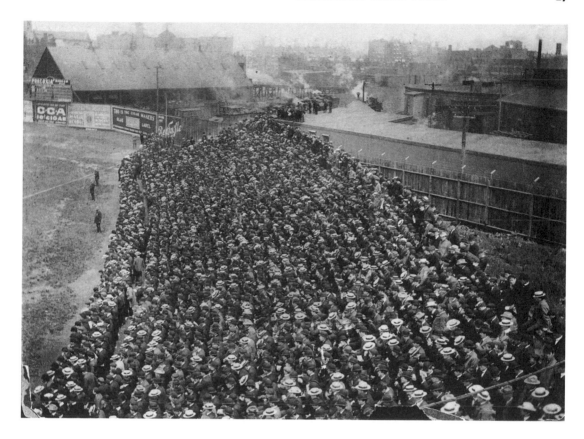

center field stretched out to 450 feet. (South End, the writer Michael Benson said, was shaped "like a bowling alley. It had only one field: center.")

The park was the home of the Boston Red Stockings, a team formed after the eighty-nine-game winning streak of the Cincinnati Red Stockings, baseball's first fully professional team, was ended in 1870 by the Brooklyn Atlantics. In the disarray that followed Cincinnati's unexpected loss, George and Harry Wright, two brothers who were the team's owners, decided to migrate to Boston and start again. They would build their Boston Red Stockings team around some Cincinnati veterans along with Albert Spalding, a star pitcher from the Forest City team in Cleveland, who would have a relatively short career as a player but who would later emerge as one of baseball's most influential executives. The Wrights would settle their new team in what would eventually become one of baseball's densest urban configurations, since the South End Grounds

Fans during a Boston Americans' game on June 12, 1903, at Huntington Avenue American League Base Ball Grounds, which was adjacent to the train yards visible in the upper central part of the photograph

would later be joined by another ballpark, Huntington Avenue Grounds, just across the railroad tracks, the only time two major league ballparks were next-door neighbors.

Huntington Grounds had an opera house, a warehouse, and Tufts Medical College across the street from it, making the district, for all the unpleasantness of the trains, a shining example of the successful integration of baseball into a dense, mixed-use urban neighborhood. It was hardly planned as such: the presence of the ballparks, the opera house, the school, the cigar factory, and the railroad in close proximity was mainly a matter of historical accident and convenience, not the product of any belief that these functions belonged side by side. Cities like Boston were growing rapidly and often haphazardly in the last decades of the nineteenth century, and what city planning there was tended to be in the city's grander districts, like the Back Bay, home to stately residences, and Copley Square, where H. H. Richardson's great Trinity Church and the city's original Museum of Fine Arts were located. South End Grounds was only a few blocks away from these elegant landmarks but in a very different world, in the 1870s its land still a part of the industrial back side of developing Boston, where sizable plots were available and an amalgam of urban functions cohabited, not always by choice. Development was mainly a matter of happenstance, not planning. And the nature of the city could change dramatically from block to block. It was a matter of course in the nineteenth-century city to find factories and residences close together, the elegant and the tawdry juxtaposed, and thus it was of little surprise to have a baseball park as part of the mix.

The location of South End Grounds within a dense urban fabric offered certain opportunities, as did most such early ballparks, to see the game free of charge from a neighboring structure. Solid fences, in some cases topped by barbed wire, blocked the view for "outlaw spectators" on the sidewalk, but what of people who could see over the fence from an upper floor of a nearby building? Preventing non-paying fans from seeing the game would be a challenge for many teams, most famously in Chicago, where neighbors of Wrigley Field would build a virtual cottage industry out of selling rooftop space in nearby houses.* One of the earliest, not to say most creative, battles in the war between adjacent prop-

* See Chapters 5 and 11 for a full discussion of Wrigley Field and the long relationship between the Chicago Cubs and their neighbors.

erty owners and ballpark owners occurred at South End Grounds. The antagonists were Michael Sullivan, who lived on Berlin Street, near Burke Street, behind right field, and Arthur Soden, James Billings, and William Conant, three men who controlled the Boston team in the 1880s and who were known to be so miserly with admission to South End Grounds that they required their players' wives to purchase tickets.

Sullivan built a viewing platform in 1887 on the roof of a stable to allow a view over the fence into the ballpark. The Triumvirs—as the three owners, who called themselves the Triumvirate, were locally known—responded by claiming that Sullivan's construction was a violation of the city's safety regulations, a conclusion that the City of Boston apparently did not share, since Sullivan's platform was allowed to remain. In response, the owners tried a physical instead of a political tactic, and added some height to the ballpark fence to block Sullivan's platform. Sullivan, in turn, built his structure up still higher. This tit-for-tat reportedly continued to the point at which Sullivan's platform, which Bostonians had come to call "Sullivan's Tower," reached a height of some eighty feet, or the equivalent of an eight-story building, well out of the reach of any solid wall the Triumvirs might build. For the next seven years Sullivan's Tower remained, a small, entirely privately built and operated viewing perch that existed in competition with the ballpark itself. If nothing else, it was a reminder of how difficult it was in the nineteenth-century city to create anything remotely resembling a controlled environment.

The original version of South End Grounds lasted only to 1888, when the Triumvirs overcame their penuriousness and reconstructed it into one of the most magnificent of all early baseball parks. The rebuilt South End Grounds had an ornate, double-decked, curving grandstand wrapped around the infield, with a pair of "witch's cap" conical towers and multiple smaller pinnacles. The architecture writer and baseball historian John Pastier called the second version of South End Grounds "the architectural crown jewel of nineteenth-century parks," and it was certainly the beginning of serious architectural ambition in the category of ballpark design. The Grand Pavilion, as the structure was frequently called, was, according to Pastier, "a virtuoso exercise in Victorian carpentry featuring carved columns, a steep and lofty double-decked grandstand built in a sweeping arc, and a sharply pitched dormered roof surmounted by six spires of various sizes and shapes."

It was one of the first baseball parks to be credited to an architect, John

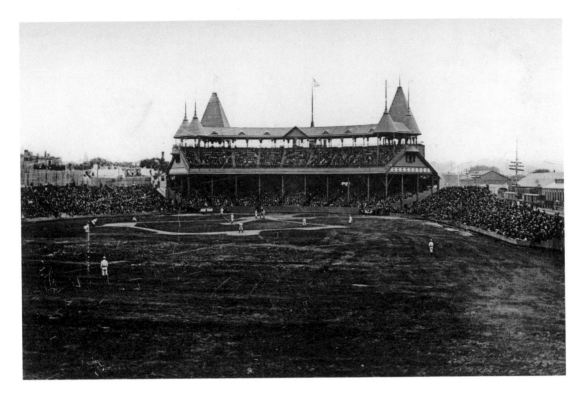

The ornate second version of Boston's South End Grounds, which was built in 1888 and destroyed by fire in 1894

Jerome Deery of Philadelphia, who initially estimated that his elaborate design would cost $35,000 to build. By the time construction began, costs had already risen to twice the original estimate. The *Boston Herald* published a full description of Deery's design, including three drawings, which it later suggested had been a deliberate tactic to assure that the increased costs would not lead the owners to abandon their plans to build "a grand stand unequaled for beauty and convenience in the country," as the *Herald* called it. Once all of Boston knew what was in store, the Triumvirs would risk a huge backlash if they did not deliver what was promised.

The third iteration of South End Grounds presented to Walpole Street a façade of brick and terra-cotta that seemed more like the entry to a castle than a ballpark. ("Sir Lancelot would have felt right at home," wrote Michael Gershman, who noted that the design did reinforce "the public view in the 1880's . . . that baseball was nearly on a par with jousting as a manly endeavor.") The grand façade of the new South End Grounds might have little connection either to Boston or to baseball, but it fore-

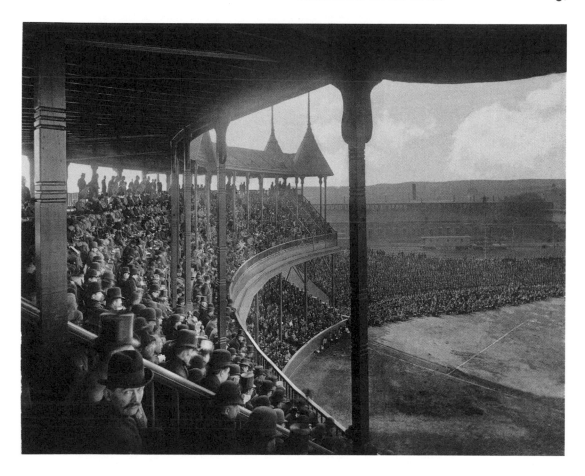

shadowed the way many of the finest ballparks in the years to follow would take on the qualities of civic buildings as they addressed the street. It was not surprising that two years after the Grand Pavilion was finished, the owners of Boston's entry in the short-lived Players League would try to compete with it in their elaborate new Congress Street Grounds. After all, observed the *Boston Globe,* a ballpark was "incomplete without a Grand Pavilion." The message the ornate Grand Pavilion sent, however, was less about the particulars of its architecture than about the fact that it *was* architecture: a true civic presence, not just a casual grandstand for entertainment. As Cammeyer's Union Grounds was the beginning of the ballpark as an enclosed space, Deery's Grand Pavilion was the beginning of the ballpark as monumental architecture. And surely both architects and team owners realized another benefit to giving the ball-

The grandstand, with its distinctive "witch's caps," of South End Grounds in 1888

park the appearance of a piece of civic architecture from the outside: the more building-like a ballpark appeared from the street, the more it would engender a sense of surprise and delight as fans got their first glimpse of the bright green grass of the field.

There was yet another message implicit in the design, less benign than the pleasure of the sun shining on the outfield grass, which was the extent to which baseball reflected social and class divisions. The Grand Pavilion's roughly 6,800 seats were occupied primarily by the same kind of "respectable" middle-class Victorian gentlemen and ladies whose patronage William Cammeyer had sought at Union Grounds in Brooklyn. The prosperous who sat underneath the fanciful towers constituted only one portion of baseball's audience, however, and to satisfy the rest, the people who could not afford seats under the lavish grandstand, the park contained large areas of open seating deep in the outfield, where the less genteel and less well-heeled could watch the game far enough away to avoid causing their more affluent fellow fans discomfort. At South End, as at many early ballparks, the "bleacher" sections—named because the intense sun was said to bleach the skins of those sitting on its rows of uncovered benches—were physically disconnected from the grandstand seating, just as the inexpensive seats in the Family Circle at the Metropolitan Opera House in New York, built in the same decade, had a separate entrance from the street, keeping the riffraff out of the main lobby. The *Boston Herald* reported that the separation between the seating classes was so total that it was not possible for bleacher customers to "obtain, by any subterfuge, admission to the pavilion."

The strict segregation reflected more than economic differences. The baseball audience formed two separate and fairly distinct cultures. Daniel Rosensweig has written of "the continual presence of a kind of ruffian culture just beyond the outfield" in baseball's early years, and described a drawing of a game in Philadelphia between the Philadelphia Athletics and the Brooklyn Atlantics showing "a small grandstand on the third-base side where the ladies sit fronted and flanked by what appears to be well-behaving men enjoying an afternoon of fresh air and harmless leisure. These men stand, sit in chairs, or even recline in their carriages parked inside the grounds in foul territory down the third-base line. Conversely on the first-base side, men from the Victorian middle-class sporting community jostle, toss objects toward the field, and make bets. . . . As in other parks, the violent behavior of this particular sector of middle-class Philadelphia society seemed to be not only tolerated but in fact sanctioned through the creation of a separate space inside the park to accommodate it. Kept at bay from the ladies and their more respectably acting suitors, these men were free to blow off a bit of steam."

No baseball team owner or ballpark builder could afford to deny the reality of the bifurcated world of baseball spectators, and none did. But some chose to embrace one of baseball's audiences over the other, and these decisions would have a major impact on the nature and the form of baseball parks as they evolved. Three of baseball's greatest early figures epitomized the split: Chris Von der Ahe, the owner of the St. Louis Browns and the builder of Sportsman's Park, and the duo of William Hulbert, the owner of the Chicago White Stockings and founder of the National League, and his successor at the helm of the White Stockings, Albert Spalding, whom Hulbert had lured away from Boston. Spalding first played for the White Stockings and then took over the team, reshaping Chicago's Lakefront Park in the process. The two teams were bitter rivals on the field, and the men were even more bitter rivals off the field. Von der Ahe's notions about what baseball should be were completely opposite from those of Hulbert and Spalding, and they gave their opposing visions physical form by constructing two distinctive and altogether different ballparks.

In St. Louis, Von der Ahe, a flamboyant German immigrant who had built several successful businesses, including a tavern and beer garden, got into baseball when he took note of the fact that a lot of his business was coming from patrons of a modest, ill-kempt baseball grounds down the street from his tavern, Grand Avenue Park. In time, Von der Ahe would take over the beer concession at Grand Avenue, squeeze out its owner, Augustus Solari (who lived in a house in right field), then take over the entire park, rebuild it with new grandstands and an upper deck, and rename it Sportsman's Park. To Von der Ahe, baseball was entertainment, not to mention a way of selling more beer, and he operated Sportsman's Park as a kind of carnival. In the first iteration of Sportsman's Park—like many early ballparks, it would be altered multiple times over the years, and have several distinct versions—he retained the former owner's house and turned it into a beer garden, apparently comfortable with the fact that this meant that tables and chairs would be within the field of play in

OLD JUDGE Cigarettes

20

Chris VonDerAhe

BROWN'S

CHAMPIONS 1886.

GOODWIN & CO. New York.

Chris Von der Ahe, the tavern owner who took on the St. Louis Browns as a way of selling more beer

deep right field, all the better to add some sense of excitement. Von der Ahe declined to cover even the portion of the beer garden that was out of the field of play on the belief that more sun made for more thirst, and greater sales of beer. The grounds also had room for other sporting events such as cricket, handball, bowling, and shooting. Long after John Stevens had made Elysian Fields in Hoboken a pleasure grounds that happened to feature baseball, Von der Ahe was using the same model in St. Louis. Sportsman's Park, people said, was the "Coney Island of the West."

There was no question which part of baseball's audience Von der Ahe saw as his market. He kept ticket prices at twenty-five cents at a time when the National League, baseball's most established professional consortium, mandated fifty-cent admission charges. More important still, Von der Ahe took pride in staging games on Sunday, the day that teams belonging to the National League were forbidden to play under the league's rigid rules, which also restricted the sale of alcoholic beverages, Von der Ahe's primary business, and the very reason he was first attracted to baseball. In his mind, baseball and beer were inseparable. Von der Ahe was a populist owner in every sense of the word—"George Steinbrenner, Charlie Finley and Bill Veeck rolled into one," the writer Edward Achorn has said—and if the fans had any doubts that the team's owner was as much a public figure as any of the players, the statue of himself that Von der Ahe would one day place in front of Sportsman's Park surely put them to rest. Von der Ahe, Achorn wrote, was "haughty, temperamental, driven to win, wildly experimental, and madly in love with a dazzling show."

That is not how anyone would describe either Hulbert or Spalding. Hulbert, strong-willed and puritanical, had organized the National League largely in the hope of bringing discipline into what he considered a disorganized and wayward collection of teams. Hulbert made himself, said Achorn, "the de facto czar of professional baseball," so determined to enforce order that he expelled the two teams that played in the league's largest markets, the Philadelphia Athletics and the New York Mutuals,

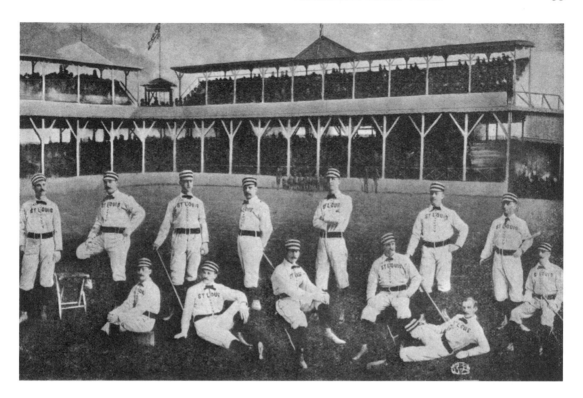

when, in an attempt to save money once they knew they were out of contention for the league pennant, they refused to make the final road trips of the season and did not play their full, agreed-upon schedules. Hulbert believed that his duty was to impose a degree of Victorian propriety on baseball, and keep the sport as far as possible from the raffish world that Von der Ahe catered to. The year before his sudden death in 1882, Hulbert ousted Cincinnati from the league for selling beer on its grounds and for allowing a semipro team to use its field for Sunday games.

Spalding was a worthy keeper of Hulbert's flame. Like many disciples, he became more zealous than his mentor; he acted as if baseball was not just a business but a calling, and he strove to establish a connection between the sport and American identity. Spalding even wrote a book entitled *America's National Game,* and he promoted the virtues of the game with the zeal of a barnstorming politician. Baseball, he wrote, "owes its prestige as our National Game to the fact that as no other form of sport it is the exponent of American Courage, Confidence, Combativeness; American Dash, Discipline, Determination; American Energy,

The St. Louis Browns from the American Association are posed in a photo collage inside old Sportsman's Park, 1884.

Albert Spalding, whose vision of baseball was the opposite of Von der Ahe's, in 1910

Eagerness, Enthusiasm; American Pluck, Persistency, Performance; American Spirit, Sagacity, Success; American Vim, Vigor, Virility."

Spalding not only controlled the Chicago White Stockings, he owned a sporting goods company that would make his name a household word, and published the annual *Spalding's Base Ball Guide*. His other business interests rendered his attempts to present the game as a noble expression of American values as not a little disingenuous. Spalding's sanctimony was all in the course of making baseball more attractive to middle-class customers who not only could afford to buy expensive seats in his ballpark but would also be likely to buy Spalding products for themselves. Fans with little money were far less welcome in his ballpark.

"Spalding worked tirelessly to reduce ballpark access to America's working poor," Rosensweig has written. It was not just the fifty-cent ticket price, but the bans on alcohol and Sunday games, which meant that the sole day of leisure that working-class fans might have could not be spent at the ballpark. Spalding presented this, according to Rosensweig, not as restrictive but as a way of showing baseball's "respect for the Sabbath."

It is easy to cast Spalding and the National League, which was established in 1876 in large part to make baseball more respectable, as exclusionary villains, and in many ways they were. But their motivations were more complex than pure snobbery, since the circumstances of baseball, which in the 1860s seemed to be growing faster than any promoter could hope for, had become more challenging by the mid-1870s. A major economic recession following the Panic of 1873 had slowed the rapid growth of the sport. Rough crowds both inside and outside baseball parks were a consistent problem, and money had become particularly scarce for the working-class immigrants whose interest had been a major factor in driving baseball's expansion. Many of them could barely afford to feed their families, let alone pay to go to a baseball game. Gambling on games was rampant, sometimes even involving the players themselves, some of whom were openly drunk on the field. Hulbert was firm in his belief that the best route to maintaining baseball as a healthy economic entity was to elevate the game by ridding it of disreputable players and marketing it to the middle-class patrons who could still afford a ticket.

The National League was created to do exactly that. The main baseball organization before the National League was established, the National Association of Base Ball Players, had been formed in 1858 as an early step in organizing what was then still a game largely played by amateurs. It had evolved into the National Association of Professional Base Ball Players by the early 1870s, but was largely ineffective in dealing with the challenges baseball had come to face by the middle of that decade. It was hardly a true league—"more a loose structure designed to award a pennant," Edward Achorn has written—and it was definitely unable or unwilling to discipline players. Hulbert wanted his new National League of Professional Baseball Clubs to assert authority over

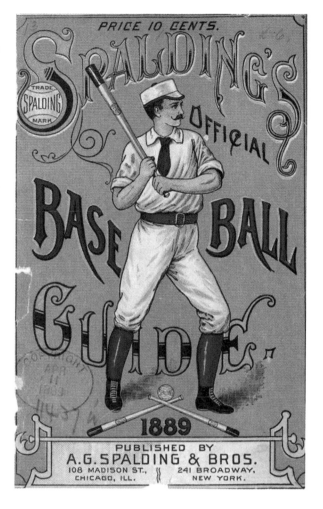

the sport and, not incidentally, to consolidate management firmly in the hands of the team owners. It was to be a league of baseball "clubs," not a league of baseball players. Not for nothing did Hulbert enthusiastically support a reserve clause, binding players to their teams, which would remain in force for nearly a century.

For Hulbert, and for Spalding after him, the process of conferring order on a somewhat disorderly sport was more than a quest for customers who could pay for a ticket in difficult times. They reshaped baseball's management structure, assuring that power remained in the hands of team owners, and they endeavored to change baseball's audience, which from the beginning had been poised between the gentility of middle-class

Spalding was an entrepreneur who built a large business around baseball.

life and the grittiness of working-class culture. While early promoters like William Cammeyer and Reuben Decker were reasonably successful at making room for both social classes, and seemed to take pleasure in catering to the different needs of both, Hulbert and Spalding believed that the "culture of ruffians" posed a threat to baseball, or at least to their ability to keep the game attractive to middle-class spectators. They saw the National League as a device for repositioning baseball on higher ground. It would be a game that, if not always played by gentlemen, would at least be attractive to gentlemen and to those who aspired to be around them.

Spalding would make the effort to elevate baseball central to his life's work. It would take many forms, since he would later play a critical role in building the myth of baseball as having emerged solely out of the American heartland, a myth that led, ultimately, to the establishment of the National Baseball Hall of Fame in rural Cooperstown, New York, the birthplace of Abner Doubleday, a West Point graduate who allegedly "invented" the sport.* The idea that baseball's most meaningful roots had to lie in rural America connects the story of baseball yet again to a far greater American myth, the vision of the nation as agrarian and virtuous, rather than as urban and transactional—it conceives of baseball as Jeffersonian rather than Hamiltonian, in other words. It was as if *rus in urbe* were not enough for Spalding; baseball had to have emerged out of the countryside alone and not to have taken form in the city if it were to be truly righteous and resonate with the deepest strains of the American character.

Von der Ahe cared little about such notions and had no patience for Spalding's platitudes; he wanted to lure the workingman into his carnival, and baseball was a means, not an end, in his quest to produce entertainment for the working class of St. Louis. The ruffians were welcome, at least up to a point, and they were encouraged to feel at home at Sportsman's Park. An early master of brand extension, he dressed the waiters in his Golden Lion Saloon, two blocks away from the park, in St. Louis Browns caps and shirts. With prizefights, rides, and shows all adding

---

* Several historians, most particularly John Thorn, have made it clear that Doubleday's connection to the history of baseball was tenuous at best, and have explained in detail how he was little more than a convenient character around whom a mythic, and largely imagined, legend of baseball as representing American virtue—particularly American rustic virtue—could be written.

to the hubbub at the park, the illusion of rusticity was not a part of the equation for Von der Ahe. He would surely have found comparisons of his ballpark to Coney Island flattering, since John Cox Stevens's Elysian Fields, not Frederick Law Olmsted's Central Park, was the antecedent of Sportsman's Park.

Then again, Hulbert probably wasn't thinking of Olmstedian rusticity either when he built Lakefront Park in Chicago in 1878 on the site of an earlier baseball grounds, Lake Park, that had been destroyed by the Great Chicago Fire of 1871. And Spalding was definitely not inspired by Olmsted's notion of Central Park as a benign mixing place for different social classes when he rebuilt and expanded Hulbert's ballpark in 1883, turning it into "the first ballpark marketed as an attraction in its own right," according to Michael Gershman. Lakefront Park could accommodate ten thousand spectators, and everything was designed to assure that the classes would not mix at all. Spalding was happy to make some room for the working poor, but like the builders of South End Grounds in Boston, he kept them at a distance: two thousand in standing room and six thousand in bleachers, the largest bleacher section in baseball. The bleachers and standing room areas were enclosed by fences, a world apart from the two thousand grandstand seats. The bleachers at Lakefront, Daniel Rosenswcig has written, served "as extremely creative forms of genial containment. They provided a way to incorporate and even profit from a potentially dangerous section of the population given to congregating just outside the walls of enclosed parks. Accommodating thousands of members of Chicago's increasingly large immigrant population instead of leaving them to congregate outside the park, Spalding was able to make enough money to provide for a comfortable segregation."

The "comfortable segregation" of the second version of Lakefront Park included not only conventional, covered grandstand seats but eighteen private viewing boxes, each provided with upholstered armchairs and served by waiters, further accentuating the class distinctions within the ballpark. For Spalding's most privileged customers, the riffraff were not only out of the way, they were all but invisible. In his quest to bring baseball upscale, Spalding in 1883 had invented the precursor of the modern skybox. No wonder that *Harper's* magazine declared the renovated Lakefront Park "indisputably the finest in the world in respect of seating accommodations and conveniences."

It was less successful as a playing field, however. The site of Lakefront was severely constrained by the neighboring tracks and city streets, and the left field wall was only 180 feet from home plate. Right field was barely longer at 196 feet. Balls hit over these short fences were considered ground rule doubles the first year the White Stockings played at the new Lakefront, but in 1884 the rule was changed and balls that were hit past the fences were classified as home runs. The team hit 142 home runs that season, more than four times the previous National League team record of 34 home runs, as clear an indication as there could be that the layout of its ballpark was more than incidental to a team's destiny. Albert Spalding's influence in the National League was not sufficient to prevent the league from deciding after that season to set 210 feet as a minimum home run distance for an outfield fence, in effect invalidating Lakefront Park's unusually generous home run fences and no longer permitting balls hit over the fence to be scored as automatic home runs. The total of home runs the following season dropped by 62 percent. The rule change effectively doomed the celebrated Lakefront, since there was no room to move the fences back and give the outfield the more generous proportions that could be found elsewhere. The White Stockings remained downtown for another few years, but within a decade the team had given up Lakefront Park and moved to the larger but less distinctive West Side Grounds, southwest of the earlier park.

It went without saying that Von der Ahe's St. Louis Browns were not welcome in the National League. In the late 1870s, many of baseball's teams were independent, with ad hoc schedules, and their income could often fluctuate as much as their scores. But Von der Ahe's notion of baseball as the anchor of what was, for all intents and purposes, a larger entertainment complex was selling plenty of tickets, and other independent teams were eager to schedule games in St. Louis to get a portion of Von der Ahe's lucrative gate. When Hulbert expelled the reconstituted Cincinnati Red Stockings from the National League after the team's president, W. H. Kennett, refused to sign the league's pledges against selling beer and playing baseball on Sundays, the Reds joined with Von der Ahe and several other independent teams to form a new league, called the American Association, to compete with the National League. Meeting in Cincinnati in the fall of 1881, the new league admitted six founding teams

and agreed on a constitution that followed some of the National League's tighter management practices, since these owners were no more willing than their straitlaced peers to cede power to the players they considered their employees. But the new league also mandated twenty-five-cent admission prices, offered the unqualified approval of Sunday baseball, and, after an initial attempt to limit the sale of beer and alcoholic beverages, agreed that these, too, would be permitted.

The new league was quickly given the nickname "the Beer and Whiskey Circuit," and it was selling plenty of its twenty-five-cent tickets, especially on Sundays, when the immigrant crowd turned out in droves. "It gave them a way to learn what America was all about: a quarter, carefully saved, could get them into the splendid spectacle of an American Association game," Achorn wrote. "Inside the park, they could see in the grandstand well-dressed and well-fed people—people who were living the American life to which they aspired—and, on the field, tough, ambitious players who were not all that far above the working poor."

Lakefront Park,
Chicago, 1878

But the crowds, if larger than National League crowds, were also rougher and harder to control. The *St. Louis Globe-Democrat,* Von der Ahe's hometown paper, noted that in the National League ballparks, "the crowds attending the ball games are made to behave, and any blackguard conduct results in prompt ejectment from the ground. In the cities where the American Association is represented, notably Louisville and Cincinnati, the hoodlums appear to rule the roost." But the Association teams were all profitable, and according to the *Cleveland Leader,* five of the initial six teams in the American Association outdrew the Chicago White Stockings, the most popular of the eight National League teams.

The new league was headed by Harmer Denny McKnight, chief executive of the Pittsburgh Allegheny team, and he turned out to be as firm a leader as the National League's Hulbert, whose death in the spring of 1882, not long after the new league was formed, seemed to tilt power even further toward the American Association. The new league expanded to eight teams, taking in the New York Metropolitans and the Columbus Buckeyes, while the National League, aware that it was losing the battle for crowds, reversed Hulbert's smug dismissal of teams from the large-market cities of Philadelphia and New York and agreed to allow the Philadelphia Phillies and a new team being formed in New York to join. The league chose not to expand: to make room, the owners decided to eject teams in Worcester and Troy that had committed no infraction other than being in cities with small populations and limited income potential. The league that liked to think of baseball as a game that represented the rural heartland had to concede that its economic future lay in the nation's biggest cities.

At the end of 1882, the two leagues were bitter rivals. One presented baseball as working-class entertainment and was largely tolerant of rowdy crowds and players. The other tried much harder to police both the game and its spectators, and strove to project an image of respectability above all. It would seem, at least at the beginning, that the American Association's populist stance and quick success would lead it to triumph over its stuffy rival, all the more because the Association's rambunctiousness contained some enlightened elements that gave it the potential of an identity more distinctive than just a rejection of the National League's Puritanism. In its first years, the Association disavowed the rigid segregation that the National League teams practiced and allowed a few African American players to join its ranks in 1884. This practice could have changed baseball history had the new league not given in to pressure from several National League players who were threatening a boycott unless all of major league baseball was segregated. It quickly abandoned its principles and agreed to include only white players on its rosters from that point forward.

Conceding to the National League's practices in an area in which it had the potential to redefine baseball, David Nemec has written, was one of the things that sealed the fate of the American Association. Despite its rapid rise, it would fail to overtake the National League, and by 1891, after only a decade, would consolidate with its older rival. It was in some ways a tortoise-and-hare battle in which victory went to the slow and steady. While the Association was not made up entirely of flamboyant owners like Chris Von der Ahe, neither did it seem to place much of a premium on conservative management. It was badly weakened by feuding owners, excessive trading of players, repeated contractual disputes, and the creation of rival leagues, not to mention by the unpredictable behavior of its best-known team proprietor, Von der Ahe, who essentially managed his team himself after his shrewd longtime manager Charlie Comiskey departed for a short-lived new organization known as the Players League. The Browns never fully recovered from the erratic decisions made by Von der Ahe, who turned out to know far more about beer than about baseball.

Baseball retained a kind of wildcat quality all through the 1880s, and Von der Ahe was far from the only eccentric owner. There was John B. Day, who owned both the New York Metropolitans, an American Association team that rented playing space at the Polo Grounds, owned by James Gordon Bennett at Fifth Avenue and 110th Street, and the New York Gothams of the National League, a team Day created by moving the Troy Haymakers from upstate New York to New York City. Day, effectively competing with himself, then set up both teams at the Polo Grounds, which after the 1882 departure of Bennett's polo club for the Bronx was available full-time for baseball. It was an unhappy cohabitation. While the Polo Grounds, adjacent to the northeast corner of Central Park and close to railroad and streetcar stops, was a fine location for baseball and Bennett had built handsome, double-decked grandstands to attract the

more genteel crowds who came to see polo matches, the field, torn up by years of active polo play, was something of a mess. There were no dugouts, and a flagpole stood in center field.

Despite the fact that the Metropolitans had strong seasons in 1883 and 1884, Day clearly favored his new National League team. He gave them scheduling priority at the Polo Grounds whenever there was a conflict, and the Metropolitans ended up playing most of their games in 1884 at a subsidiary field on the East River, officially called Metropolitan Park, which David Nemec described as "a small and windy facility on the East River that was known by New Yorkers as 'The Dump' because it resided on the site of an old city dump at 108th Street." Metropolitan Park was probably the worst advertisement that ever existed for the idea that baseball benefits from being integrated into an urban fabric. It faced a group of factories across the East River that spewed noxious fumes toward the field, leading *Sporting Life* to observe that the Metropolitans were attracting fewer fans with their twenty-five-cent admission fee than other New

York teams were getting when they charged fifty cents. It was, according to pitcher Jack Lynch, a place where "a player could go down for a grounder and come up with six months of malaria."

Day seemed so determined to humiliate the Metropolitans that he could have been the model for Rachel Phelps, the Cleveland Indians owner in the 1989 film *Major League* who did all she could to make her team lose. When the Mets won the American Association pennant in 1884 and then proceeded to lose three straight games in the best-of-five World Series to the Providence Grays, the National League champions, Day all but abandoned the team. He shifted its capable manager, Jim Mutrie, to the Gothams, released two of its best players, and engaged in a complex sleight-of-hand maneuver involving sending Mutrie and the players to Bermuda for ten days to assure that no other National League team would sign them during the requisite waiting period after their

Club owners are billed above their players in an 1894 lithograph of the Polo Grounds.

release from the Mets. To make things still worse for the Metropolitans in 1885, Day scheduled many games for the morning when they would attract sparse crowds, and when they played at the Polo Grounds he refused to allow the team to use the regular diamond. He created an awkward and clearly inferior secondary diamond in deep left field, with a canvas fence separating it from the main playing area—surely the only time a single ballpark has contained two distinct, intersecting playing fields.

In 1885, the American Association pressured Day to divest himself of the team he was so eager to undermine, and he sold it to Erastus Wiman, owner of the Staten Island Amusement Company, which also owned the Staten Island ferry, for a reported $25,000. Wiman wanted to move the Mets to the St. George Cricket Grounds in his "Palace of Eden" amusement park on Staten Island, a move that would have echoed the early years of baseball's presence in Hoboken, when John Stevens's ferries took fans to and from his suburban ball field. Denny McKnight, the Association president, was firmly opposed to the notion of the team leaving Manhattan for the rural precincts of Staten Island. Taking a leaf from William Hulbert's book, he ejected the Mets from the Association and admitted a Washington, D.C., team in its place. Wiman sued and won reinstatement after the court ruled that membership in a baseball league is "as sacred as any property."

The Mets moved to Staten Island, where their attendance fell still further, as McKnight had predicted, and the team, weakened by the months of legal wrangling, declined. So did the Association, and so did McKnight himself, who was also fending off accusations of conflicts between his ownership of the Pittsburgh team and his role as Association president. His authority diminished, the other team owners fired him, and then, in an act of vindictiveness, they also ordered him to give up his interest in the Pittsburgh team, at which point McKnight, effectively thrown out of baseball, moved to the West and took over a cattle ranch.

The Gothams did not last much longer than the Mets at the Polo Grounds. Day lost his lease after the 1888 season, when the City of New York decided to cut 111th Street through the site and the original Polo Grounds was demolished. The team, by then the Giants, moved in 1889 to Manhattan Field, a tightly sited park on Coogan's Bluff, in Upper Manhattan beside the Harlem River. The land was less than ideal, given that the playing field was far from flat, and center and right fields had the steepest embankments within the field of play of any major league ballpark. A year later the Players League built Brotherhood Park on a more expansive site just beside Manhattan Field, so close that once a home run hit by Mike Tiernan of the Giants landed in the other park. When the Players League folded just a year later, the Giants took over the larger park, which soon, in honor of the team's earlier home downtown, became known as the Polo Grounds. Manhattan Field was used for a few years as a cricket grounds, and by 1911 had been converted into a parking lot to serve a new, expanded version of the Polo Grounds.

Sportsman's Park had a much longer life than the early New York ballparks—it would be rebuilt and expanded multiple times, including a 1909 iteration that had one of baseball's first steel and concrete grandstands, and in various versions it would last until 1966. But Von der Ahe himself came to a sorry end. Never cautious about overplaying his hand, he eventually lost control of the St. Louis team, and died broke. Even before that, however, he had lost the support of many of his early boosters, including his old friend Al Spink, the founder of *The Sporting News,* who first encouraged Von der Ahe to invest in baseball. Spink was so offended by some of Von der Ahe's excesses at Sportsman's Park that in 1896 he commissioned an article for *The Sporting News* entitled "The Prostitution of a Ballpark," claiming that Von der Ahe had turned his park into a "resort of disreputable men and women," and encouraging a hostile takeover to wrest from him control of his team and his ballpark. It would not be necessary: within a couple of years, Von der Ahe's financial empire collapsed, done in by poor investments, personal scandal, and lawsuits following a disastrous fire at Sportsman's Park, and the St. Louis Browns passed into court-ordered receivership.

Von der Ahe blamed his downfall on the National League, which he felt was still intent on destroying him, years after it had taken over his American Association. The Association was long gone by then, but even though it was no longer a legal entity, the ripples of its presence were still felt. The American Association had redefined the game, and for all that its absorption into the National League was, at least in the literal sense, a defeat, many of the Association's innovations became a permanent part of baseball. Under the terms of the consolidation, the National League agreed to permit Sunday games, and shortly thereafter it also allowed all teams, at their discretion, to sell alcoholic beverages. So even as the National League solidified its position as the preeminent governing organization of baseball, the ongoing identity of the sport after the two leagues consolidated was shaped as much by the rogue tone of the American Association as it was by the National League's own traditions of propriety.

Baseball may have been reflective of the American character, as Albert Spalding and the National League liked to claim. But that character was far messier and more difficult to define than they were inclined to admit. If the opposing natures of Chris Von der Ahe and Albert Spalding could not be reconciled in life, their divergent visions of the sport, as well as the ballparks they built, would nevertheless both shape the future of baseball.

From Wood to Steel and Stone

WHETHER BASEBALL PARKS through the 1880s were ostentatious Victorian piles like the Grand Pavilion at South End Grounds in Boston, or disheveled settings for carnivals like Sportsman's Park in St. Louis, or exercises in economic segregation like Lakefront Park in Chicago, they had one thing in common: they were constructed entirely, or almost entirely, of wood. Even structures as elaborate as the Grand Pavilion were in some ways just expanded versions of the grandstands that were built by William Cammeyer at Union Grounds in Brooklyn: rows of wooden stands, with a roof to protect their occupants from the summer sun or rain, a roof that made its presence known not only through the protection it provided, but also through the forest of columns needed to support it, which managed to interfere, at least partially, with the view from almost every seat.

That the first ballparks were built out of wood was not surprising. Ballparks grew out of simple wooden grandstands, and took on the accoutrements of architecture haltingly and gradually. Wood was an easily obtained material, modest in cost and commonly used for almost every kind of construction except the grandest civic buildings. And since the earliest ballparks were barely conceived as civic buildings at all, let alone as elaborate ones, there seemed little need, at first, to consider any other building material. The age of ballparks like South End Grounds and Lakefront Park coincided with the construction of great resort hotels of wood, like the Hotel Del Coronado, outside of San Diego, in 1888, and Mohonk Mountain House in New Paltz, New York, in 1870, extravaganzas of timber that underscored the extent to which these decades viewed wood as a natural material for even the largest public buildings of a certain type. And while wood construction could not span great distances, meaning that every grandstand was burdened with a multitude of columns intruding upon the view of the field, that was a problem common to most large gathering places in the late nineteenth century: theaters built of brick and masonry, for example, often had iron columns compromising the view of patrons underneath balconies.

But wood presented another problem, far more serious than its inability to span long distances. Wood also burned, easily and frequently. Fire was the most determined enemy of the early ballparks, and the reason that so many of them were reconstructed, sometimes repeatedly. While it was not the only spur to rebuilding—the growing popularity of baseball was often incentive enough to build bigger, and many wooden ballparks were casually expanded several times—fire was behind so many of the multiple iterations of the early wooden ballparks that it is hard not to conclude that the era of wooden ballparks was also the era of combustible ones.

The age of ballpark fires might be said to have begun with Chicago in 1871, where the loss of the original Lake Park after just a single season was no more than a footnote to the enormous fire that destroyed so much of the city. After that came fires in Brooklyn's Washington Park in 1889 and the first Eclipse Park, in Louisville, in 1892, among others, followed by the burning of four major city ballparks in 1894: South End Grounds in Boston, West Side Grounds in Chicago, Union Park in Baltimore, and Huntingdon Grounds (later Baker Bowl) in Philadelphia.

The fire in Boston was particularly dramatic, and architecturally devastating, since it destroyed the most ornate structure yet built for baseball, the Grand Pavilion of South End Grounds, only six seasons after its completion. The fire began during the third inning of a game on May 15, 1894, between the Boston Beaneaters (who later became the Boston Braves) and the Baltimore Orioles, and it started out in the right field bleachers. Boston's right fielder, Jimmy Bannon, saw the flames, ran to the bleachers, and tried at first to stamp them out with his feet, then used his cap. He was unsuccessful, and moments later, an apparent wind shift caused the fire to blow up into a major conflagration, spreading to the left field bleachers and then into the Grand Pavilion itself as fans ran in panic. The game was halted and the players fled the field, with barely time to retrieve their clothes from the clubhouse before that, too, was engulfed in flames. The fire did not stop with the Grand Pavilion: it jumped quickly across the street to the old wooden tenement houses that clustered on the blocks east of the ballpark, and continued to spread across the Roxbury section of Boston. Within an hour the fire had covered twelve acres. By

Fires in wooden ballparks made frequent headlines.

the time it was brought under control it had destroyed roughly two hundred buildings and left 1,900 people homeless.

The origins of what became known as the Great Roxbury Fire were never determined, but it was clear that the widespread damage was due in part to a slow response from the Boston fire department and to the difficulty of bringing water to the site of the fire. The nearest working fire hydrant was some distance from the ballpark. While there was a fire hydrant at South End Grounds, apparently the owners of the Boston team had never paid the required fee to have it connected to the city's water system, and it was useless the one time it was needed. The odd mix of extravagance and parsimoniousness of the Triumvirs, as the three owners of the team were known locally, was well established, and it probably came as no surprise to Bostonians to discover that while the Triumvirs had built the most lavish park in baseball, they had also failed to insure it properly, and had purchased only $45,000 worth of insurance for a structure that would cost roughly $80,000 to replace.

They did not waste time getting started on a new version of the ballpark, however, and the third iteration of South End Grounds was completed in only two months, in time for a game on July 20. But the speed of construction of the new South End Grounds was surpassed only by the modesty of its conception. Since the owners did not invest more than their limited insurance proceeds in the new park, the new South End Grounds was only a pale echo of the Grand Pavilion. It was built partly of brick for greater fire safety, but there was no way to hide the fact that it was little more than a plain, one-story grandstand with a pair of small spires taking the place of the Victorian extravaganza that had been lost, a structure so captivating to Bostonians that at its opening the *Globe* had proclaimed on its front page that the Boston Tea Party, the battle of Bunker Hill, and Paul Revere's ride would "fade into nothingness" beside South End Grounds' "beautiful, cathedral-like grand stand."

If Boston responded to fire by scaling back its ambitions, Philadelphia did the opposite. When a fire set off by a plumber's torch destroyed the Huntingdon Grounds in North Philadelphia, the undistinguished home of the Philadelphia Phillies built in 1887—it survived only a year longer than the Grand Pavilion in Boston—the team replaced it the following season with the nation's first ballpark constructed of steel, brick, and concrete. The new Huntingdon Grounds, officially called Philadelphia

National League Park and later known as Baker Bowl for William F. Baker, who owned the team from 1913 until 1930, not only employed the latest materials, it was structurally innovative as well, using steel to cantilever a large portion of the upper deck over the lower deck. The grandstand design significantly reduced the number of view-blocking columns, opening up vistas and making the new Huntingdon Grounds baseball's most overt symbol of modernity. As the park neared completion, Alfred J. Reach, the former baseball player and sporting-goods entrepreneur who was co-owner of the team, issued an extensive public statement in the form of an invitation to Philadelphians to help inaugurate the new ballpark. It is worth quoting at length, since it may be the most comprehensive statement of architectural intentions any major league team owner has ever issued:

The new structure is mainly of brick and steel, containing no wood or other inflammable material except the platforms and seats. New massive brick walls of stretcher and press bricks, laid in red cement, support and enclose on four sides the lower deck. Street front, field front and gables are of brick.

There are twenty-one platforms on the Huntingdon Street side and seventeen on the Fifteenth Street side, holding 3,750 chairs and promenades with standing room for 1,000 additional patrons. The upper deck has nine platforms and a broad promenade divided into sixteen sections including eighteen boxes, the total capacity thereof being 1,750 seats with standing space for about 800 extra.

Underneath the lower deck is an immense asphalt and granolithic pavement upon which are laid out the entrances, ticket offices, toilet rooms, restaurants, etc., all separated by heavy brick walls. There is a wide passageway connecting the right and left field bleachers; also, a long avenue of racks for bicycles to be stored and checked. At the field front, protected by heavy wire screens, are two stone platforms holding over 400 chairs for those who like to get in on the ground floor.

Connecting the different decks or floors are three separate sets of iron stairways, wide and massive, built in the centre and two end towers. They extend from pavement to roof. Although the structure may be said to be fireproof (an approximate term), a 6-inch main runs from the street into the centre tower with branches and connecting hose on every floor, ready to deluge every portion of the entire Pavilion with any required quantity of water, should occasion ever require its use.

And now a word as to the architectural form of our edifice:

Our former Pavilion was considered a marvel because, unlike all other so-called Grand Stands, it had but one row of iron posts, and they 24 feet apart, to obstruct the view of the spectator. The new Pavilion will have no posts at all in front of two-thirds of those seated on the lower deck, and none at all in front of all of those seated on the upper deck. In other words nine platforms of the upper deck project beyond any post into the air, and over the heads of those below. This is only rendered possible by the adoption of the Cantilever system, first suggested, after a completion of plans, by the well-known architect, John D. Allen, of 107 Chestnut Street. The novelty of the idea made it at first seem chimerical. True, we had heard of Cantilever Bridges, and had gazed at the greatest of them over the Firth at Edinburg, and had seen the embryonic principle illustrated in a balcony of two or three over-hanging platforms, but to have nearly 30 feet of heavy iron girders, braces, platforms, etc., with the same extent of iron roof and trusses, projecting out and beyond supporting columns or posts, seemed not only a risk of capital but the more serious risk of life and limb to those upon and under such a gallery. Architect Allen, however, not only gave his personal guarantee as to its practicability and safety, but has during its progress and since its completion verified his guarantee by the severest tests (hydraulic included) to which any such edifice could be subjected . . .

There are fifteen of these cantilevers supporting the upper deck and roof. . . . The resistance of this anchorage is about 90,000 pounds to each cantilever. In addition there is the weight of six platforms and the promenades of both decks with whatever "live or moving loads" may be on them, to add to the above already gigantic figures, as counterpoises to any possible weight or pressure on the other side of the fulcrum.

It would therefore be impossible to play seesaw with one of our cantilevers, even with three times the live weight, that could ever be crowded on them and even if at the same time 3 feet of snow were on the roof and the wind blowing 50 miles an hour. The greatest possible load that could be crowded upon one truss could not exceed 30,000 pounds, and even this is minimized by the fact that the entire structure is in continuous thread and network of steel, diffusing its strength to its weakest parts, and transmitting its loads, by the law of gravity to the ground. The builders of this magnificent steel and iron structure are Parvin & Company, the well-known Philadelphia engineers and contractors.

In dedicating the Pavilion and its fixtures, on May 2, 1895, to the greatest of athletic sports, the Philadelphia Ball Club will ask that its title as pioneer in original, beautiful and appropriate architecture be confirmed by the verdict of its patrons, and that the public at large will appreciate the enterprise, which adds so novel and unique a structure to the many other ornamental edifices of our beloved city.

For all of Reach's high hopes for his new park, it had an odd history. Its field was awkwardly shaped, constrained by a tight urban site, and badly rutted, thanks in part to a bicycle track that ran around the periphery so that the park could also be used for bicycle races. The site was a former dump, and there was a rise in center field below which a railroad tunnel ran. (For years, the park was nicknamed "The Hump.") The playing field was defined in part by a structure containing clubhouse facilities for home and visiting teams in center field. More intrusive still was a sixty-foot-high combination of solid masonry wall and pipe and wire screen running from the clubhouse to the right field foul line, creating an exceptionally tight right field, a precursor of the more famous, and more affectionately tolerated, "Green Monster" of Fenway Park in Boston. But the nameless wall in Philadelphia was actually twenty-three feet higher than its Boston counterpart would be and thirty feet closer to home plate, and dominated its small playing field to an even greater extent—even more after the team sold advertising rights to Lifebuoy soap, which posted an enormous billboard across it proclaiming THE PHILLIES USE LIFEBUOY.*

---

* The common retort among Philadelphians was to repeat the slogan on the wall and add, "And they still stink."

*Philadelphia's Baker
Bowl hosts the Boston
Red Sox and a full
house in October 1915.*

In many ways, this advanced park was particularly ill-fated. In 1903, a section of the left field seating area collapsed, killing twelve people. (It was not the steel cantilever structure that failed, but a projecting balcony at the rear of the wooden stands, overlooking the street, that had become overcrowded with people who had rushed to view a disturbance outside the park.) While William Baker's name is more closely linked to the park than that of his predecessor who built it, Baker and other later owners of the Phillies maintained the park poorly, and in 1927 another section of the stands collapsed, reportedly due to rotting timbers. The park became "increasingly seedy as the years went by," wrote Michael Benson. "As a cynical sports writer of the 1920's put it, 'National League players will be pleased to learn that the visiting dressing room at Baker Bowl is being completely refurbished for next season—brand new nails are being installed on which to hang their clothes.'" The park, which never seated more than twenty thousand, was widely mocked as inferior to the fully steel and masonry ballparks that followed it, and its small

dimensions highly favorable to hitters seemed to inspire disdain for the Phillies rather than affection.

Baker Bowl made another kind of baseball history in 1923, when the Phillies pressed charges against an eleven-year-old boy named Robert Cotter for keeping a baseball hit into the bleachers.* For the crime of catching a foul ball and placing it in his pocket, Cotter was kept in the city house of detention overnight, setting off an outcry. In his ruling, a local judge took direct aim at the Phillies, comparing its management unfavorably to that of their local rivals, the Philadelphia Athletics. "I never heard of Connie Mack or Tom Shibe throwing small boys into prison because they took a ball that was batted into the bleachers," the

---

* Until the 1920s, balls hit into the stands were presumed to be the property of the team, and guards were sent to retrieve them from the fans who had caught them. In 1921, a thirty-one-year-old New York stockbroker, Reuben Berman, was sued by the Giants for refusing to return a ball at the Polo Grounds. While that case was decided in Berman's favor, it took some time for the principle that fans could keep balls (fair or foul) they retrieved to become established policy across all major league teams.

One of the legendary advertising signs of baseball, at Baker Bowl in Philadelphia

judge wrote. "They were boys. . . . Such an act on the part of a boy is merely proof that he is following his own natural impulses. . . . I wouldn't brand this boy a thief just to help Mr. Shettsline [the Phillies business manager] save a $1.50 ball."

If the Phillies park ended the nineteenth century with a burst of structural innovation, the Cincinnati Reds opened the twentieth century with an ornate, if nostalgic, look backward. The lyrically named Palace of the Fans, completed in 1902, was technically a steel-reinforced concrete reconstruction of Cincinnati's wooden League Park, which had burned in 1900. Designed by John G. Thurtle, it was the most flamboyant piece of ballpark architecture yet, and the first and only ballpark to be inspired by the grand and celebratory classicism of the Beaux-Arts, which had become the favored architectural style for courthouses, museums, city halls, and banks since the "White City" of Beaux Arts buildings at the World's Columbian Exposition in Chicago in 1893. The Palace, too, was white, and it had grandstands supported by Corinthian columns. The center of the structure, behind home plate, was marked by a monumental classical frieze beneath a triangular pediment, with the word CINCINNATI engraved across its face. The wide, bow-fronted seating boxes, more like opera boxes than ballpark seating, were marketed as "Fashion Boxes";

beside them were elongated bars at the edge of the field, extending along the first- and third-base lines, called Rooters' Row.

John T. Brush, the owner of the team, was determined to create "the first baseball palace" in Michael Gershman's words. But Brush's conception was true to its name: the design favored the comfort of the fans over the comfort of the players. There were benches for the players instead of dugouts, and no dressing rooms. Visiting teams had to change in their hotel rooms. The park's true façade was not toward the street, but toward the field, where its classical grandstands created an image of monumental grandeur that was altogether new to baseball.

It was not, alas, to last. The most grandiose grandstand in baseball turned out to be mainly a façade, and it was poorly maintained by the owners who took over from Brush less than a year after the park opened. (He sold the team to a consortium including two of the city's political bosses, who reportedly told him that if he refused to make a deal with them they would order a new city street run through the ballpark site.) The new owners clearly had none of the pride that had led Brush to envision the grandstand as a statement of elegance for Cincinnati, and before long there were reports of cracked girders and unsafe floors, as well as crumbling bleachers. Brush emerged sufficiently unscathed from his maltreatment by Cincinnati's politicians that only a month after losing the Reds he moved East, his ambitions undiminished, and purchased the

The ornate classical grandstand of Palace of the Fans, home to the Cincinnati Reds from 1902 to 1911

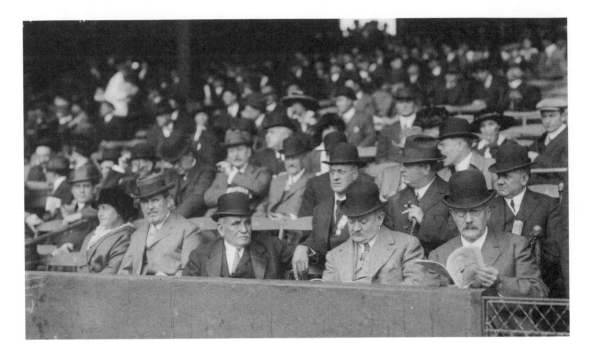

Ben Shibe (third from the left) and other baseball executives at the 1913 World Series in Shibe Park, Philadelphia

New York Giants from Andrew Freedman. The park he left behind did not fare as well. In 1911, after only nine seasons and another change of ownership, the new management team decided to demolish the Palace of the Fans and construct a new ballpark on the same site. In place of the park Brush had built rose Redland Field, which eventually became Crosley Field, where the Reds would remain until 1970.

The short life of Palace of the Fans was, in a sense, a curtain-raiser for the first true palace of baseball, built seven years after Palace of the Fans opened and two years before its demise: Shibe Park, the home of the Philadelphia Athletics, just five blocks away from Baker Bowl in North Philadelphia. If the outlandishness of the Cotter case of the stolen foul ball made the Phillies seem like a less dignified operation than the Athletics, the ballpark the Athletics would build in 1909 only accentuated the distinction between the images of the two Philadelphia teams, neighbors in North Philadelphia but otherwise a world apart. Shibe Park lacked the structural innovation of Baker's cantilevered grandstands, but it was in every other way a more serious work of architecture. Shibe represented the most elegant reconception of the ballpark since Boston's Grand Pavilion, and along with Forbes Field in Pittsburgh, it was the most fully

realized architectural statement baseball would make in the first decade of the twentieth century.

Shibe—named for Ben Shibe, the owner who built the park, and many years later known as Connie Mack Stadium in honor of Shibe's onetime partner and the team's longtime manager—was designed by William Steele and Sons, a construction firm known for its expertise in steel and concrete work. (Steele had built Philadelphia's first steel and concrete skyscraper, the Witherspoon Building, a dozen years before, and was among the innovators of "ready mix" concrete, mixed on job sites in trucks with rotating drums.) The park was constructed of steel, reinforced concrete, brick, and terra-cotta. From the street, the most remarkable thing about it was that it looked like a building, not a sporting venue: an ornate, French Renaissance façade faced both Lehigh Avenue and Twenty-first Street, with a round tower, topped by a cupola, marking the corner. (Mack's office was at the top, beneath the dome.) There were storefronts built into the base of the building, facing the streets. John Pastier described Shibe Park best: "a richly eclectic yet tasteful extravaganza in a French Renaissance revival style. Its embellishments included a copper-trimmed green slate mansard roof with thirty-two pedimented

Entrance to Shibe Park, Philadelphia, 1909

dormer windows, a circular corner entrance and four-story office tower topped by an arcaded octagonal cupola and dome plus several flag poles, cornices, belt courses, two monumental arcades each composed of seventeen tall Ionic pilasters flanking sixteen arches, a rusticated stone base, banded red brick walls, and light-colored terra-cotta trim. To remind observers bedazzled by all this magnificence that they were actually entering a ballpark . . . there were bas-relief busts of team owner Ben Shibe and manager Connie Mack."

If the façade resembled anything, it was not a ballpark at all, but Carrère and Hastings's monumental Bicentennial Buildings, constructed for Yale University in New Haven seven years earlier. Like Shibe, the Bicentennial Buildings consisted of two wings set at a 90-degree angle to form an L, with a round tower as a hinge at the corner. Yale's exercise in Beaux Arts grandeur could not have been more different from Shibe in terms of function: it had a concert hall in one wing and a vast dining hall in the other. But the L enclosed a large, open quadrangle, rectangular like the open space of the field at Shibe. That Shibe was set into a rectangular site in the even grid of Philadelphia streets, without any of the eccentric diagonals that defined the playing fields of many ballparks both before and after it, made it look from the outside even more like a building first and an athletic field second. Now, more than forty years after its demolition, it is still the building-ness of Shibe that impresses. It was, more than any ballpark before it, a statement about the role of the ballpark as a civic building, as a public gathering place, and as a civic institution worthy to take its place beside museums, courthouses, and concert halls. Shibe, who made his fortune manufacturing sporting goods, including baseballs,* wanted the ballpark to be "a lasting monument."

Reversing the pattern of Palace of the Fans, the interior of Shibe was somewhat more conventional than the street façade. It is no accident that most of the archival photographs of Shibe show the ballpark from

---

* Shibe was a longtime partner in the sporting goods business of Alfred J. Reach, who was the co-owner of Philadelphia's National League team, the Phillies. According to Bruce Kuklick in *To Every Thing a Season: Shibe Park and Urban Philadelphia, 1909–1976,* Reach preferred making and selling baseballs to owning a team, and willingly sold his interest in the Phillies when Shibe invested in the Athletics, then a new franchise, to avoid having the partners own opposing teams.

the street, while images of Palace of the Fans show the structure as it appeared from the field. But the seating areas, if not as lavish as the exterior, were huge, with accommodations for twenty-three thousand, the most of any ballpark up to that time. The original grandstands, later expanded multiple times, held seating for ten thousand, with broad over-hangs to maximize shade. There was no advertising on the twelve-foot-high, green-painted concrete wall that surrounded the outfield, and the park had an early version of an electric scoreboard.

Ben Shibe spent just over $300,000 to construct his park, far more than any previous ballpark had cost. The excitement generated by its opening on April 12, 1909, which attracted a crowd of more than thirty thousand paying customers—which means a vast number of them were standing—extended through the season, when the Athletics booked a total attendance of 675,000, the highest of any team outside of New York. The park was grand, but every aspect of its monumentality had a clear business purpose: to attract more fans, and to accommodate them.

"For magnates like Shibe, baseball was a revenue-based enterprise. The construction of a huge building to house the business reflected its com-plexity," wrote Bruce Kuklick. "Shibe also wanted a grand showplace as a symbol of his worthiness as an American entrepreneur. He proudly and repeatedly stressed the financial appropriateness of building Shibe Park, 'a shrewd business move.'" Shibe, bigger and more ornate than the ballparks that had come before it, did not inspire universal admiration, however. Kuklick observed that the "imperial and impersonal look" that

Fans view the Philadelphia Athletics from neighboring rooftops during a game in the 1909 season at Shibe Park.

Shibe sought also meant "a loss of intimacy and the inconvenience fans accepted in walking great distances. The new parks 'depersonalized' the game, separated players from fans, and destroyed much of the previous era's informality when customers and athletes were cheek-by-jowl"—an observation that would have a certain historical irony, since precisely those criticisms would be directed half a century later at the sprawling suburban stadiums of the postwar era when they replaced the ballparks of the Shibe generation.*

The ballpark's presence within the grid of city streets meant that it was not just in the lavishness of its architecture that Shibe Park echoed Boston's South End Grounds; there was also a good view of right field from the neighboring row houses, many of whose owners along Twentieth Street built bleachers on their roofs and, like Sullivan with his tower in Boston, charged admission. In 1935, Mack, having already closed off the left field side with expanded double-decker grandstands, built a high wall in right field to block the neighbors' view. The result was a fully enclosed playing field shaped something like a rectangle. While there were small diagonal sections cutting off the corners beyond third base and first base, it nevertheless appeared from home plate and the grand corner entry almost like a vast diamond outfield embracing the smaller diamond of the infield.

At the end of June 1909, just a few weeks after the opening of Shibe Park, the other great ballpark of 1909, Forbes Field, at the other end of Pennsylvania in Pittsburgh, was ready for play. More understated as a work of architecture than Shibe, it was in some ways more luxurious in its accommodations, and certainly in its location in the midst of Schenley Park in the posh Oakland section of Pittsburgh. Barney Dreyfuss, owner of the Pittsburgh Pirates, joined with Andrew Carnegie to purchase a seven-acre section of the former Schenley estate as the site for a new ballpark, breaking with the pattern of placing baseball parks in random parts of the city where land was available and large plots could be economically assembled. For all their intimate connection to the urban fabric, early twentieth-century ballparks were almost never on prime downtown real estate: there were rarely available parcels large enough, and in any event,

* See Chapter 7 for a fuller discussion of postwar stadiums, which generally placed fans much farther from the playing field than they were at Shibe.

land in the central business district in any city big enough to support a major league team was simply too expensive. Better to be where the city was developing and land prices were manageable. The fans, who were as likely to work in outlying factories as in downtown offices, probably lived closer to these neighborhood ballparks than to the downtown core.

Shibe Park, for example, was in a largely undeveloped area of Philadelphia near the city's smallpox hospital, the presence of which had depressed real estate values in that part of the city and slowed its growth; Ben Shibe knew that the hospital was planning to close, which would have raised prices to the point at which it might have been difficult to assemble the park's large site. Shibe's builder, Joseph Steele, purchased numerous plots in a series of separate transactions to avoid suspicion that the team owner had a large project in the works, and managed to assemble the entire site of nearly six acres for $67,500 before the hospital's closing was announced. Not the least of the attractions of the site at Lehigh Avenue and Twenty-first Street was its easy access to streetcar lines, a key component of ballpark location decisions in many cities. Shibe's site also had the benefit of being close to the Pennsylvania Railroad's North Philadelphia station.

Forbes Field, shown here just after its opening in 1909, was constructed adjacent to Schenley Park in Pittsburgh.

In Pittsburgh, Dreyfuss, possessed of both a partner with deep pockets and what was effectively virgin land, did not have to assemble his
site in stealth. But he had other problems, such as a ravine that divided
the site in two and had to be filled in before construction could begin.
And he had to deal with concerns that the location was too distant from
Pittsburgh's center, leading some locals to refer to it as "Dreyfuss's Folly."
The anxiety of Pittsburghers notwithstanding, the site, a ten-minute trolley ride from downtown, was no farther from the city's core than most
baseball parks were. And the Oakland neighborhood, which already had
a Carnegie library, would in time become the city's main cultural center,
with several museums, the University of Pittsburgh, and what would
become Carnegie Mellon University. In some ways being part of that
kind of mix, with the added benefit of an upscale residential neighborhood nearby, fulfilled many of the early aspirations of baseball to be seen
not just as sport, but as having a degree of cultural standing. What made
Forbes Field's location unique was not its distance from the city's business
core, which most ballparks shared, but its presence amid museums and
parkland. No other city could claim a major league baseball park as a part
of its cultural mix, either in 1909 or anytime afterward. The geographical
intersection of the ballpark with other cultural institutions would have
no examples other than Forbes Field at Schenley Park.

The location, as far from rough-and-tumble as Pittsburgh could offer,
turned out not to be a problem for baseball fans. It was only a ten-minute
trolley ride from downtown, and the park attracted a crowd of more
than thirty thousand at its opening. The Pirates played there for the next
sixty years. The designer, a civil engineer named Charles Leavitt, came
up with multiple innovations to speed circulation at Forbes, including
elevators and ramps instead of stairs and a wide internal promenade. The
grandstand had three tiers, and the asymmetrical playing field was open
on one side to offer fans a view of the formal landscaping of adjacent
Schenley Park. The aesthetic of Forbes may have been less showy than
that of Shibe, but it was hardly plain: there was a façade of buff-colored
terra-cotta with the monogram PAC, for Pittsburgh Athletic Company,
set into square cross-hatching, steelwork painted a light green, and a red-
tinted slate roof. The geometries were low-key but proto-modern, and
the sense of restraint was heightened by what was possibly the park's most
radical element of all, Dreyfuss's decision to defer to the landscape of the

neighboring Schenley Park and keep Forbes Field free of all advertising billboards.

Dreyfuss clearly believed in open space, since he wanted Forbes to feel expansive not just to the fans who were able to look toward the landscape of Schenley Park, but to the players on his field, who he made certain would have no close-in fences to hit over. The owner was said to have "hated cheap home runs and vowed he'd have none in his park," and the outfield distances at Forbes were long: 360 feet in left field, 462 feet in center, and 376 in right. "Forbes would be one of the toughest major league parks to hit home runs out of," Michael Gershman wrote. But the generous dimensions made for an unusual number of triples.

Neither of the distinct interpretations of elegance that the two Pennsylvania ballparks of 1909 represented was equaled by the next major park to be completed, White Sox Park on the South Side of Chicago, known for most of its life as Comiskey Park in honor of its builder, the White Sox owner and Chris Von der Ahe's former manager in St. Louis, Charles Comiskey. Comiskey Park was the third major park to be built entirely of steel and masonry, and with 28,800 seats at its opening in 1910, it was

Exterior of Forbes Field, Pittsburgh, 1909

Z. T. DAVIS
ARCHITECT

the largest park in the major leagues, with a large playing field to match. It was a rare exercise in symmetry, with both left and right field foul lines set at 362 feet. The site itself was not symmetrical, however, so to achieve perfect balance between left and right fields, the stands in their original form were built at unequal depths, as John Pastier observed.

Comiskey's architecture was by Zachary Taylor Davis, with an assist from White Sox pitcher Ed Walsh, who was surely the first active player to have been drafted as an adviser to help plan the layout of a ballpark. It should be no surprise, then, that Comiskey was known as a pitcher's park.

Despite the carefully wrought order of its field, Comiskey was something of an architectural anticlimax, with neither the subtlety of Forbes Field nor the drama of Shibe Park, and the park's South Side location—the site of a former garbage dump not far from the Chicago stockyards—had neither the energy of the densest urban sites nor any degree of scenic appeal. To be fair, however, Comiskey was probably not the easiest of clients for Davis. While he encouraged both Ed Walsh and Davis, who had never designed a ballpark, to visit Shibe Park and Forbes Field—Davis would end up copying Forbes's ramp system—Comiskey rejected Davis's initial plan for a Roman classical façade as too expensive, and went for a plain red-brick exterior instead. A proposal for cantilevered upper decks

Ed Walsh, a player, advised Charles Comiskey on the design of his ballpark.

Zachary Taylor Davis, architect of both Chicago ballparks

was also turned down for budgetary reasons, giving Comiskey Park more supporting columns than most stadiums in the age of steel and concrete would have. Years later, owner Bill Veeck would paint the outside white, an act that would have desecrated either Shibe or Forbes. At Comiskey, however, Veeck's coat of paint had a far more benign effect, giving a dull building a welcome degree of brightening.

In New York, where the baseball park began, there would in time be construction to equal and surpass the great ballparks that were going up in other cities, but not yet. Most activity remained centered in Brooklyn and at the original Polo Grounds and Metropolitan Park in Upper Manhattan, as well as at St. George's on Staten Island. The first ballpark construction of the twentieth century in New York centered on the dispute between the established National League and the upstart American League, which was formed out of the Western League, an association of secondary teams. The American League was run by Ban Johnson, a former sportswriter from Cincinnati who had clashed consistently with

Exterior of Comiskey Park, 1914

John T. Brush when he owned the Cincinnati Reds. Johnson was eager to have an American League team in New York, and Brush, who had moved to New York to take over the Giants of the National League, was determined to keep the other league out of the city.

Johnson went so far as to line up a pair of political operatives with connections to Tammany Hall—Frank Farrell, a pool hall owner, and Bill Devery, a former police chief who was known as a major gambler—to buy the bankrupt Baltimore Orioles, an American League team, and move the franchise to New York. Whether it could find a place to play baseball was the issue. The bitter rivalry between Brush and Johnson led Brush's friend Andrew Freedman, who had sold Brush his stake in the New York Giants, to use his position as a director of the Interborough Rapid Transit Company, the builder of New York's first subway, to block a proposed American League ballpark Johnson wanted to build at 142nd Street and Lenox Avenue, adjacent to a subway terminus. Freedman, determined to help Brush keep the American League out of New York, scuttled the deal on the verge of its approval by the IRT board of directors, and subsequently convinced his colleagues on the board to block several other potential sites on the premise that they were needed for subway expansion.

Meanwhile, Farrell and Devery, the owners of the team, had brought in a former deputy city buildings commissioner, Joseph Gordon, as the team president and public face. Gordon, who had once served as president of the New York Metropolitans, knew New York real estate, and he discovered a site that the subway system had not yet coveted, a high, rocky bluff overlooking the Hudson River at 165th Street. It had views

American League Park, New York.

of the Palisades and New Jersey beyond, but it had little else to recommend it, according to *The New York Times,* which described the site as a combination of swampland and rocky ridge, with more than a hundred trees in the way of the playing field.

The team leased the land for ten years for $10,000 per year, and began to build a ballpark. The costs of clearing and leveling the land were roughly $200,000, so substantial that the owners spent little on the structure itself. Hilltop Park, as the ballpark was informally called—its official name was American League Park of New York—was a throwback, constructed almost entirely of wood. It was not yet finished when the relocated team, renamed the New York Highlanders, took to its new field on April 30, 1903, defeating the Washington Senators 6–2. Over the years it was altered and expanded multiple times, but it never acquired any real allure or even, for that matter, any significant character, and it was not surprising that as the end of the ten-year lease approached, the team's owners considered writing off their entire investment and abandoning the park to the owner of the land, the New York Institute for the Blind. By 1909, there were reports that Frank Farrell had acquired land on Kingsbridge Road in the Spuyten Duyvil section of the Bronx for the construction of a new ballpark for the team.

The truism that in New York, everything ultimately comes down to real estate definitely applied to the Highlanders. The Institute for the Blind declined to renew the team's lease, making a move essential; by 1910, however, relations between the two leagues had warmed considerably, and the Giants made their large ballpark, the Polo Grounds, available for occasional Highlander games that were likely to attract more

Hilltop Park in Upper Manhattan, the original American League ballpark in New York, home to the New York Highlanders

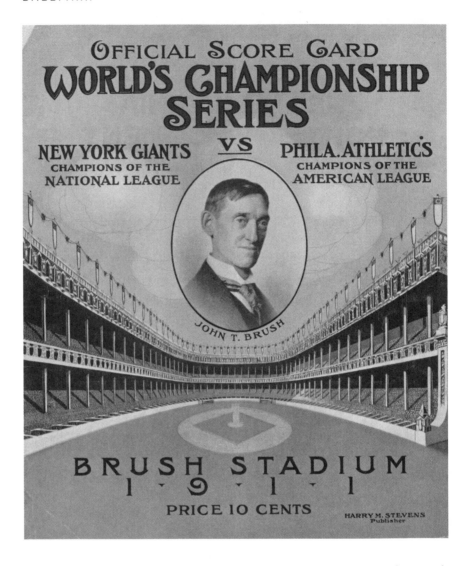

Official score card, World's Championship Series, New York Giants vs. Philadelphia Athletics, 1911. John Brush, owner of the Giants, tried to popularize Brush Stadium as a name for the Polo Grounds.

fans than could fit into Hilltop Park, which seated only sixteen thousand. When the Polo Grounds burned just before the 1911 season, the High-landers returned the favor by offering Hilltop Park to the Giants for their home games, and at the same time began site preparation for a new Highlanders Ballpark at 221st Street and Kingsbridge Road.

The Giants moved quickly to rebuild their ballpark, and a new Polo Grounds was ready by the middle of the 1911 season. John T. Brush made an effort to rename it for himself, and scorecards for the 1911 World Series, played between the Giants and the Philadelphia Athletics, list

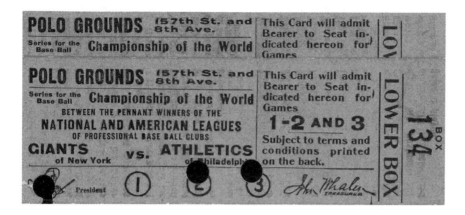

the venue as Brush Stadium. The name Polo Grounds, having already survived for more than two decades since the Giants actually played at a polo grounds, was too deeply ingrained in the team's culture to be abandoned, and Brush's attempt to change its name came to naught, surely not helped by the fact that Brush—perhaps the only real advocate of the name change—died just a year after the elaborately reconstructed Polo Grounds opened.

Brush did, however, manage to give the rebuilt park some hints of the fan-oriented luxury that he had provided in Cincinnati. The box seats in the upper deck had Italian marble, there was decorative iron scrollwork on the end seats of each row, and the park's semicircular grandstands were decorated with American eagles, wings outstretched, and with the coats of arms of National League cities. Brush's determination to market the Polo Grounds to prosperous fans led to an advertisement from the New York Telephone Company urging business executives to spend a day at the ballpark. "Instruct your office to call you at the Polo Grounds if you are needed," the ad said. "Then leave your name and seat number with the operator. If [you are] called on the telephone, a messenger will summon you."

The long, narrow shape of the field at the Polo Grounds, defined by the large semicircular grandstand around the infield, was often likened to a bathtub. The diamond was positioned at the center of the long, deep playing field, and its foul lines were short, 279 feet in left field and 257 in right field. By contrast, center field, 483 feet for most of the park's existence, was unusually deep.

Ticket to the World Series, 1911

The speed with which the Giants were able to reconstruct the Polo Grounds must have been frustrating to the Highlanders, whose real estate dramas seemed unending. The Kingsbridge Road site on which the team planned to build its new ballpark was on landfill over the former bed of the Spuyten Duyvil Creek, which had been straightened and joined to the Harlem River to create a more navigable waterway. It was a big enough site for a stadium and had ample mass transit connections, but these advantages were offset by engineering challenges that proved more daunting than the ones the team had faced a decade earlier at Hilltop Park. The old creek did not take well to being filled in, and the promised start of construction was delayed repeatedly as engineers tried to stop the flow of water into the site. Although the team revealed plans in the fall of 1911 for a steel and concrete stadium that would seat thirty-three thousand and would have direct connections to the subway, construction had not even started by the promised opening day in the spring of 1912. Later it was promised for 1913, and then 1914. Finally, in the fall of 1914, the team abandoned the project.*

The Highlanders played their last games at Hilltop Park in 1912, and in 1913 the team, continuing its recent tradition of mutual hospitality with the Giants, relocated to the Polo Grounds for what was expected to be a

Box seats at the pre-1914 Polo Grounds, occupied by Frank Farrell, owner of the New York Highlanders

* According to an unsigned posting in a blog entitled *The Second Division,* which is the most thorough source of information about the aborted plan to build a stadium in Kingsbridge, it was the creation of the short-lived Federal League that doomed the project, not the engineering challenges, which the writer believed had finally been surmounted by 1914. But the team's financial situation was not secure, and the added competition from the new league seemed to significantly enhance the risk of the building project for Farrell and Devery, denying the team an opportunity to build a ballpark that would have been a contemporary of Fenway Park, Ebbets Field, Wrigley Field, and the other important early ballparks of steel and concrete.

year or two until the stadium at Kingsbridge was ready. The site of Hilltop was sold and the stadium was demolished in 1914, only eleven years after its opening,* while the team, lacking another home field, would remain at the Polo Grounds for another decade. The move out of Hilltop Park was not the only thing the Highlanders would do in 1913 that would set a new direction for its future. The team also took on a new name that would become one of the most celebrated in all of sports: the New York Yankees.

* The site became the home of the Columbia University Medical Center and Columbia-Presbyterian Hospital. The precise location of Hilltop's home plate is marked by a small five-sided memorial plaque within a courtyard of the medical center, added in 1993.

The Polo Grounds was located adjacent to the Harlem River Speedway, a public road used primarily for equestrians and carriage drivers and left unpaved until 1922.

4

The Golden Age

I F 1894 WAS THE YEAR of fires that signaled the era of the wooden ballpark was nearing its end and 1909 the year that Shibe Park and Forbes Field suggested a blueprint for the future, then 1912 was the year when the first generation of steel and concrete ballparks fully hit its stride. On April 11 of that year, Redland Field in Cincinnati, later known as Crosley Field, opened on the site of the decade-old Palace of the Fans, the exuberant classical folly that had one of the shortest existences of any noteworthy twentieth-century ballpark. Nine days later, on April 20, two of the greatest ballparks ever built, Tiger Stadium and Fenway Park, opened at the same time, and their impact would be both broad and deep.

It was not an accident that there was a burst of ballpark construction in those years. Ban Johnson, the head of the American League, had made it his business to lobby team owners to build new facilities, eager for the greater seating capacity and improved sightlines that a steel and concrete ballpark could allow. Wooden ballparks were a thing of the past, Johnson argued in 1911, and said he expected that every city with a major league team would have an up-to-date ballpark with "well-kept fields of such dimensions that a fast runner may complete a circuit of the bases on a fair hit to their limits in any direction, and sited with mammoth fireproof stands, crowded to their capacity. . . . In another year—two more at the farthest—every scheduled game in the American League will be contested on grounds owned by the home club and provided with concrete and steel structures for the accommodations of the patrons."

Many owners hardly needed Johnson's campaign to be persuaded of the need to update and expand their facilities, of course, and there would be plenty of construction throughout the major leagues, not just in his American League. What was clear was that the age of wooden firetraps was over, as was the notion of a short-lived, quirky design experiment like Palace of the Fans. The steel and concrete parks of 1912 would last far longer, and have vastly more impact on the history of baseball: Crosley Field would remain the home of the Cincinnati Reds until 1970, and Tiger Stadium, originally called Navin Field and later Briggs Stadium, would house the Detroit Tigers for even longer, and would remain in active use until the end of the twentieth century. Fenway's reach is even greater still, since it continues in use well into the twenty-first century and there is no sign that its active life will ever come to an end. Discreetly renovated, it is now the oldest ballpark in major league baseball, and arguably the most beloved.*

The only ballparks that challenge Fenway in terms of its emotional impact, not to mention its intimate connections to the culture of its home city, are two that were built almost immediately after it: Ebbets Field, in Brooklyn, completed in 1913, and Wrigley Field, originally Weeghman Park, on the North Side of Chicago, which opened the following year, in 1914. Ebbets, almost as ambitious a work of architecture as Shibe Park in Philadelphia, was demolished in 1960, an act that in the annals of ballparks ranks with the destruction of Pennsylvania Station in New York as the devastating loss of an irreplaceable landmark. Wrigley, like Fenway, still goes on, significantly if respectfully renovated, the second-oldest major league ballpark in active use. If it was never as beautiful a structure as Ebbets Field, Wrigley Field's ongoing life vaults it, like Fenway, into the realm of the immortal ballparks. What Fenway, Ebbets, and Wrigley share is not so much an architectural sensibility—they were never the same in appearance—as an intimacy, since their different layouts all have the ability to make fans feel connected both to the

---

* See Chapter 11 for a fuller discussion of the renovation of Fenway after the Boston Red Sox abandoned a plan to replace it.

field and to each other. Not for nothing have writers tended to group the three parks together as baseball's great "jewel boxes." Yet the jewel boxes are not the entire story of the intense period of ballpark construction between 1912 and 1914. Taken together, the quintet of 1912–14—three lost ballparks, Tiger Stadium, Crosley Field, and Ebbets Field, and two extant ones, Fenway and Wrigley—if not quite so breathtaking as their immediate predecessors, Shibe Park and Forbes Field, still constituted a dazzling, two-year-long climax to the first golden age of ballpark design.

CROSLEY FIELD

It would be a stretch to think of Redland/Crosley Field as architecturally significant; its design, by Harry Hake, was less grandiose by far than the Palace of the Fans, even though it was larger and had the potential to be a more lucrative home for the team. As a piece of construction, Redland was a fully modern work of concrete and steel; as a piece of design, it was more of a hybrid. The main portion of the structure was a curving, boomerang-shaped, double-decked grandstand that gave the field a vaguely proto-modern air, all the more because it was the only one of the

A night game at Crosley Field in Cincinnati, the first ballpark to have nighttime baseball

1912 parks that was originally constructed with an upper deck as well as a lower one. But projecting out from the curving exterior was a traditional wing of brick, containing the team's administrative offices, looking almost like the leftover stub of an older structure around which the ballpark had been constructed. It had the virtue of blending in with the older brick factory buildings that had come to occupy the West End neighborhood at the corner of Findlay Street and Western Avenue, however, many of which would become perches for advertising signs visible to fans.

When the field was new, it had an exceptionally large outfield. The 360-foot distance to left field was the smallest dimension; right field was 385 feet, and center 420. The enormous field was not amenable to home runs, and in the winter of 1926–27 it was shortened, not by moving the fences in, but by moving home plate twenty feet toward the outfield. That allowed for the addition of roughly five thousand seats, mostly in new field boxes. Still, it was an odd way to solve the problem in that it pulled the game farther away from the grandstand, where most of the seats were, and it did not address what may have been Redland's most notable eccentricity, the incline in left field that began fifteen feet from the fence and rose four feet. It was known locally as the "terrace," a euphemism that seems intended to suggest that there was something intentional, not to say elegant, about an outfield on a slope that required outfielders to run slightly uphill to catch fly balls.

The Reds were the oldest fully professional team in baseball, but for all of their long and distinguished history, they floundered badly at the box office during the Depression years, and there was talk of the team abandoning Cincinnati and moving elsewhere. In 1934, the local industrialist Powel Crosley, Jr., who manufactured radios, refrigerators, and, for a time, automobiles, purchased the team to keep it in Cincinnati. The park was renamed Crosley Field, and altered further, with home plate once again moved toward the outfield. That was not sufficient to make the park home-run friendly, however, and at two different points in the 1940s and 1950s the team experimented with a screen in front of the expansive right field bleachers, which were called the Sun Deck for day games, and the Moon Deck at night. (There were no left field bleachers—the pattern of surrounding streets precluded them.)

Crosley brought in Larry MacPhail as general manager in 1934, and MacPhail, whom Lawrence Ritter described as "blustery, abrasive, brilliant, one of baseball's great innovators," staged the first night game in the major leagues on May 24, 1935, against the Philadelphia Phillies. The move was controversial. Many teams were reluctant to play under lights: this was, after all, a game of the outdoors, always played on grass under the sun. MacPhail was limited to seven night games that first season. To give the event some gravitas, the team invited President Franklin D. Roosevelt to throw a switch in the White House to turn on the new lights. At the appointed moment Roosevelt lit Crosley Field, night baseball was born, and the game was never quite the same again.

TIGER STADIUM

Tiger Stadium, originally called Navin Field after Frank Navin, the team owner who built it, and then Briggs Stadium after Walter Briggs, a later owner who expanded it, was built on the site of Bennett Park, a ballpark with a wooden grandstand and a peaked roof that the Detroit Tigers had opened with their first game in 1896. Bennett Park had the distinction of being one of the few wooden ballparks that did not burn down. It was demolished after Navin decided that his successful team, which had

View of Navin Field, the original version of Tiger Stadium

won three American League pennants in succession in 1907, 1908, and 1909, could support more fans than the fourteen thousand that could fit into Bennett's grandstands and bleachers. Like the Cincinnati Reds, but unlike most other teams that built new ballparks of steel and concrete, the Tigers did not seek new land to accommodate their new facility. Navin was content to keep the fans at the corner of Michigan and Trumbull in the Corktown neighborhood, just west of downtown, the only home grounds that the Tigers would have for more than a century.*

Navin did, however, expand the irregularly shaped site, acquiring neighboring row houses whose owners, like those in so many other cities, had constructed rooftop bleachers in the hope of siphoning off some fans and earning income for themselves. Navin demolished the houses and their so-called wildcat bleachers and then, with a more generous site to play with, rotated the diamond 90 degrees, placing the new field's home plate in what had been Bennett Park's left field.

Navin Field was never as architecturally ambitious as Shibe Park, as sophisticated as Forbes Field, or as willfully shaped as the Polo Grounds. Its most notable feature as a work of architecture was a casual, even almost ramshackle air, its exterior more like a large, rambling, somewhat irregularly shaped industrial structure. The design was one of the earliest efforts of the Osborn Engineering Company of Cleveland, a firm that had designed League Park in its home city in 1910 and would become a major force in ballpark design through the twentieth century, consistently producing workmanlike ballparks that tended to make up in amiable practicality what they lacked in flamboyance.

Not that Navin Field was without character. It was, John Pastier has written, "remarkably intimate, with upper-deck seats very close to the field," and after the park was expanded in stages from its original twenty-three thousand seats to an eventual fifty-three thousand, it had, Pastier observed, "many interesting anomalies such as an overhanging right-field upper deck, subtle structural shifts and jogs, and upper-deck walkways that projected out over the sidewalk. It was a textbook example

* If Bennett Park and Tiger Stadium are viewed as one site, if not as one field, the Tigers could be said to have played their home games in the same place for 104 years when they departed Tiger Stadium after the 1999 season, giving the team the longest unbroken run of any major league team in one location.

of adaptive and pragmatic design, and its accretions gave it convincing character." Tiger Stadium, Pastier concluded, "may have been the most underrated of the classic parks."

"Accretions" is an apt word, since Tiger Stadium grew in fits and starts, more opportunistically than in response to any aesthetic vision. The intermediate stages, irrelevant in the case of many ballparks, are worth recounting here. There was the original version in 1912, with only a single-deck grandstand wrapping around the infield, separate and slightly disconnected grandstand sections reaching toward the right and left field corners, and a bleacher section in right center field. In 1923, the main portion of the grandstand wrapping around the infield was given an upper deck. In 1934, the year the Tigers won the American League pennant for the first time since 1909, the empty left field fence was replaced with a large, temporary bleacher section. Two years later, in 1936, the new left field bleachers were removed and replaced with an extension of the two-story grandstand along the left field side of the ballpark. Two years after that, when the city of Detroit agreed to close Cherry Street on the left field side of the stadium, the grandstand was extended all the way to left center field, totally enclosing the stadium.

Aerial view of Tiger Stadium from 1935

Tiger Stadium also had an exceptional bleacher section, which had upper and lower decks, the only double-decker bleacher area in baseball. An enormous bleacher section made sense in a manufacturing city in which blue-collar workers made up much of the fan base, but Tiger Stadium's bleachers were in many ways a throwback to the early years of wooden ballparks when rigid economic segregation was the order of the day. The section had a separate entrance, concession stands, and restrooms, and for a time was cut off from the rest of the stadium by barbed wire fencing to prevent its occupants from mixing with the holders of more expensive seats.

The final form of Tiger Stadium—or Briggs Stadium, as it was called from 1938, when Walter Briggs took ownership of the team, to 1961—showed the same irregular quality as the construction process. The diamond, for reasons that have never been explained, was rotated roughly 4 degrees off from the grandstand, so the foul lines were not parallel to the front edge of the grandstand, as in most ballparks. There was a 125-foot-tall flagpole at the far end of center field, 440 feet away from home plate but still technically in the field of play. And then there was the overhanging upper deck in right field, which was constructed in the 1930s among the early expansions that went on during the Briggs era. It did at least have a clear reason for being, namely the closeness of the stadium to Trumbull Avenue, which ran along right field. There was no room to erect a grandstand of optimal depth without cutting too deeply into the playing field, so when the stadium was expanded, the lower deck remained relatively shallow. But the upper deck was extended roughly ten feet over the lower deck, since that did not, at least technically, compromise the playing field. It did create some spectacular upper-deck seating, with fans in the front rows all but suspended over the outfield. Their pleasures came at the expense of the fans below, since the projection of the upper deck made for numerous supporting columns and an extended roof limiting views from the lower deck. Even relatively close to the front the experience for almost everyone in the right field lower deck was like being under the balcony in the rear of a theater, where the seats had views only straight ahead and not upward.

Some of the stadium's physical quirks, like the fact that the added upper deck did not extend as far back as the lower deck beneath it, giving the façade facing Trumbull Street an uneven configuration, had no impact on the game, and merely added to the somewhat improvisational air of Tiger Stadium's exterior. The overhang, however, had the potential to affect the game considerably under certain circumstances. With the upper deck ten feet closer to the batter than the lower deck, a high fly ball that normally would have been easily caught could, instead, land on the upper deck and be scored as a home run, even though it might have been hit a shorter distance than a line drive that went below the upper deck and could be caught to cause an out. For many years, there were two separate distance markings at the right field foul pole: 315 feet at the upper deck, and 325 feet at the lower. There are no records as to how many home runs may have been scored over the years by left-handed batters who hit ordinary fly balls into the upper deck. But there were surely many, and it was beyond a doubt that Tiger Stadium's eccentricity favored certain kinds of batters over others.

FENWAY PARK

Fenway Park was no more an object of beauty than Tiger Stadium: it was an urban ballpark, through and through, a workaday park that never had the aspirations of grandeur that drove the designs of Shibe Park or Forbes Field. That it would become a cherished icon was less a result of Fenway's architecture than its benign quirkiness, its remarkable and rich history, and its evolution after a 1934 renovation into a place that possessed two unique elements: the "Green Monster" wall in left field and the soft, surprisingly deep paint color, a kind of somber grayish green, at once warm and aloof, that washes over almost every surface of its interior.

John Updike famously called Fenway "a lyric little bandbox of a ballpark," adding, "Everything is painted green and seems in curiously sharp focus, like the inside of an old-fashioned peeping-type Easter egg."* Yet the park would probably not have moved Updike to such rapture in its

---

* Updike's lines about Fenway appeared in his piece about Ted Williams's final game, "Hub Fans Bid Kid Adieu," in *The New Yorker* of October 22, 1960. It is one of the most admired short pieces on baseball ever written, and the description of Fenway is among the most famous ever written about any ballpark. Updike's words are painted on the wall of the Red Sox headquarters inside Fenway Park.

original state, since most of Fenway's most prized elements were not there when it opened in 1912. It was built by John Taylor, whose family owned the Red Sox and had numerous other Boston business interests, including *The Boston Globe* and substantial real estate in the neighborhood of the Fens, the old marshes beside the Charles River that had been filled in with the expectation that they would be converted into profitable parcels for development. Another portion of the area had already developed into a cultural center, with a new home for the Museum of Fine Arts as well as Isabella Stewart Gardner's villa, which in time became one of Boston's most fabled museums; both buildings faced the park designed by Frederick Law Olmsted that was the area's centerpiece.

The portion of the region closest to Kenmore Square had no such symbols of refinement. It was on the other side of the park from the cultural institutions, and it was the last sector of the area to develop. The Taylors were not indifferent to giving it a boost. Locating a new ballpark there was an easy way to put a substantial chunk of the unused land to productive use, and naming it Fenway would connect it in Bostonians' minds to the elegant park and cultural center that were reasonably close by, if not really in the same neighborhood, and would remind everyone that this was the direction in which the city's development was headed.

It would serve another use for Taylor, who intended to sell a majority interest in the team. He did not own the land beneath the Huntington Avenue Grounds, where the Red Sox had played since 1901; in fact the annual rent he paid to its owner, the Boston Elevated Company, was so substantial that in some years, Glenn Stout speculated, the company may have made as much money off the Red Sox as the Taylors did. Huntington Avenue's small grandstand seated only 2,500, and the team's lease was due to expire. It made no sense to renew it, Taylor decided, and instead came up with a plan to build a new ballpark himself, sell an interest in the team, and earn the certain profits of a landlord rather than the uncertain ones of a team owner. Taylor realized that if he could package the team with a lease for a new ballpark he would have a far more valuable enterprise, and, better still, he and his family could use the revenues from the sale of an interest in the team to finance the ballpark themselves, without having to use any borrowed money. "That meant that even after they sold the team they would still participate in any increase in profits, as well as pay rent to themselves and receive an annual payment for the park from a new investor. There was virtually no way they could lose money on the deal," Glenn Stout has written.

In June 1911 Taylor announced his intention to build a new ballpark on an eight-acre parcel of land that his father, General Charles Taylor, had acquired four months earlier for $120,000 at a public auction. Bounded by Lansdowne Street on the north, Ipswich Street on the east, and Jersey Street on the west, the parcel was close to other real estate the Taylor family owned. They formed the Fenway Realty Company to market their other holdings—not for nothing did the ballpark carry the same name as the family real estate enterprise—and the plan to use the promised ballpark as a form of promotion was so successful that by September 15 they were able to announce the sale of a half interest in the Red Sox to James McAleer, a Ban Johnson crony who had been managing teams in Washington and Cleveland, and Robert McRoy of Chicago, another Johnson loyalist, for $150,000, $15,000 more than the Taylors had paid for the entire team seven years before. Fenway Park had barely broken ground, but Taylor had already managed to use it to more than double the value of the team and fund much of the ballpark's construction.

The Taylors hired James McLaughlin, a thirty-seven-year-old local architect who had never designed a ballpark (and never would again), to draw up plans. His buildings, Glenn Stout has written, were "essentially utilitarian [but] at the same time . . . were precise, balanced, aesthetically pleasing and built to last." He had already gained a certain reputation for designing schools and other public buildings in Boston, and he was known to favor brick. He was in almost every way an average architect of his time—a professional, an active member of his community, and a man who saw architecture as a matter of meeting functional challenges in an aesthetically pleasing but not intellectually challenging way. If he knew of Frank Lloyd Wright and other modernist architects who were beginning to challenge traditional ways of designing buildings, he probably did not agree with them. By all accounts McLaughlin did not have any interest in rethinking architecture, and he did not seek to design monuments that would be remembered for the ages.

That at Fenway he would be responsible for something that would indeed be remembered for the ages was the result of factors that had little to do with McLaughlin's design ideas. The most important contribution McLaughlin made to Fenway Park was the brick façade facing

Jersey Street.* It is a lovely piece of design, with some surprisingly elegant detailing that suggests the Arts and Crafts style of Gustav Stickley, but it is low-key, never grandiose, and it is as notable for its comfortable, old-fashioned quality and for the ease with which it blends into its urban streetscape as for any of the particular design elements McLaughlin brought to it. The brick façade feels neither too plain nor too fancy; McLaughlin, to his credit, navigated skillfully between the excessively utilitarian stance that marked Tiger Stadium and the Renaissance extravaganza represented by Shibe Park.

McLaughlin's façade is almost like a small brick building slipped into the side of the grandstands; unlike Shibe Park, Ebbets Field, and many other ballparks, Fenway never had a grand entry directly behind home plate. Another thing that it lacked, at least for several decades, was an upper deck. Taylor vacillated about whether to build a single- or a double-decked grandstand, concerned that the cost of constructing an upper level would not be justified by additional ticket sales. He ultimately compromised by building a single deck and having McLaughlin design foundations that could support the eventual addition of an upper deck. It would not be until 1946 that the upper deck would finally be built, although there would be numerous changes to the seating layout before then, including the addition of 11,600 seats, mainly in new right field bleacher sections, in September 1912 to allow for expanded crowds when the Red Sox ended their first Fenway season in the World Series.

The first season was an extraordinary debut. For all of Fenway's modesty as a work of architecture, it attracted crowds from the beginning: the opening game on April 20, 1912, postponed three times due to bad weather and played when the nation was still absorbing the shocking news of the sinking of the *Titanic* just a few days before, was still a sellout, and the crowd of more than twenty-four thousand, many of whom took

---

* This was the ballpark, and the team's, official address. The section of Jersey Street facing the ballpark was renamed Yawkey Way in 1977 in honor of Tom Yawkey, who owned the Red Sox from 1933 to 1976. In 2018 the city of Boston changed the name back to Jersey Street in response to the widely held belief that Yawkey was a racist who did not deserve the honor of having an official city street named for him. Under Yawkey's ownership the Red Sox were the last major league team to integrate. They did not field a black player until 1959, twelve years after the Dodgers hired Jackie Robinson. The address of Fenway Park, once 4 Yawkey Way, is now 4 Jersey Street.

advantage of the fact that the new park was easily accessible via the city's streetcar system, saw Boston edge out a 7–6 win over New York, already an established rival. The park had gone up in just four and a half months of construction time at a cost of $600,000, which broke down to $24 per seat. More remarkably, the speedy construction would be repeated just a few months after the opening, when the new owners decided that the ballpark was too small, and called back James McLaughlin, the architect, and asked him to design additional seating. The Red Sox were doing so well that a World Series appearance was looking likely, and McLaughlin increased the capacity of Fenway by nearly 50 percent. He filled in the open space in right field with additional bleachers, extended the grandstand area to the left field wall, added bleachers in the outfield along Lansdowne Street, and squeezed in a number of extra rows elsewhere in the ballpark to increase its capacity to 36,100 in time for the series.

Fenway's brick façade, ca. 1915

The somewhat ad hoc nature of Fenway's expansions, while hardly unique in baseball, would give the park an even more chopped-up feeling

than many ballparks. While A. Bartlett Giamatti could refer to his boy-hood visits to Fenway by saying that "I knew that as a building [Fenway] was on the level of Mount Olympus, the Pyramid at Giza, the Capitol, the Czar's Winter Palace, and the Louvre—except, of course, that it was better than all those inconsequential places," the reality was that Fenway was the opposite of a grandiose work of civic design intended to make a monumental statement. But its very casualness, its unevenness, would come in time to represent not discordancy but charm. It would inspire not only Giamatti's hyperbole and Updike's ode but observations like that of Martin F. Nolan, the longtime political reporter for *The Boston Globe,* who called Fenway "a crazy-quilt violation of city planning prin-ciples, an irregular pile of architecture, a menace to marketing consul-tants. . . . It works as a symbol of New England's pride, as a repository of evergreen hopes, as a tabernacle of lost innocence. It works as a place to watch baseball."

However informal Fenway's appearance was, its design was hardly ran-dom, and the uneven, oddly shaped building plot meant that James

Fenway bleachers, in preparation for the 1912 World Series

McLaughlin had to solve a number of notable planning and organizational problems, made even more challenging by the fact that the original parcel did not include a couple of small corner plots. The site the Taylors had acquired was ample, but not expansive, certainly not when compared to Redland Field in Cincinnati or the Polo Grounds in New York. But neither was it excessively cramped, particularly for the dead-ball era, as baseball historians called the first two decades of the twentieth century, when the balls in common use did not respond as energetically as would later ones to the impact of the bat, and were often dulled further from overuse.* The age of the power hitter had not yet begun, and home runs and high-scoring games were comparatively rare. Relatively close-in fences at least increased the modest chance that a ball would be hit out of the park.

The uneven shape of Fenway's outfields was not just the inevitable product of the pattern of streets surrounding the park but was also the result of conscious design decisions, primarily the preference to give the playing field the same orientation to the sun as at Huntington Avenue Grounds, Glenn Stout has written. A symmetrical field with that same orientation could have been created but would have ended up being even tighter, given the uneven shape of the ballpark's plot. McLaughlin produced an asymmetrical park out of a desire to maximize the use of the Taylors' trapezoidal site.

And thus was Fenway's tight left field, which eventually gave birth to the Green Monster, born. It began as a small wooden wall, largely to keep the field enclosed on the Lansdowne Street side, where the road ran so close to the outfield that there was no room for a grandstand, or even a full complement of bleachers. When the park was new several rows of bleachers were shoehorned in front of the wall, even though the main function of the wall seemed to be to serve as a billboard for advertising that could be seen from the rest of the ballpark. There was also a slight rise in the field itself; the 15-degree incline to the left field wall became known as Duffy's Cliff, after the Red Sox left fielder George "Duffy" Lewis.

---

* In those years, mainly as a cost-saving measure, balls were reused until they were badly worn, which was why fans were required to throw back balls hit into the stands.

The bleachers burned in a small fire in 1926 and were never replaced.*
By the 1930s, Fenway Park was in poor condition, and Tom Yawkey, who
purchased the team in 1933, embarked on a major program to upgrade
the place, replacing wooden seats with steel and concrete ones, and taking down the original 25-foot-high wooden wall and replacing it with a
37-foot-high metal one.† The 1934 renovation—which was interrupted
by a substantial fire, after which Yawkey was widely admired for increasing the number of construction workers on the job to guarantee that he
would meet his promise to have the park ready for the 1934 season—
was, for all intents and purposes, a reconstruction. Other than the brick
façade, relatively little of James McLaughlin's original park remained visible, though the underlying structure was intact. But it was Yawkey's
renovation, carried out by the Osborn Engineering Company, that
established much of the classic image of Fenway, including the "Dart-
mouth Green" paint covering much of the ballpark's interior facing the
field,‡ which, beyond suggesting a connection to nature and the grass
of the field—returning, it could be said, to the *rus in urbe* dreams of
the nineteenth century—also had the advantage of smoothing over the
many rough spots of a ballpark that had grown randomly over the years
and had no discernible pattern to its design. The color knitted the place
together and made it seem not ramshackle, but whole and intentional.

Michael Ian Borer has observed that the nostalgia that was to envelop
Fenway in later years—a nostalgia that the ubiquitous green paint played
a share in creating—was nowhere apparent during the early years of the
Depression, when Yawkey bought the team. The park was a mere two
decades old, but it had not been well maintained and was already looking tired and rundown. The absence of an upper deck made it seem even
more old-fashioned than it was. "There were no impassioned pleas for

---

* Seats were added to the top of the wall in 2003, and became so popular that they were restricted to single-game sales rather than sold as season tickets, with buyers chosen by lottery.
See Chapter 11.

† The wall was not painted green until 1947, when the advertisements were removed. The
nickname "Green Monster" did not become common until the 1950s.

‡ The formula behind the precise shade of Fenway Park's green paint, a deep, rich color with
neither the brightness of Kelly green nor the darkness of forest green, is proprietary to the
Red Sox, although a consumer version of it is available from Benjamin Moore.

Fenway Park's preservation before Yawkey's reconstruction project got under way during the blustery winter of 1934," Borer has written. "No one waxed poetic about the aura, magic, or authenticity of the dilapidated and decaying ballpark. There were no campaigns to 'save' the ballpark, no nostalgic memoirs, and no public laments."

EBBETS FIELD

If Fenway Park was built by owners who saw it as a way of turning their ownership of a baseball team into what today would be called a real estate play, Ebbets Field was the product of an owner who wanted to memorialize himself and his team, in that order. Charles Ebbets, a New Yorker with an energetic entrepreneurial streak, had started as an employee of the team and obtained some stock in 1890 when he was thirty-one. By 1898, when he was not quite forty, he had both been elected to the New York

Ebbets Field, Brooklyn

City Council and obtained effective control of the team. That was also the year that Brooklyn gave up its status as an independent city and merged with New York City, and its major league baseball team became, at least symbolically, all the more important as one of the few remaining elements of Brooklyn's civic identity. The team, officially incorporated as the Brooklyn Baseball Club, had been known at various times as the Superbas, the Robins, the Grays, and the Bridegrooms (the last when seven of its members were married in the same year), and when the team moved in 1891 from Washington Park in South Brooklyn to Eastern Park in the developing East New York section, hard by some streetcar tracks, it added another nickname to the list, one that would imprint into baseball history the connection between baseball and the city: the Trolley Dodgers.

That name would stick, at least in shortened form, when all the others faded into history, although it would not become official and appear on the team's uniforms until 1932; until then, their jerseys contained just a single word, "Brooklyn." Ebbets was not a fan of the Eastern Park location, which had been chosen, Michael Benson has written, because one of the team's stockholders owned land in East New York and, like the Taylors at Fenway Park, thought the presence of baseball would be a good way to promote it. Eastern Park cost the team $7,500 in annual rent, and despite the presence of nearby streetcars, the outlying neighborhood was a long distance for many fans to travel. In 1898, as soon as he became president of the team, Ebbets organized a move back to a new Washington Park, much closer to the center of population in Brooklyn, where he managed to get backing from two streetcar companies to build a new, expanded wooden grandstand on a site adjacent to the old Washington Park. It was still far from ideal—there was seating for only 18,800, and the stench from nearby factories and the putrid Gowanus Canal regularly wafted into the ballpark. Even though the team was not playing well and did not finish in the first division after 1902, Brooklyn was full of loyal fans, and especially when the team played their arch rivals from Manhattan, the New York Giants, the ballpark was often overcrowded. It was clear that the current park was not a long-term solution and that there would be a need for further upgrades.

After considering a major reconstruction, Ebbets decided to look elsewhere to build the larger, more modern ballpark he craved. Beginning in 1908, he started to purchase land at the edge of Crown Heights on the far side of Prospect Park, in an area known as Crow Hill or, more col-

Charles Ebbets

loquially, as Pigtown. It was no more elegant than Gowanus—it was actually something of a garbage dump—but it would turn out to be a wise choice. While it was farther from Brooklyn's population center than Washington Park, it was more convenient than East New York. The site—bordered by Franklin Avenue, Bedford Avenue, Sullivan Place, and Montgomery Street—was served by multiple streetcar lines, and would eventually be reachable on two different subway lines as well. And it was within blocks of the new Brooklyn Botanic Garden, a former ash dump being redesigned by the Olmsted Brothers, the eminent landscape architects.

This was clearly a rising neighborhood, and Ebbets, with limited funds and a wariness of being taken advantage of by local landowners, craftily purchased forty separate parcels of land through various dummy corporations, hiding his identity and his intentions from the sellers. The process took several years, and Ebbets, a colorful figure not known for his reticence—when he addressed a banquet of baseball owners at the Waldorf-Astoria in Manhattan in December 1909, he told them that for all the explosive growth that the sport had experienced in the previous decades, "baseball is in its infancy"—he revealed not a hint about the plan that was already under way. By then Shibe Park and Forbes Field had opened, Comiskey Park was in construction, and the age of steel and concrete ballparks had clearly begun. But Ebbets had not yet finished assembling his site, and he was still two years away from making any announcement about his intentions. By 1911, he had squeezed his budget of $200,000 for land acquisition and hadn't yet assembled all of the pieces.*

---

* Michael Gershman, in *Diamonds,* writes that Ebbets had already exhausted his budget for land acquisition. Bob McGee in *The Greatest Ballpark Ever* writes that Ebbets had spent somewhat less than $200,000 when his land assemblage was nearly complete. It is clear, however, that Ebbets's finances were tight.

Later, Ebbets would end up selling a half interest in the team to Ed and Steve McKeever, brothers who were prominent Brooklyn building contractors, for $100,000. Unlike the Taylors in Boston, who sold off part of their team in a financial transaction intended to allow them to withdraw from day-to-day management of the team and function primarily as landlords, Ebbets was simply overextended and in need of money. His ambitions were grander than the Taylors', and his resources more limited. In a way, his deal turned out to be the opposite of what the Taylors had done in Boston, since his arrangement with the McKeevers called for him to continue as the primary operating executive of the ball club. A separate company, the Ebbets-McKeever Exhibition Company, was set up to construct, own, and manage the ballpark. The field would carry Charles Ebbets's name, but the McKeevers would be the money behind it.

Like the Bostonians, Ebbets turned for design advice to a young architect who was rooted in the community, but had no experience designing ballparks. Thirty-eight-year-old Clarence Randall Van Buskirk had a well-established architecture practice in Brooklyn, and that was apparently enough for Ebbets, who took him to see other ballparks so that they could shape a vision for the new field together. Ebbets clearly counted on Van Buskirk not only for design expertise, but for discretion. When he first retained the architect, the plan to build a new park was still not public. Ebbets explained to his architect only that he wanted a new and expanded ballpark, and did not tell him at first whether he would be designing for the site of the existing field at Washington Park, or for some other location.

Ebbets presumably figured out—or Van Buskirk told him—that an architect cannot create a meaningful design without knowing where it is to go, and soon enough, Ebbets decided that he would have to trust Van Buskirk enough to explain that he wanted to build his new ballpark on a site in Crown Heights that he was still in the process of assembling. The architect became part of a very small circle that actually knew what Ebbets was planning. According to Bob McGee, Van Buskirk would sometimes arrive at the team offices with plans hidden inside his suit jacket to assure that no one could catch a glimpse of what he was working on until he was behind closed doors and seated at Ebbets's desk.

The secret apparently held until the evening of January 2, 1912, when Ebbets, with his characteristic flair for drama, decided to announce his plans at a banquet for baseball luminaries and journalists at the Brooklyn

Club. In the presence of Grantland Rice and Damon Runyon, among others, Ebbets gave a talk that began by conceding the problems his team was having on the field.

"Brooklyn has supported a losing team better than any other city on earth," he said. "No place has such loyal and cheerful fans, and no one realizes it more thoroughly than myself. Such a patronage deserves every convenience and comfort that can be provided at a baseball park, and that is what I hope to provide. It is a plain case of expressing my appreciation to those who have stuck by me even when the outlook was at its worst."

And he went on to reveal Van Buskirk's designs for the "Proposed New Grand Stand for the Brooklyn Base Ball Club," which was for a site that took virtually everyone by surprise. The *Brooklyn Citizen* had predicted that Ebbets was about to announce a new park on the site of the old Washington Park, and there had been speculation about other sites all over Brooklyn. But as William Granger wrote in the *Citizen,* "the location had been so well concealed that [of] all of the guesses made as to the location of the new park not one was even close." The Crown Heights area Ebbets had chosen had barely begun to develop, and when Ebbets broke ground on March 4, 1912, there was almost nothing else in the immediate vicinity of his site save for "a couple of shacks and rough terrain, rutted gullies, small hills, cow paths, and goat trails," according to Bob McGee.

As Van Buskirk's design for Ebbets Field evolved, it became clear how important the actual location was: it is among the most site-specific of all ballparks, its irregular shape precisely filling out the uneven block created by the four surrounding streets—all mapped but some not yet paved— which did not all meet at right angles. It is hard not to think that both Ebbets and Van Buskirk were taken with Shibe Park in Philadelphia, even though Shibe's plot was more regular, since, like Shibe, Ebbets Field is oriented around an urban corner, which it addresses with a monumental gesture of civic architecture that surely seemed, if nothing else, an act of optimism when there was not yet an urban context to address. But it would come, and as the Brooklyn borough president Alfred E. Steers told the crowd at the groundbreaking, "In my mind this huge ball field will do much toward developing this section of Brooklyn. Already the trolley, elevated and subway line owners are getting in touch with the situation and are planning to have better transit facilities. By the time the stadium is built, there will be a big change in the transit situation. Just wait and see when the Superbas"—the nickname by which the team was then most commonly known—"start playing in their new park."

Steers went on to celebrate baseball in tones worthy of Albert Spalding. "A man who is not interested in baseball is not a human man," he said. "Something is wrong with him. We cannot have too much baseball in these strenuous business days. Out of the offices, the factories and the stores there come into the sunshine and open air thousands and thousands of our citizens. It is a great sport, a clean sport, a healthy sport and an honest sport. . . . I tell you what I want to see, and that is for Brooklyn to proudly take her place at the top of the baseball world, as she did when I was a boy and used to peek through holes in the fence. And I think Mr. Ebbets will give us the best team in the country, and it will play right here in this park."

Steers's oration, for all its hyperbole, did underscore the deep connection between Brooklyn and baseball, and the extent to which the borough's identity was tied to its major league team, the descendant of the many local teams that had helped build popular interest in baseball decades before. It did feel to Brooklyn that all of the emotion, all of the energy, and all of the history of Union Grounds, Capitoline Grounds, and Washington Park was somehow being funneled into this new project; even though Brooklyn's other fields would remain, the borough conferred a symbolic importance on Ebbets from the beginning as the culmination of Brooklyn's rich baseball history. Fenway Park earned iconic status gradually, over many generations; Ebbets Field was born with it.

For all that Van Buskirk was clearly influenced by Shibe Park, Ebbets was not as ornate as Shibe. No ballpark's exterior would be; in place of Shibe's lush French Renaissance ornament, Ebbets offered a flatter façade, decorated with arches and pilasters and large, Federal-style double-hung windows with multiple square panes. There were concrete gargoyles, and bas-relief medallions of baseballs, showing a degree of wit that was absent from the more palatial Shibe. Indeed, if Van Buskirk's well-crafted, carefully wrought façade resembled anything, it was a cross between a civic building and a handsome, turn-of-the-century factory building. In this factory, the ornamental detail made it clear that the product was baseball. The rounded corner entrance, topped by team offices, was similar in con-

*Entrance to the rotunda
at Ebbets, 1914*

cept to the one at Shibe, but Van Buskirk's was actually more expansive than the one in Philadelphia, and included a grand rotunda inside the round front door, a formal vestibule for the ballpark that surpassed what was beneath Shibe's elegant cupola.

The rotunda was eighty feet in diameter, twenty-seven feet high at its center, and punctuated by a chandelier crafted out of facsimiles of baseball bats with illuminated globes in the form of glass baseballs. The room would have a mosaic tile floor patterned with the stitches of a baseball, and Italian marble columns. *The New York Times,* noting that the new ballpark was expected to cost $750,000, said it would "rank with the best parks in the country," and other press praised Ebbets for choosing a site that would be so accessible by public transportation.

Ebbets had at one point promised that the ballpark would be ready by the middle of the 1912 season, an optimistic schedule given that construction did not even start until March 4. He did not meet the goal of completion by mid-season, or even the end of the season, and the schedule was not helped by his recurring cash shortages. It was only after the deal was made with the McKeevers that he was able to speed up construction and have the park ready in time for the start of the 1913 season. But nothing stopped Ebbets from indulging in his fondness for pageantry. He held an elaborate cornerstone-laying ceremony on the morning of July 6, 1912, when he once again brought out the borough president, who this time called the ballpark "this great monument to baseball, to Brooklyn, and to New York City." More original, and certainly more relevant to working-class Brooklyn's close relationship to the team, were the remarks of the Reverend James M. Farrar, who told the crowd that "the bleachers alone define pure democracy. . . . Mr. Ebbets has done a great work for Brooklyn and for baseball." After the cornerstone had been laid, Ebbets took his guests to the Consumers Park restaurant nearby, and then on to Washington Park, where they watched the Superbas lose to the Giants.

Ebbets Field finally opened on April 5, 1913, with an exhibition game against the Yankees. This time Brooklyn won, if only by a single run, and the *Brooklyn Eagle* could only respond with joy. "Rejoice, ye Brooklyn fans," the paper exulted, "and deliver thanks, for our own Superbas fittingly dedicated Charles Hercules* Ebbets' magnificent stadium, the greatest ball park in these United States, by soundly trouncing Frank Chance's Yankees yesterday afternoon to the merry tune of 3 to 2 in the presence of 25,000 wildly enthusiastic rooters who jammed every available inch of space in this immense stadium—the greatest outpouring of baseball fanatics that ever turned out to witness an exhibition game."

Such hyperbole would prove to be standard so far as reporting about Brooklyn, its team, and its ballpark were concerned. The team was colorful but not always high-functioning, and the same could be said about Ebbets Field itself. The corner rotunda, conceived as an elegant means of entry, turned out to be such a bottleneck that additional gates had to be installed on either side of it under the grandstands. Somehow neither Van Buskirk nor Ebbets realized that funneling thousands of people through a single room was not the most practical means of getting them in and

---

* Ebbets's real middle name was Henry, but his accomplishments as a young man earned him the nickname of Hercules, which, like the nickname of his team, eventually stuck.

out, especially since the twelve gilded ticket windows were all inside the rotunda so that fans queuing up to buy tickets blocked those who already had tickets from getting in. The first regular season game had been played in bad weather and did not attract a sellout crowd, but when the Giants came to Brooklyn to play a weekend game on April 26, forty thousand fans tried to gain admission, and the result, according to Bob McGee, was a "near riot."

Van Buskirk was clearly better at façade design and ornamentation than at planning—he had included only twelve turnstiles—and he also neglected to include a press box, an omission that, curiously, Ebbets appears not to have noticed or been troubled by; it would not be added to the stadium until 1929. A mistake corrected much more quickly was what was advertised as a "megaphone device," a primitive microphone that was intended to broadcast the home plate umpire's calls. Unfortunately it projected not just balls and strikes but a lot of more colorful language from batters and catchers, and for the sake of decorum this experiment in advanced technology was quickly abandoned. More lasting elements of Ebbets Field's character, surely, were the colorful billboards that decorated much of the outfield, such as haberdasher Abe Stark's HIT SIGN WIN SUIT advertisement, thirty feet long but only three feet high;* Tanglefoot flypaper's billboard announcing that its product had caught 50,000,000,000 flies; and Schaefer Beer, whose *h* lit up when there was a hit, and whose first *e* was illuminated to denote an error.

Crowds of people lining up to watch a baseball game at Ebbets Field

---

* According to Philip J. Lowry in *Green Cathedrals,* the sign was hit only once, by Woody English of the Dodgers, on June 6, 1937. In *The Greatest Ballpark Ever,* Bob McGee claims that English hit the sign three times, and that Johnny Hudson, an infielder who was on the team between 1937 and 1940, hit the sign three times as well.

Where the ballpark also succeeded was in spurring development in the neighborhood around it, although the area's growth was undoubtedly due even more to the arrival of new subway lines, historically a key impetus to new construction in New York neighborhoods in the early decades of the twentieth century. But the combination of subways and a ballpark was potent, and by 1916, Bob McGee reported, block after block of row houses were going up in almost all of the surrounding area, as construction filled Crown and Carroll Streets, President Street, Sterling Street, Lefferts Avenue, and Lincoln Road. Ebbets may have purchased an old garbage dump, but within three years he had a ballpark situated in a largely built-up neighborhood. Frank Graham, in *The Brooklyn Dodgers: An Informal History,* reported that many players lived in the new housing being built near the ballpark, enhancing the sense of intimate connection between the team and its Brooklyn neighborhood. Players and their wives "were reportedly often seen pushing their baby carriages on surrounding streets or in Prospect Park."

· · ·

Haberdasher Abe Stark's famous advertisement, HIT SIGN WIN SUIT, *seen here (at bottom of scoreboard) at the 1955 World Series between the Brooklyn Dodgers and the New York Yankees*

And so Ebbets Field went on, an extraordinary balance between the grand and the quirky. Once the nickname of the Dodgers became official, the team's most frequent moniker was "da Bums," based on the Brooklyn Bum created by the *World-Telegram* cartoonist Willard Mullin in 1937. At around the same time, the Brooklyn Dodgers Band, which became known as the Sym-Phony, set itself up in the stands when a group of musicians from Williamsburg managed to sneak musical instruments into the park. Eventually the zany band, which included a tuba, snare drum, bass drum, a trombone, and a trumpet, obtained regular seats in Section 8, Row A, and its off-key mock performances became an Ebbets staple. So was the cowbell rung by Hilda Chester, who called herself "Mother of the Dodgers," and sat in the center field bleachers.

The playing field itself might seem almost like an afterthought, given that Ebbets Field was a state of mind as much as a place for baseball. The shape of the field was a bit eccentric, although not more so than that of many of its peer ballparks. Ebbets did have an unusually small foul terri-

Dodgers fans roar, in this 1951 photo from the Brooklyn Eagle.

tory, putting many balls out of play that would have been caught in other parks, and a fairly short right field at 301 feet; left field was 419 feet, and center stretched to 450. What really made Ebbets's right field notable, however, was not its short distance but the concave walls on its fence that would often cause balls to bounce up at odd angles. Like most ballparks, Ebbets was altered frequently, including a substantial reconstruction in 1931 under the direction of the McKeevers that added roughly six thousand seats in a new double-decked grandstand extending from behind third base out into left field, bringing the capacity to thirty-one thousand. It was designed not by Clarence Van Buskirk, who had abandoned his practice and left Brooklyn for Michigan in 1914 after his wife sued him for divorce, but by Otto C. Poderwils, an architect from Queens.

Out of all of this came baseball, sometimes great, sometimes mediocre, but almost always endearing. Charles Ebbets possessed both Chris Von der Ahe's showmanship and Albert Spalding's view of baseball as an exalted pastime. Ebbets was crowd-pleasing and high-minded both. He built himself a sumptuous office atop the ornate entry rotunda, but he was more often found in seats at the edge of the field, where he would hold court amid Brooklyn fans. Ebbets presided over his namesake park for only a dozen years—he died in 1925—but the tone he set remained in the field that would forever bear his name.

WRIGLEY FIELD

In the beginning it was not Wrigley Field, and it was not even for the Chicago Cubs. The ballpark at the corner of Clark and Addison on the North Side of Chicago was erected by Charles Weeghman, a self-made restaurateur who loved baseball, saw it as a means of promotion for his businesses, and actively supported the Federal League, a short-lived attempt to challenge the hegemony of the American and National Leagues.

Weeghman owned the Chicago Whales, a team that, like the seven other Federal League clubs, had been formed by luring established players away from existing teams with the promise of higher salaries. This strategy allowed the Federal League to pose a more serious threat to baseball's existing league system than many other "outlaw leagues" set up in the years before World War I, such as the United States Baseball League, which was started in 1912. The Federal League openly disregarded the reserve clause, which bound players to the teams that had signed them and denied them the right to sell their services to the highest bidder. In 1913 Chicago was having discussions with Joe Tinker, the Cincinnati star

Charles Weeghman,
ca. 1914

shortstop who was resisting a trade to Brooklyn, and had refused to sign with Charles Ebbets's team, reportedly demanding $10,000 per year instead of the $7,000 Ebbets had offered. In late December 1913 Charlie Murphy, the owner of the rival Cubs, told the *Chicago Daily News* that he considered the Federal League "a joke from start to finish. I don't think Tinker will sign with the Federal League. . . . There is no one in the league who knows anything about baseball. Besides, they have no money."

Three days after that, Weeghman, who had been hovering in the background, took over full control of the team, and Tinker signed with the Whales for $36,000 for three years. Murphy had, in effect, dared the Federal League to make good on its desire to buy the services of the best players, and Weeghman had called his bluff, giving Tinker a contract worth even more than he was said to have asked for.

Weeghman's determination to make his team the equal of Murphy's Cubs and Comiskey's White Sox extended, naturally enough, to wanting his own turf. The day after he bought control of the team he told the *Chicago Tribune* that he intended to build a new grandstand of steel and concrete "to cost about $100,000 or $125,000 if necessary." Weeghman looked to the North Side of Chicago, Stuart Shea has written, so the Federal League team could be "far enough away from the White Sox and Cubs to build their own identity and not suffer in comparison to the existing parks." The North Side had the advantage of being a developing area, well served by public transportation, and largely residential. It did not have a baseball team, and while many of its residents were fans of the city's existing teams, neighborhood loyalties always ran strong in Chicago, and the possibility of establishing a new fan base was tempting. Most important of all, the North Side had a large plot of land at the corner of Clark and Addison that just happened to be available.

Weeghman leased the land for ninety-nine years, with a curious stipulation that he not spend more than $70,000 on improvements, a provision that his stated budget for the new ballpark already violated. No matter; Weeghman soon announced that he was prepared to spend $250,000 to build a ballpark, violating not only the lease provision but his own declared budget, for what he hoped—and at that point it was only a hope—would be not only the home of the city's third baseball team, but the anchor of the third national baseball league. He managed to fend off several attempts made by organized baseball to stymie the project, including, in January 1914, an offer to the owners of a small adjacent parcel that Weeghman needed to get complete control of the land for his ballpark. "The episode shows just how desperate organized ball was to keep the Federal League out of the picture by thwarting its strongest franchise," Stuart Shea has written.

That same month Weeghman hired Zachary Taylor Davis, the architect who had designed Comiskey Park, to draw up plans. Davis's design for the North Side was less grandiose than Comiskey, and seemed from the beginning to acknowledge the ballpark's location within a residential quarter of mostly small-scale buildings. His original design called for a large, single-deck grandstand, with structural provisions to allow for the addition of an upper deck, and for storefronts to be integrated into the exterior.

Weeghman, like Charles Ebbets a natural promoter, held both a groundbreaking ceremony and a banquet to mark the start of construction in March. He announced that his plans included placing potted plants atop the brick right field wall along Sheffield Avenue, something he never quite got around to doing, but which presaged the celebrated ivy that would come to the ballpark's outfield years later. The idea behind the plants, however, had little to do with nature; Weeghman was meticulous about the level of cleanliness in his restaurants, which stood in contrast to the messy, greasy dives that were often his competition, and he figured he could similarly distinguish his ballpark if it were a cleaner, more carefully tended environment than other places where fans watched baseball.

That was not hard; most ballparks, even the ones that showed some degree of architectural ambition, offered little in the way of amenities for the majority of fans. There were no concession stands, restrooms were generally filthy, and the stands often looked as if they were cleaned between seasons, not between games. Weeghman, who had grown rich by delivering customers sanitary places to eat, "saw—as few other baseball men did at the time—that a pampered customer would, more likely than not, return," Stuart Shea has written. Not the least of his innovations was in setting up food kiosks behind the stands to reduce the jostling among vendors roaming the aisles.

Weeghman Park was constructed with impressive speed: the field and grandstand were put together within a couple of months, a feat enabled in part by the relative simplicity of Davis's original design, which had eighteen thousand seats and a single deck. The grandstand was broad and deep, and it seemed almost flowing in shape. While the park would be altered frequently over the years—beginning with an adjustment to the outfield fences in 1914 after only three games, when it was determined that they were too close in, and made home runs too easy to achieve—the basic configuration of the main seating level, and the unusual sense of both breadth and intimacy that it offered, would remain. So, too, would the sense of connection to the park's immediate surroundings: this was a ballpark with a street address, a ballpark woven into the urban fabric. Almost every seat in Weeghman Park offered not only a close view of the playing field, but of the row houses that lined Waveland and Sheffield Avenues overlooking the outfield, buildings that seemed, in their way, almost as much a part of the stadium's architecture as the grandstand itself.

Those houses would come to play an ongoing role in the life of the ballpark, if only as a kind of foil to it. They would in time become known, collectively, as the Wrigley rooftops, reflecting the name the ballpark assumed in 1926; but even when it was Weeghman Park people would gather atop houses on Waveland Avenue to look into left field, and on Sheffield to look into right. This, of course, was not the only major league ball field into which neighbors could claim a free view, and owners had been grumbling about losing income to denizens of adjacent rooftops since the days of the wooden ballparks. But the extent to which Weeghman Park was tightly woven into an urban fabric of residential streets filled with townhouses with roofs at just the right height to offer generous views across the playing field meant that rooftop viewing would be more identified with this ballpark than anywhere else.*

Weeghman's construction of the ballpark at Clark and Addison would

---

* The Wrigley rooftops were accepted as a local curiosity, almost a piece of Chicago folklore, until the 1980s, when many of them were upgraded to include built-in bleachers instead of folding chairs. At that point the management of the Chicago Cubs began to see them as a competitive nuisance, and in 2002 the Cubs instigated legal action against the owners of the houses on the grounds that they were providing and profiting from unlicensed access to the team's games. Eventually the Cubs acquired most of them, which the team operates as "Wrigley Rooftops LLC."

be the high point of the Federal League. By the fall of 1915 the league would fall apart, its teams defunct and its players scattered. Weeghman's team, the Chicago Whales, had won the Federal League pennant after a tight race in 1915, but the lively competition within the league was no more than a temporary distraction from a deeper problem, which was that after two full seasons, the Federal League had a limited fan base and had made almost no real inroads into the duopoly of the American League and National League. The Boston Red Sox and Philadelphia Phillies, playing in the 1915 World Series, ignored Weeghman's pleas to have his Chicago Whales play the winner. Instead of acknowledging the Federal League's growth by inviting it in, the two other leagues decided in late 1915 to offer it money to go away. With startling suddenness—enhanced, surely, by the sudden death of Robert Ward, the wealthy owner of the Brooklyn Federal League team—the Federal League collapsed. Several of its owners accepted buyout funds from the major leagues, and some, including Weeghman, were given the opportunity to become major league owners themselves.

Weeghman emerged out of the reshuffling as the owner of the Chicago Cubs, into which he managed, in effect, to merge much of the Chicago Whales. The Cubs played at the West Side Grounds, a small ballpark in poor condition in a less desirable part of the city. Weeghman's first decision was no surprise. It would have a huge impact on the future of baseball: he moved his new team to his two-year-old ballpark on the North Side, which from 1916 on would become the home of the Chicago Cubs.

In the winter of 1916, Weeghman made another big decision. He sold a portion of the Cubs for $50,000 to J. Ogden Armour of the Chicago meatpacking company, who in turn brought in another Chicago tycoon, William Wrigley of the chewing gum company. Both men took seats on the board in preparation for the team's opening day game against the Cincinnati Reds in Weeghman Park on April 20, 1916, which Armour observed with the gift of a bear cub, named Joa for his initials, who would spend the season on view in a cage at the corner of Clark and Addison, just outside the ballpark gates. Weeghman commemorated the opening in a more businesslike way, expanding the seating capacity of the ballpark by another three thousand seats just in time for the game, which the Cubs won, 7–6, in the eleventh inning. Weeghman's additional seats did not satisfy demand, however: the following day, the *Chicago Tribune* would observe that hundreds of fans watched the game "from

the roofs and windows of flat buildings across the street from the ball park."

Charles Weeghman's restaurant business had made him famous and successful, but it never brought him the serious riches of corporate tycoons like Armour and Wrigley, and he was often short of cash, his financial position made all the tighter by his habit of signing new players at generous contracts. Two years after the Federal League's collapse Weeghman had not abandoned its policy of paying players well, and neither had he given up his inclination to put more funds into the maintenance of his ballpark than many major league owners did. In 1918, just two years after taking over the Cubs, in a year that should have been a triumph for him—the Cubs won the pennant, and played against the Boston Red Sox in the World Series—Weeghman's finances descended into a serious crisis. World War I and the 1918 influenza epidemic had been cutting into the customer base at his restaurants and lunch counters, severely crimping his cash flow,* and it turned out that he had been plugging his financial holes by gradually selling off shares of the team to William Wrigley, who turned out to be far less of a silent partner than

Wrigley Field was constructed in 1914 as the home of Chicago's team in the new, short-lived Federal League and first named Weeghman Park after Charles Weeghman, the team's owner.

---

* The war also resulted in a shortened 1918 season, and a revised World Series schedule between the Cubs and the Red Sox. To reduce train travel, the first three games were played in Chicago, and the final four, if necessary, were scheduled for Boston. Boston won in six games.

he had been expected to be. In November 1918, Wrigley told Weeghman, according to Harry Neily of *The Sporting News,* "If I help you out, you must retire from baseball and devote all your time to business." By then Wrigley held all, or most of, the cards, and Weeghman stepped down from his position as owner and public face of the Cubs.

He did not even get to enjoy the thrill of watching the World Series in the ballpark that carried his name. Walter Craigshead, the young business manager of the Cubs, was surely aware of Weeghman's declining financial situation, and came up with the idea of asking Charlie Comiskey, the owner of the White Sox, if the home games of the series could be played in Comiskey Park on the South Side, which had roughly twice the seating capacity of Weeghman Park. Comiskey agreed, and Weeghman, whose cash squeeze left him in no position to argue against some added revenue, went along with the plan.

By the 1919 season, Weeghman was gone, and Wrigley effectively in charge, although he did not fully consolidate his ownership until 1921. The field was renamed Cubs Park, and it began to change, albeit gradually. A limited amount of advertising crept in, just enough to make it clear that something other than the name had changed. Though Wrigley was a promoter by nature, he made no great push to commercialize the team or the park. "Baseball is too much of a sport to be a business, and too much of a business to be a sport," he was fond of saying. But his instruction to Weeghman was more telling: he saw baseball as an indulgence that he

William Wrigley, Jr., ca. 1920

could afford to support as Weeghman no longer could. He treated the Cubs and their ballpark as a long-term investment, not to say almost as a civic resource, and if he saw any short-term commercial possibilities in the team, it was that they might help him sell more chewing gum. And so Wrigley made deals in the 1920s to allow Chicago radio stations to broadcast Cubs games for free, knowing that hearing games on the radio would be a powerful magnet, ultimately expanding the universe of both Cubs fans and chewing gum consumers.

Shortly after he took over the team he hired a sportswriter, Bill Veeck, Sr., as the Cubs president. Veeck and Wrigley—the "Two Bills," in local parlance—were both promoters, and Wrigley took particular pleasure in offering free tickets to Cubs Park through special events such as "Ladies Days," when "mothers, daughters, sisters, wives, grandmothers" were all offered free admission to "the prettiest baseball grounds in the world," as newspaper ads put it. The Ladies Days were a huge success: one day in June, George Will reports, thirty thousand women showed up for free admission, which, even with some expansion of the park's seating capacity, left relatively few seats for paying customers.

Wrigley and Veeck also offered standing room on the edge of the outfield, behind ropes held by uniformed ushers. According to George Will, the crowd, presumably supported by the ushers, figured out how to create an unusual form of home field advantage: they would step back as a mass when the visiting team hit a fly ball, expanding the field of play; when the Cubs were up, they would push forward, "turning a probable out into a home run."

William Wrigley died in 1932, and his son, Philip K. Wrigley, took over. Veeck in time was succeeded by his own son, Bill Veeck, Jr., who would ultimately own the Chicago White Sox, but in the 1930s worked closely with the younger Wrigley to oversee the park, which by then had been renamed Wrigley Field. Wrigley was not particularly interested in investing his money in hiring the best players, but he and Veeck took seriously the notion that they were in charge of "the prettiest ball grounds in the

world." Veeck would later write of learning from his boss that "a team that isn't winning a pennant has to sell something in addition to its won-lost record to fill in those low points on the attendance chart. His solution was to sell 'Beautiful Wrigley Field'; that is, to make the park itself so great an attraction that it would be thought of as a place to take the whole family for a delightful day."

This, George Will has written, "became the Cubs' conscious business model: if the team is bad, strive mightily to improve . . . the ballpark," a strategy that Will would also call "a beautiful setting for ugly baseball." And that led to Veeck's most enduring innovation, and the most iconic single design element of Wrigley Field, although it was never seen by either Charles Weeghman or William Wrigley: the ivy on the outfield walls. Veeck installed it in 1937, taking the idea from Perry Stadium, an attractive, vaguely Art Moderne minor league ballpark constructed in Indianapolis in 1931.* Philip Wrigley was reportedly so excited about the

---

* Perry Stadium, later called Bush Stadium, was used as a stand-in for both Comiskey Park and Crosley Field in the 1987 filming of *Eight Men Out*. In 2013 it was converted into 138 loft condominiums, a novel form of adaptive reuse for a baseball park.

Wrigley Field's exterior, with its unmistakable sign, added in 1934

notion of adding green to his ballpark that he tried to up the ante by ordering trees to be planted amid the bleachers, an attempt at beautification that failed utterly, since the wind from Lake Michigan stripped away all the leaves, making the bleachers resemble "the Russian steppes during a hard, cold winter. Nothing but cement and bark," Veeck would write.

But the ivy—originally mixed with faster-growing bittersweet, which it eventually crowded out—was as successful as the trees were not. It became as identified with Wrigley Field as the neighbors' rooftop viewing platforms, the curving red metal marquee sign reading WRIGLEY FIELD HOME OF CHICAGO CUBS—which had been added to the front of the ballpark, at the intersection of Addison and Clark, three years earlier, in 1934—and the green, hand-operated scoreboard. With its soft leaves flowing over a brick wall, the ivy summed up, in its own way, the weaving together of country and city that was at the very essence of the idea of every baseball park. The ivy walls were Chicago's expression of *rus in urbe,* and they were Wrigley's own.

Chicago Cub Jon Jay (30) chases a home run ball in a 2017 game against the Milwaukee Brewers.

5

Aspiring to Monumentality

WHEN A COMBINATION of structural and financial challenges meant that the New York Yankees, once the New York Highlanders, were unable to get their new ballpark built at 221st Street and Kingsbridge Road near the northern tip of Manhattan* in the years before World War I—a project that would have given the Yankees a home contemporary with the parks of the golden age, Ebbets Field, Fenway Park, and Wrigley Field—they had little choice but to continue to play at the Polo Grounds as tenants of the New York Giants. The Yankees had hosted the Giants at their former home, Hilltop Park, when the Polo Grounds was being rebuilt after a fire; by the time the Giants' field was ready, the Yankees had lost their lease on Hilltop Park, which would soon be demolished, so the Giants could be seen as merely returning the Yankees' hospitality. But it was not a relationship of equals. The Giants held the upper hand in almost every way: not only did they own the ballpark and have a stronger balance sheet than the Yankees, they were a far mightier team on the field. It was no accident that when Colonel Jacob B. Ruppert, one of New York's most powerful brewery owners and a politically

* See Chapter 3. The park the Highlanders tried to build for several years was in Marble Hill, adjacent to Inwood, in a section that is now considered part of the Bronx.

well-connected former congressman, wanted to buy a baseball team, the Giants was the organization he first tried to acquire.

Harry Hempstead, who had controlled the team since his father-in-law, John T. Brush, died in 1912, had no interest in selling New York's dominant sports franchise, but the team's longtime manager John McGraw introduced Ruppert to Tillinghast L'Hommedieu Huston, a successful engineer and builder with whom he wintered in Havana, and encouraged the two men to join forces to buy the Yankees instead. In January 1915, they did, paying $460,000 to the unlikely duo of Frank Farrell, a professional gambler, and Bill Devery, a former city police commissioner, who had owned the team for a dozen years, during which they had invested little and amassed a record of 861 wins and 937 defeats. "It was an orphan club, without a home of its own, without players of outstanding ability, without prestige," Ruppert would say of his purchase.

He and Huston would change all of that. They were far more active owners than Farrell and Devery, and their ownership would reshape not only the Yankees, but baseball itself. Their most dramatic move did not come until they had owned the team for almost five years, when they made a second purchase, this one from Harry Frazee, a Broadway theater producer who owned the Boston Red Sox and was perennially short of cash. In exchange for $100,000 and a $300,000 mortgage on Fenway Park, Ruppert and Huston obtained the services of a young Boston pitcher named George Herman Ruth, who arrived in New York in time for the 1920 season and in his first season as a Yankee hit fifty-four home runs. With Babe Ruth, the Yankees were a different team. In 1921 they would win their first American League pennant and would play in the World Series for the first time. Their National League opponent was their landlord, the Giants, which made the 1921 series the first World Series played entirely in one ballpark. (The Giants won the best-of-nine series in eight games. Ruth, injured, played only a minor role.) The two teams would win their respective league pennants again in 1922, and again the World Series—for the first time a best-of-seven series—was played entirely at the Polo Grounds, and again the Giants won.

From the beginning of his career as a Yankee, Babe Ruth would attract fans, and Yankee attendance at the Polo Grounds, which had averaged 345,000 over the course of a season in the years before Ruppert and Huston owned the team, exploded to over a million in 1920 and 1921. Ruth,

baseball historian Lee Allen wrote, was "as much a tourist attraction in New York City as the Statue of Liberty, Grant's Tomb and the Fulton Fish Market." As landlords, the Giants were profiting from the Yankees' new allure, but that was hardly enough to prevent the Giants ownership from resenting the reversal of its underdog tenant's fortunes. The Giants were still the dominant team—the World Series results in 1921 and 1922 proved that—but the tide was turning, and it was clear that the relationship between the two teams was not conducive to a long-term cohabitation. Shortly after buying the Yankees, Ruppert and Huston had made a proposal to purchase the Polo Grounds as well and replace it with an enormous new stadium that would seat one hundred thousand and be shared by the two teams, but it was hard to understand quite what was behind it, other than perhaps an impulse to irritate the Giants by demonstrating that the Yankees now had a rather bigger view of themselves. With every upward tick in the Yankees' success it had become more and more obvious that the only thing the Giants really wanted was to be rid of their newly ambitious tenant altogether.

As far back as the fall of 1920, at the end of Babe Ruth's first season, the Giants, by then owned by Charles Stoneham and McGraw, had made it clear to the Yankees that they would need, sooner or later, to find

Ban Johnson, president of the American League, with Babe Ruth, 1922

another home. They did not want baseball's biggest star playing in their ballpark for another team. Ruppert and Huston did not disagree. They were more than ready to give the Yankees a field of their own, and they had already begun to look at sites around the city. They considered the land at 221st Street where the team had tried and failed to build almost a decade earlier; it was still in the possession of Frank Farrell, who was in ill health and was eager to sell it, but Ruppert thought the location was too far uptown and would be difficult for fans to reach. He and Huston looked at land near the Queens end of the Queensboro Bridge and at a site over the Pennsylvania Railroad tracks on the far West Side of Manhattan, where they were prepared to build until the War Department of the federal government rejected the notion of building over the tracks on the grounds that it would interfere with an undisclosed plan to set up antiaircraft emplacements there, meaning that the ballpark would somehow jeopardize national security.* When they learned they could not build at the railyards, Ruppert and Huston turned back uptown to a site in Upper Manhattan owned by the Hebrew Orphan Asylum on Amsterdam Avenue at 136th Street, which they liked enough to sign a contract to purchase. This, too, fell through when the orphan asylum could not promise to vacate in time to meet the Yankees' schedule.

To move quickly, the team needed vacant land, or land that could be made vacant easily and quickly. That finally came in the form of a twelve-and-a-half-acre site in the South Bronx, owned by the estate of William Waldorf Astor and occupied by a large, little-used lumberyard. The Yankees bought it for $675,000. It was, for better or for worse, just across the Harlem River from the Polo Grounds, and while it was not in Manhattan, there was something appealing to Ruppert and Huston about putting the grand ballpark they envisioned right in the Giants' line

---

* The rationale for the bizarre argument that the open tracks were in some way necessary for national security was never fully explained. The Yankees' flirtation with it would be the beginning of a long history of consideration of the midtown railyards as a potential location for sports facilities, and the site would be proposed again almost a century later as a location for a new Yankee Stadium and for a replacement for Madison Square Garden. It would also be considered for a football stadium for the New York Jets and as the site of a stadium to house the Olympics in 2012. The Jets stadium did not win planning approval and the 2012 Olympics ended up going to London. The site became Hudson Yards, a mixed-use development of office towers and condominiums. (See Chapter 11.)

of sight. The two rivals would face each other across the Harlem River, and while John McGraw would dismiss the building site as "Goatville" and say of the Yankees that "before long they will be lost sight of. A New York team should be based on Manhattan Island," the site was barely more distant from the commercial center of Manhattan than the Polo Grounds, and it was just beside the Grand Concourse, the Bronx's most aspirational boulevard, and near some of the city's most rapidly growing middle-class neighborhoods. It was hardly the nether reaches.

The timing of the new ballpark, if slower than the Giants might have wished, turned out to be ideal for the Yankees. The Bronx in the early 1920s was in the midst of a major transformation, with each passing month less of an outlying, semi-rural section of the city and more of a dense agglomeration of middle-class apartments filled with likely fans. The site may have been farther from the city's midtown and downtown commercial centers than Ruppert and Huston would have liked, but the presence of much of the team's new and growing fan base in a developing part of the city an easy walk or subway ride away more than made up for that. New subway lines were making the Bronx the residential neighborhood of choice for people ready to take a step up from the tenements of the Lower East Side, and the Yankees' new ballpark had the potential to become at least as much a local magnet as Ebbets Field was for its urban surroundings in Brooklyn. If the site at 161st Street and River Avenue was relatively undeveloped when the Yankees selected it, soon it would be adjacent to one of the city's most rapidly urbanizing areas, easily accessed by new subway lines. And yet, knowing that they had almost twice as many seats to fill as the Dodgers, which would require building a fan base that was truly regional and not just neighborhood-based, the Yankees used some of their new land to provide roughly two thousand parking spaces for fans who chose to come by automobile, a small number by contemporary standards but an advanced amenity in the 1920s. It made Ebbets Field and the Polo Grounds, which had almost no parking, seem old-fashioned. As generous as it may have seemed when conceived, however, the parking space the Yankees allocated turned out not to be enough, and when the stadium opened there were reportedly thousands of cars parked haphazardly on neighboring streets, making Yankee Stadium, among other things, a clear precursor of the coming suburbanization of baseball.

"Cap" Huston's engineering background led him to become so deeply involved in planning the Yankees' new facility that, according to Robert Weintraub, he considered drawing up the plans himself. He and Ruppert decided instead to hire the Osborn Engineering Company, a Cleveland-based firm that had begun as a bridge builder and had turned to sports facilities in 1909 with the construction of Swayne Field in Toledo, a minor league ballpark with a double-decked grandstand that John Pastier cites as the first minor league park to aspire to the quality of a major league ballpark. Osborn's best-known early parks were League Park in Cleveland of 1910, the 1911 reconstruction of the Polo Grounds, and Navin Field (Tiger Stadium) of 1912; it was effectively the first architecture and engineering firm in the nation to become known as a specialist in ballpark and arena design. If Osborn was not known for buildings as ornate, or as distinctive, as Shibe Park, Forbes Field, or Ebbets Field, its work was solid, functional, and generally handsome, if understated.

Ruppert and Huston made it clear that they wanted Osborn to do something that went beyond all previous ballparks. The brief given to Osborn by "the Colonels," as Ruppert and Huston were called—each man had a National Guard commission and liked to use his military title in civilian life—was far grander than any previous client from the world of sports had put forth: at a time when most baseball parks could accommodate between 30,000 and 35,000 fans, they wanted to more than double that number, with 85,000 seats;* when most ballparks considered two decks to be more than sufficient, they wanted to have three levels, running all the way around, covered by projecting roofs.

It was no accident that Ruppert and Huston wanted to call the Yankees' new home a stadium, not a ballpark: their inspiration was not the rustic enclosures with which the baseball park began, but the grandeur of the Roman Colosseum. In 1913, the year that Ebbets Field was finished, New York had also completed Grand Central Terminal; the city

---

* Some sources put the seating capacity of the original design as 100,000 seats. It is not clear whether the design was ever developed fully enough to plan seating precisely, and it is possible that the 100,000 number was circulated partly as a marketing ploy, to make the stadium the Yankees were planning seem even more grandiose than it was. Depending on the width of seats and how they are configured, it is possible that 100,000 seats could have been fit into a structure of roughly the same size as the one envisioned for 85,000 seats.

had inaugurated Pennsylvania Station three years and the New York Public Library two years earlier. So far relatively little of the city's imperial grandeur had filtered down into the realm of baseball, but perhaps by 1921 the time had come. And if so, Ruppert and Huston felt that they were the people, and the Yankees the team, to do it.

In response to Ruppert and Huston's aspirations, Osborn came up with a design that would have been far more than an ornate architectural counterpoint to the bright, green rural fantasy of a playing field, the way the structures of Shibe Park or Ebbets Field were in their elegant balance between building and field. In the original scheme drawn up by Osborn, Yankee Stadium was to have been nothing like a park at all, but rather an unrelenting piece of monumental architecture that would have fully surrounded the playing field, its structure in effect squeezing out any remnant of the rural yearnings that had defined earlier ballparks.

It did not turn out quite that way in the end. Eighty-five thousand seats were deemed too many, in part because the notion of a fully enclosed stadium really did seem too grandiose, too monumental, even for the increasingly self-assured Yankees. And while the Colonels were prepared to spend more money than any of their peers had yet put into a ballpark, Ruppert and Huston were not in a position to offer a blank check, however many seats Babe Ruth might have been able to fill.

Whatever its financial implications, the decision to pare back the design was a welcome piece of luck, since the fans in an eighty-five-thousand-seat stadium would have had a very different kind of experience from what baseball fans had traditionally come to expect. Yes, this was to be a stadium and not a ballpark, but Ruppert and Huston, perhaps prodded by Osborn, realized during their planning process that to squeeze out all vestiges of the ballpark would be dangerously self-defeating. Establishing a new tone of monumentality that would make Yankee Stadium something bigger and more intimidating than any pre-

Yankees owner Jacob Ruppert, commissioner of baseball Judge Kenesaw M. Landis, and Yankees co-owner Tillinghast Huston at opening day of Yankee Stadium, April 18, 1923

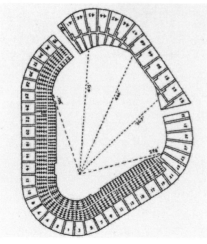

Osborn's original design for Yankee Stadium called for a fully enclosed structure with more than eighty thousand seats.

vious ballpark did not have to mean losing all traces of *rus in urbe,* and nor did it have to mean cutting off the field from the outside world. An early press release made reference to the Yale Bowl, the fully enclosed, partially sunken football stadium that had been completed in 1914 in New Haven, and spoke of the play inside it as being "impenetrable to all human eyes, save those of aviators." Happily, that is not what happened at Yankee Stadium. While fully surrounding a baseball field with seats would have rid owners of the pesky problem of occupants of neighboring structures watching the game for free, it would also have meant a field that felt entirely closed to the world, and to the life of the city around it. And it would have cut the playing field off from sunlight as well, assuring that at many times during the playing season, most of the field would be in shadow by late afternoon. While the game would still be played under the open sky, it would have risked giving baseball, a game deeply connected to the great outdoors, something akin to a sense of being played indoors.

It is not clear exactly what saved Yankee Stadium, in the end, from the overkill of Osborn's original design, which, however magnificent, was also an exercise in unbroken monumentality that drove out all vestiges

of baseball tradition. The decision to carry the enclosed, triple-decked masonry structure only to the foul poles and build a relatively conventional set of bleachers in the outfield allowed the stadium to be nearly as grand as originally envisioned, yet to be open and connected to the city at the same time. Since the great wooden grandstands of the 1880s, the best ballparks had balanced elaborate structure with a sense of openness to their surroundings. It mattered little what those surroundings actually were, and whether they were sufficiently green to create the illusion of rusticity. The field itself would always suffice for the presence of nature; what mattered most was not whether the world outside the fence was urban or rural but that spectators experienced the sense that the ballpark continued into the world beyond the outfield. The most important thing, in other words, was that the space of the ballpark itself was not finite, but appeared, visually at least, to be open, so as to allude, at least symbolically, to the notion that the outfield extends into infinity. No ball field is truly infinite, of course, and bleachers and walls have always given fields enclosure. But there is a difference between the low enclosure

Entrance to Yankee Stadium. Manhattan Post Card Co., ca. 1930

of bleachers and walls, over which open space appears to flow outward, and the total enclosure of a high, multi-level grandstand extending all the way around the field, so there is no longer any visual relationship to the world outside. Had Yankee Stadium been built according to its original, fully enclosed design, it would have been a far different place, less connected to the classic ballparks out of which it came than prefiguring the fully enclosed mega-stadiums of the mid-twentieth century, like the Astrodome.*

As built, Yankee Stadium managed to navigate between the hauteur that Ruppert and Huston clearly wanted and the openness that baseball tradition dictated. The outfield beyond the bleachers was open, and while there were a few glimpses of neighboring buildings in the tradition of urban baseball parks—and there would be more as the neighborhood continued to develop, and new buildings were built along River Avenue and other surrounding streets—the more striking element was the presence of the elevated tracks of the new Lexington Avenue subway line, slipping past the edge of the outfield, its trains offering just enough sense of movement and activity to be enlivening from within the ballpark, but never so much as to be distracting from play. And riders, of course, got a spectacular, if momentary, peek at the verdant green of the playing field and the grandiose structure of the triple-decked stands.

The masonry façade of the stadium, with its high, arched windows, was slightly simplified from Osborn's original scheme, but it still had an aura of monumental grandeur to it, its relative plainness projecting just enough austerity to suggest that this was a building whose designers wanted it to be respected more than liked. Ebbets Field was warm and eager to please; Yankee Stadium was cool, as if it had nothing to prove. You were supposed to be impressed by it, and more than a little awed.

It did have one exceptionally likeable, not to say quirky, feature: the graceful copper cornice that ran like a classical frieze all the way around the inside top of the structure. There was nothing else like it in any other ballpark, and its intricacy and rhythmic sequence of arches gave the stadium its most distinct architectural element, a filigree that was a welcome counterpoint to the formidable solidity of the exterior. To the

---

* See Chapter 7 for a discussion of the Astrodome and the fully enclosed, multi-use stadiums built for both baseball and football.

extent that the stadium had personality, it came from the waving lines of the cornice, which became, far more than any element of the exterior, the building's architectural signature; compared to everything else about Yankee Stadium, it was an element of grace, almost whimsy.

The Colonels had hoped to have the stadium ready for the 1922 season. It soon became clear that this was impossible, less because of the challenges of construction than the difficulty of getting necessary political approvals. The Giants, despite their eagerness to have their tenants move on, also realized that they would be able to charge an exploitative rent for 1922 if the Yankees' new field was not ready, and did not mind the public embarrassment that the Yankees would suffer if they had to throw themselves on the Giants' mercy because they still did not have a ballpark of their own. Robert Weintraub has surmised that the gambler Arnold Rothstein, a close associate of John McGraw's and the owner of

Yankee Stadium's famous decorative cornice

a minority share in the Giants, whose connections to the Tammany Hall political machine of New York were stronger than Ruppert and Huston's, had intervened to cause the city to delay giving routine approval to the closing of Cromwell Avenue and 158th Street, which ran right through the middle of the site of the new stadium. Until the city agreed that the streets could be closed, the Yankees were unable to turn a single spade of earth.

There were more routine complications, too, such as the fact that the Astor family, which still owned parcels of land adjacent to the site they had sold to the Yankees, needed to grant approval for the street closings as well, and most of the Astor heirs lived in England and were not easy to reach. By the time all the approvals had come through, there was no possibility of having the stadium ready for 1922. The Yankees went back to the Polo Grounds, signing a one-year lease extension that upped the rent they paid the Giants by 25 percent, from $60,000 per year to $75,000.

On May 3, 1922, two weeks after the 1922 season had begun, the Yankees finally signed a contract with the White Construction Company to build the new stadium. The agreed-upon cost was $1.1 million. The contract followed a letter the Colonels had sent to White a few weeks earlier, stating, "We own a plot of land in the Bronx at 161st and River Avenue containing about 240k square feet. We MUST play ball there next spring . . . and we must have the completed stadium by April 18, 1923. Are you interested?"

Signing the contract, of course, was only the beginning, and the start of construction work only meant the opportunity for new kinds of delays and frustrations. If this was not quite the same as the situation that a different Yankee ownership had experienced a decade earlier, when multiple attempts to build at 221st Street on a plot of land formerly including Spuyten Duyvil Creek were foiled by foundation issues, the Yankees had a new set of problems to contend with as they tried to build the largest baseball park ever constructed. Eliminating the portion of the stadium that enclosed the outfield certainly helped to simplify construction, as did reducing the middle seating level to a relatively shallow mezzanine with less depth than the first and third levels, which meant that while the stadium technically had three separate decks, only the first and third had the depth of traditional grandstands. The mezzanine was tucked under the upper grandstand.

Some of the challenges had to do with sheer volume. The building—and it was a building—surrounding the field required 30,000 cubic yards of concrete and 2,500 tons of structural steel, 1,000 tons of reinforced steel, 500 tons of iron, and more than four miles of steel piping and 2.5 million feet of lumber, Robert Weintraub has written. Once it was time to prepare the playing field, 16,000 square feet of sod were trucked in from Long Island and spread over 13,000 cubic yards of topsoil, which was enough to handle the needs of a field that, like the stadium's seating capacity, was larger than anything else in baseball. The outlying point of center field was 490 feet from home plate, and left field was almost as deep, at 460 feet. (Right field was somewhat smaller, with the foul pole at 295 feet and a maximum distance of 368 feet.)

As with every large construction project, there were changes along the way, which inevitably caused delays. The most troubling, according to Weintraub's account, was a decision to dispense with the original plans in building the bleachers to a lower standard than the rest of the project. In a more successful rejection of baseball park history than their abandoned plan to enclose the field on all sides, the Colonels decided to have the bleacher section built with concrete footings, exterior walls that matched the rest of the stadium, and ramps, bathrooms, and refreshment stands that were the equivalent of the rest of the stadium. It was a gesture toward equality that raised the budget for the bleachers from $116,000 to more than $250,000 and threw the project further off schedule. By the time of the 1922 World Series at the Polo Grounds, the stadium was roughly a third complete, and "the colonels despaired of being able to finish in time for opening day," according to Weintraub.

Seating would be a continual problem, since it seemed always to be in flux. The letter the Colonels sent to White Construction, the builder, before the contract was signed referred to plans being prepared by Osborn Engineering "for a stand that will seat about 75,000"—fewer seats than Osborn's original design had called for, but more than what was actually built, so it is clear that at least some elements of the design were still undetermined when the contract was signed. In fact, there are conflicting accounts as to how many seats the stadium actually did contain when it opened on April 18, 1923, and in any event the number would vary again and again due to frequent renovations, which would also reduce the enormous size of the outfield multiple times over the years to make the stadium more conducive to home runs. *The New York Times,* writing just before opening day, rounded the number off to an even 70,000, which was almost surely high in terms of actual seats, which other sources put at 58,000. The Yankees announced a crowd of 74,217 on opening day, which was later revised down to 60,000, probably a more accurate estimate, given standing room and the fact that the bleacher section, while inexact in its capacity, was not fully elastic. There were 18,000 reserved seats, all of which were sold out in advance, with general admission available on game day. According to some reports, 25,000 people seeking general admission were turned away.

The *Times* treated the opening as the major civic event that it was, and not just because Al Smith, the governor of the State of New York, was there to throw out the first ball at 3:30 p.m. and John Philip Sousa was there with his band to play his classic marches, a performance that was compromised, according to some reports, by the size of the field. The new stadium, Robert Weintraub wrote, "was so vast that all of the pageantry—even Sousa's marches—was swallowed up." The *New York Post* noted that "only snatches of the tunes reached the crowd near the home plate."

The prospect of inaudible music did not trouble *The New York Times,* which greeted its readers on the morning of April 18 with enthusiasm bordering on awe. "In the busy borough of the Bronx, close to the shore of Manhattan Island, the real monument to baseball will be unveiled this afternoon—the new Yankee Stadium, erected at a cost of $2,500,000, seating some 70,000 people and comprising in its broad reaches of concrete and steel the last word in baseball arenas," the paper proclaimed.

The *Times* noted that Yankee fans "have been waiting for this day ever since the American Leaguers packed bags and baggage and moved out of that antiquated wooden home of theirs on Washington Heights back in 1912. From a small stand of wood to the greatest steel and concrete park in baseball is a long jump, even when it takes eleven years to do it."

Appropriately, the Yankees hosted the Boston Red Sox for the first game, then as later the team's most important American League rival. What mattered most to Yankee fans, of course, was not the new playing field itself, but whether Babe Ruth would christen it properly with a home run scored against his old team. "I'd give a year off my life to hit one today," Ruth reportedly said before the game. In his first time at bat, Ruth hit a fly ball that was easily caught. Then, in the bottom half of the third inning, with two men on base and the Yankees ahead 1–0, he came up to bat again. The count was 2-2 when Ruth hit the ball, bringing forth from the crowd, the great sportswriter Grantland Rice wrote, "the greatest vocal cataclysm baseball has ever known" as Ruth produced his, and Yankee Stadium's, first home run. Rice described it as follows: "A white streak left Babe Ruth's 53-ounce bludgeon in the third inning of yesterday's opening game at the Yankee Stadium. On a low line it sailed, like a silver flame, through the gray, bleak April shadows, and into the right field bleachers, while the great slugger started on his job around the towpaths for his first home run of the year."

The Yankees won 4–1, and shortly after the game Ruth drove himself back to his apartment in the Hotel Ansonia on the Upper West Side in his new Pierce-Arrow, his route eased by police who cleared a path for his car. Most of the fans left by more conventional modes of transportation, but it boded well for the new stadium that their departure was nearly as smooth as Babe Ruth's had been. Multiple exits and the presence of enormous ramps instead of narrow staircases allowed the huge crowd to leave the stadium in just eleven minutes, according to Major Thomas Birmingham, one of the construction engineers. Even with its huge capacity Yankee Stadium "was emptied . . . in quicker time than the Polo Grounds ever was," *The New York Times* noted. The crowds clogged the narrow subway stairs and platforms, but that was to be expected, and the Yankees were not responsible for the design of the transit system. So far as what the team did control, it had succeeded in building a stadium that worked for crowds, and worked for Babe Ruth. It was indeed "the house that Ruth built," as Fred Lieb wrote in the *Evening Telegram.* From its opening day, Yankee Stadium did what was expected of it.

If Yankee Stadium had thrown down the gauntlet of monumentality, the major league teams and their cities did not seem at all eager to pick it up. While several teams responded to the Yankees by expanding the seating capacity of their ballparks—*The New York Times* would report that the total number of seats in all major league ballparks would increase by ninety-three thousand in 1923, a sign that merely having Yankee Stadium

Lou Gehrig of the
New York Yankees
addresses his teammates
and fans during his
famous farewell speech
on Lou Gehrig Day,
July 4, 1939, at Yankee
Stadium

under construction had some effect*—no one could say that the Yankees unleashed a new era of monumental ballparks. Adding seats to the Polo Grounds or Wrigley Field did not have to change their essential natures, and did not; indeed, part of what made the wave of ballpark renovations in the 1920s and 1930s a positive development was that the feeling of most existing ballparks was not altered significantly as they were renovated to accommodate larger crowds. Indeed, many of the renovations of classic ballparks in those decades added elements that would build, rather than diminish, their identities, such as the upper decks, ivy walls, and red marquee sign of Wrigley Field, or the upper deck of Fenway Park and, even later, its characteristic green paint.

* The *Times* article, which appeared on February 3, 1923, was headlined "Big League Parks to Hold 461,000; Total Capacity of Grounds Will Be Increased by 93,000 for 1923 Season." The article cited expansions in the Polo Grounds—clearly made in response to the construction of Yankee Stadium by the Giants' longtime tenant—and on the Cubs' field in Chicago. Of course the majority of the 93,000 seats added were the ones in Yankee Stadium.

The main reason the monumental example of Yankee Stadium was not followed by other teams was that most teams already had ballparks that were relatively new and, especially with their expanded seating capacities, well suited to handle the needs of the next generation. The surge in baseball park construction that preceded Yankee Stadium meant that even though the decade of the twenties was a boom period in America's major cities, with the enormous volume of construction of everything from skyscrapers to movie palaces in almost every downtown reflecting an ever-rising economy, the one building type that was quiescent was the ballpark. Cities were building apartments, hotels, office buildings, churches, and civic structures of every type as fast as architects could draw up plans, but Yankee Stadium would be the only major league park built for the entire decade.

Only one city decided to be an exception to the trend of indifference to Yankee Stadium's grandiose aspirations: Cleveland, which by 1920 had become the nation's fifth-largest city. Like many midwestern industrial cities, Cleveland seemed destined to grow forever, and its leaders, more than those of many other cities, seemed inclined to express their confidence through building. In 1902 the city commissioned Daniel Burnham, Arnold Brunner, and John M. Carrère, three of the nation's most distinguished architects, to create a master plan for downtown that led to a major array of civic buildings around a vast central mall built on landfill beside Lake Erie; among them were new Beaux Arts structures for a federal courthouse, a county courthouse, a post office, City Hall, the Cleveland Public Library, and a civic auditorium. The civic center mall had originally been planned to include a new railroad station at its center, unifying multiple rail lines, but there was serious opposition to this part of the plan from real estate interests pushing to place the train station at Public Square, closer to the city's commercial center, where it could also connect to planned rapid transit lines. The Public Square advocates won in a public referendum, which led to the construction of Terminal Tower—at its completion in 1930 the second tallest building in the United States after the Woolworth Building in New York (a title it held only briefly, since the Chrysler Building opened that same year).

Cleveland did not lack for self-assurance, then. But with the railroad station having gone to Public Square downtown, the grand civic center mall lacked a centerpiece, and the administrator in charge of physical education for the Cleveland City School District suggested a lakefront

stadium that might serve all the region's schools. William R. Hopkins, the Cleveland city manager, had another idea. He knew that Cleveland was one of the few cities whose major league team played in a ballpark that was neither new nor well respected, and Hopkins had no interest in wasting the prime land in the heart of the civic center on high school football games. The Cleveland Indians were in flux—their owner, Jim Dunn, had died in 1922, and the team was managed on behalf of Dunn's widow by Ernest S. Barnard, who had been charged with finding a new owner. But even the team's uncertain status, Hopkins and Barnard reasoned, could be used to justify their notion that the city should build a stadium. The team would not be in a position to do anything itself until its ownership was settled, and the certainty that an attractive new facility was on the horizon might make the team more valuable.

League Park,
Cleveland, Ohio,
between 1900 and 1910

League Park, where the Indians played, was a steel-and-concrete reconstruction from 1910 of a wooden ballpark structure from 1891. Even after a second expansion in 1919 it seated only twenty-two thousand, the smallest capacity in the major leagues. The site was so awkward it was almost a parody of the notion of a ballpark whose design emerged out of the pattern of its surroundings: thanks to the refusal of three adjacent property owners to sell back in the 1890s, the field was "essentially a rectangle, with right field and left center as the short sides," in the words of Michael Gershman. Right field was originally only 240 feet from home plate, which renovations later pushed out to a still tight 290 feet. As at Ebbets Field, the right field wall was too close to the field of play to leave room for any seats. But this was even tighter than in the Brooklyn park, with more of the field devoid of seats. And Cleveland's wall had more unusual challenges than the scoreboard and Abe Stark's famous HIT SIGN WIN SUIT billboard at Ebbets. The lower portion of the League Park right field wall was concrete, the upper portion was marked by a screen, and another portion had protruding steel beams. Depending on which part of the wall a ball hit, it might bounce back hard, bounce softly, or rebound in any direction at all. League Park was, in a sense, a glorious eccentricity, but its architecture—it was the first major league ballpark constructed by the Cleveland-based Osborn Engineering Company—made it look as much like a factory as a civic building, and its site was too constrained to allow any meaningful improvements. There was nothing about League Park to encourage a new owner to invest further.

In 1926, Hopkins went to Osborn Engineering, which by then had completed Yankee Stadium, and asked Osborn to come up with a plan for a stadium that would seat at least eighty thousand, putting it in the category of the original, unbuilt scheme for the Yankees. Hopkins saw no reason not to make it that big, since he envisioned that the stadium would be leased to the Indians for the baseball season and would be booked with other events for the rest of the year, filling the city's coffers with money.

Hopkins had in mind not a baseball park into which other events would be dropped, but the first truly multi-purpose stadium, a vast coliseum that would host every possible kind of sporting and musical event. In a time when professional baseball teams built and owned their own ballparks, his belief that the stadium should be a public facility, built and owned by the city, was just as innovative as his notion that it should house multiple sports and events. In the 1920s, cities did not underwrite the construction of sports stadiums. Owners did. Hopkins's belief that there would be public benefit to the city in constructing a major league stadium itself would unwittingly set the tone for an entire generation of future ballparks, sometimes with troubling results.

Cleveland voters approved a $2.5 million bond issue to construct the stadium in 1928, and by 1930, construction was under way on Osborn's design, which had been tweaked by another Cleveland firm, Walker and Weeks, who were brought in as consulting architects and proposed to give the vast, circular structure a façade of stone to match the Beaux Arts civic buildings of the mall, several of which they had designed. When that proved too expensive, they switched to tan brick with some trim details of aluminum, a revised exterior that gave the stadium a hint of the Art Moderne style, making it feel connected to the architectural trend of the moment but out of place amid the classical civic structures that were its neighbors.

The stadium, known variously as Cleveland Municipal Stadium and Lakefront Stadium, would hardly have been a natural fit on the mall whatever its façade looked like. At 115 feet it was the height of a ten-story building, and it sprawled over more than twelve acres. Its plans showed the dangers of designing with an absolutely clean slate: with none of the constraints of the immediately surrounding streets, which had dictated much of the design of earlier ballparks, the designers were without the limits that had given so many other ballparks their distinctive qualities. Since they felt they had all the room in the world, and wanted the stadium to work for multiple sports, the designers included a full-size running track around the periphery of the field, either unaware of or indifferent to the fact that this would contradict a priority of baseball park design, the desire to get as many fans as close to the field as possible. The track pushed everyone, including those at field level, farther away. The playing field itself was symmetrical, which, while not unique—the Polo Grounds, too, was essentially symmetrical—seemed to further contradict baseball tradition, and certainly underscored the absence of the traditional constraints of a ballpark's immediate surroundings. More to the point, the field was enormous, measuring more than four acres, prompting Babe Ruth to remark, "A guy ought to have a horse to play the outfield here." Four stair towers poked out from the round exterior, and there were just under eighty thousand seats, more individual seating than

in any other arena in the world. (The only stadiums that could accommodate more people had benches, or bleachers, and not individual seats.)

Cleveland got the monumental structure it sought; beside Municipal Stadium, Yankee Stadium seemed almost modest. But Cleveland would discover that monumentality came at a price. Not only did Clevelanders have mixed feelings about their new facility—only eight thousand turned out for the concert marking the formal opening on July 2, 1931, despite good weather, meaning that 90 percent of the seats were empty—the city and the Cleveland Indians were not able to agree on terms of a lease, and for all of the 1931 season, the Indians remained in League Park. The stadium did not turn an operating profit until 1942, and then only if debt service on its bonds was not counted. The lakefront site had other problems, too: it was cold, windy, and largely inaccessible by public transportation. Indeed, it had little to offer besides the symbolic value

Municipal Stadium in Cleveland, Ohio. The tall building at the upper right is the Terminal Tower on Union Station.

of being part of the civic center mall, which emerged more out of a view of urban planning as a kind of abstraction than out of an understanding of how the city worked. For all the inconveniences of League Park, it was firmly embedded in the city, not least because it was located along streetcar lines. (League Park's builder, F. D. Robison, not only owned the predecessor team to the Indians, the Cleveland Spiders, but like many other team owners also controlled the local streetcar company.)

By late July 1932, the city and the Indians had agreed on a lease, and on July 31, 1932, the team played its first game at Municipal Stadium, against Philadelphia, which beat the Indians 1–0. The game was played before a full house, but that seems to have been motivated mainly by curiosity about the new stadium, since it was rarely repeated. The equivalent of a sold-out game at League Park would fill barely more than a quarter of the seats at Municipal Stadium, and after a dreary 1933 season of playing to empty stands, the Indians returned to League Park for their midweek games, using Municipal Stadium only for weekend and holiday doubleheaders, when they could be assured of larger crowds. (Beginning in 1939, when lights were installed at Municipal Stadium, they played night games there as well.) For a dozen years, then, the Indians occupied two home fields. It was not until 1947, when Bill Veeck owned the team and found the conditions of League Park too rundown to justify even midweek games, that the Indians returned to play full-time at Municipal Stadium.

Babe Ruth was right: the field was vast, too vast, which made it such an unwelcome spot for hitters that in 1947, presumably as a condition for the Indians' return to full-time play there, a new inner fence was constructed across the outfield to bring home run distances in by 50 to 75 feet. The bleachers were so distant from home plate that they were never reached by a home run ball. If the stadium felt right for any sport, it was football, which fans expected to see from a greater distance,* and which seems more suited to the monumentality that Hopkins and his architects sought. For years, the local nickname for the stadium was "the Mistake by the Lake," and with good reason: not only was it unprofitable

---

* The Cleveland Browns played at Municipal Stadium from 1946 until the team departed Cleveland for Baltimore in 1995, becoming the Baltimore Ravens, after which the stadium was demolished and the site used for a new stadium for a new Cleveland football team, which assumed the old name of the Browns.

for most of its life, a precursor to the unwise subsidies to professional sports that so many other cities would, in time, come to adopt, it was physically disconnected from the city of which it was a part. Despite its presence beside so many other civic structures, its nature was more suburban than urban. A planning process intended to enhance Cleveland's civic grandeur ended up, paradoxically, creating one of the least urban of city baseball parks—an isolated, bleak structure remembered more for its harsh winds blowing off the lake than for anything it might have done to elevate Cleveland as a city.

Cleveland, seeking to outdo every other city's baseball park, succeeded mainly in spending enormous amounts of public money to violate almost every tradition of the urban baseball park. Municipal Stadium had neither *rus* nor *urbs;* for all the hugeness of its field, looking upon it offered little sense of connection to nature, and almost no meaningful integration with downtown Cleveland. It may have been in the city, but it was not of the city. What Cleveland's enormous stadium did do, however, far more than any of its creators might have envisioned, was foreshadow how it would be cities, not team owners, that would pay for baseball parks in the years after World War II, and the enormous, circular forms that these ballparks would take.

While Cleveland's initiation of the municipally financed stadium was driven mainly by William Hopkins's desire to complete an ambitious work of urban design, the civic center mall, and not by a wish to subsidize professional sports teams, the mechanism of public finance that he used to get the Cleveland stadium built would nevertheless become a form of subsidy to private businesses. And it would become a far more impactful legacy of Cleveland Municipal Stadium than its architecture.

6

Leaving the City

FOR MORE THAN A DECADE, as the Cleveland Indians shuttled back and forth between the funky, antiquated League Park and the new, enormous, and austere Municipal Stadium, they were not only straddling the old world of baseball and the new, they were living both in the American city as it had been and the American city as it was becoming. League Park, like Fenway Park, Ebbets Field, Crosley Field, Navin Field, and so many other ballparks that had been built or rebuilt early in the twentieth century, exuded qualities that characterized the older cities of which they were a part: they were dense, lively, curious mixes of the eccentric and the grand. They were disheveled, scrappy, and for the most part good-natured places, constructed on the premise that there was something valuable in the notion of even so expansive a public space as a baseball park being tightly woven into the urban environment. Baseball parks were a part of the urban fabric because, up until the middle of the twentieth century, everything was a part of the urban fabric.

That this might change was first apparent in the 1920s and 1930s, as the automobile began to remake urban centers from places defined by dense webs of active, pedestrian-oriented streets to places of parkways, highways, and freeways. At first, this transformation was slow and barely noticeable, in part because the Depression made it hard for many people to acquire automobiles and for private entrepreneurs to initiate large-scale construction projects. It is no accident that other than Cleveland's publicly financed Municipal Stadium, there were no major league baseball parks opened in the 1930s, a decade whose most notable construction achievements so far as baseball was concerned were the renovations of a few older parks and the building of a few excellent minor league ballparks, such as Riverview Stadium, a tiny 1937 gem of Art Deco in Clinton, Iowa, that like several others in that era was a project of the federal government's Works Progress Administration.*

By the postwar years, however, it was another matter. Prosperity brought not only a building boom, but a sense that the world had changed: the city of dense, walkable neighborhoods, made up of a tight web of streets, had begun to seem old and tired. The suburbs, with the promise of a backyard and a barbecue for all, increasingly beckoned. The federal government, through a combination of mortgage support and an ambitious program for building interstate highways, effectively subsidized the move of middle-class families from rental apartments in older city neighborhoods to new suburban communities of developer-built tract houses. Neighborhoods like the ones that surrounded Yankee Stadium, Ebbets Field, and the Polo Grounds in New York, not to mention League Park, Tiger Stadium, and their equivalents in so many other cities, began, at first slowly and then more rapidly, to lose their middle-class families to places like Levittown, where bland suburban sprawl replaced the cohesive urban fabric.

The lure of the new was powerful, especially in the postwar years; the world really was remaking itself, and the old neighborhoods that had baseball parks at their heart began to seem tired, their shabbiness obscuring their strengths as social vehicles to bring people together. Baseball parks were the least of it, since only a handful of neighborhoods could claim them, but they symbolized the value of the public realm at a time when the very notion of the public realm was in decline. In the city, public space was privileged over private space, and the baseball park was,

---

* Better known than Riverview Stadium, if not as elegant, is Durham Athletic Park, a minor league park built the following year, in 1938, and set amid the industrial quarter of Durham's tobacco warehouses. It was used in the 1988 movie *Bull Durham*, one of the greatest of all baseball films.

in many ways, the greatest public space of all. It was certainly the one that accommodated the most people, and created the greatest number of opportunities for shared social experience. When it was closely integrated into the urban fabric, the public nature of day-to-day life among city streets flowed naturally into the public experience of being at the ballpark.

In the suburbs, the equation was reversed: private space was privileged over public space, which meant that the ballpark as it had grown up over past generations did not fit naturally into the scheme of things. It wasn't a big, beautiful garden in the middle of a city to which it felt inextricably connected, but an island of public space amid an ocean of private spaces and places. While Cleveland's Municipal Stadium beside Lake Erie wasn't technically suburban—it was in the midst of a civic mall and surrounded by other civic structures—it was isolated from downtown Cleveland, from the city's residential and commercial neighborhoods, and from public transit. To visit the new Municipal Stadium you had to have what amounted to a quasi-suburban experience, even though you were still within the city. It foreshadowed a kind of suburban isolation that would define many of the new stadiums that were built after World War II, just as the decline of League Park and its surrounding neighborhood made it easy to think that the old ballparks and the areas they were in were disposable: in both the rejection of its old ballpark and the design of its new one, Cleveland's decisions in the 1930s and 1940s predicted the movement toward what John Pastier has called "the suburbanization of baseball" in the postwar decades.

To be fair, it was not only the rush to the suburbs that led to an interest in building new ballparks. For all their boisterous appeal, most of the older ballparks, like the neighborhoods of which they were a part, seemed out of sync with the fresh, clean modernity to which the United States aspired in the 1950s. James Murray, writing in *Sports Illustrated* in August 1956, took note of the uncomfortable seats, dirty and inadequate restrooms, and multiplicity of seats with obstructed views that were common in all of the older ballparks, and imagined a husband being told by his wife after he proposed an evening at a baseball game, "The ball park? That filthy hole? Not on your life!" The following spring, *Sports Illustrated*'s annual baseball preview offered a "Spectator's Guide" to the coming season. Yankee fans were warned about "fantastic traffic snarls," and also about taking seats toward the rear of the lower and middle decks, "since overhang obscures all balls hit skyward." At Comiskey Park, readers were reminded that parking and restrooms were inadequate, and that "hot tempers often erupt, so brawls are frequent." Fans at Comiskey also had to contend with the foul odors from nearby stockyards, while attendees at Connie Mack Stadium in Philadelphia often found their cars vandalized, according to the writer David G. Surdam.

The desire for something new was not entirely irrational, then, and it was not only a matter of accommodating an increasingly automobile-centered culture. Still, the next new major league ballpark would not be built until more than twenty years after Cleveland Municipal Stadium opened. It would also be in the Midwest, and also built with public funds. The county of Milwaukee, Wisconsin, which had a minor league baseball team, the Brewers,* wanted to attract a major league team, and decided that a new ballpark would be the way to do it. County planners settled on the expansive site of an abandoned quarry west of downtown, accessible more from freeways than city streets, and hired Osborn Engineering to design a stadium that, like Cleveland's, could work for both baseball and football.

That requirement alone assured that the stadium would not be ideal for either sport. That said, as John Pastier has written, County Stadium "reflected Osborn's ongoing search for an ideal baseball layout free of urban constraints, this time unencumbered by a running track [as at Cleveland Municipal Stadium] and weighted far more toward baseball's demands than football's." County Stadium was surrounded by fourteen thousand parking spaces and was, even more than Cleveland, the antithesis of a classic urban baseball park. Still, if its site felt disconnected from anything other than suburban sprawl, the stadium was a decent place in which to both play and view baseball. Simple and straightforward, with generally good sightlines and a capacity of 36,011 (which was later expanded), its modesty and understatement made it seem in some ways more like the old urban ballparks that it followed than the new suburban ballparks that it prefigured. It felt open to its surroundings, even if the view from the upper grandstand was mainly toward a sea of parking.

---

* Milwaukee had once had a major league team, also called the Brewers, which played at the city's Lloyd Street Grounds in 1901, but it did poorly and moved after a year to Missouri to become the St. Louis Browns.

*County Stadium in
Milwaukee, Wisconsin,
amid a sea of parking,
1957*

The county's gamble worked: the Boston Braves, tired of being the perennial second team in a city dominated by the Red Sox, moved west in 1953 and became the Milwaukee Braves. Four years later, in 1957, they beat the Yankees and won the World Series, but their triumphant years in Milwaukee would be fairly limited. Attendance declined after their World Series win, and in 1965, after only a dozen years in Milwaukee, the Braves would move again, this time to Atlanta, claiming that Milwaukee was not able to provide a large enough fan base to be a suitable home.

County Stadium also served as a part-time playing field for the Green Bay Packers, whose home base was in the small city of Green Bay, 120 miles to the north of Milwaukee, but who played several home games in Milwaukee in the years before their own stadium, Lambeau Field in Green Bay, was expanded to meet NFL standards. The belief that a stadium could work equally well for baseball and football was becoming increasingly common in the 1950s, as the next stadium to be occupied after Milwaukee, Memorial Stadium in Baltimore, made clear. It had

been built as a multi-purpose stadium in 1950 on the site of Baltimore's old Municipal Stadium, primarily to house the Baltimore Colts football team and the city's minor league baseball team, the Orioles, with the hope, as at Milwaukee, that a big new ballpark would attract major league baseball to the city. Here, too, the gamble paid off. When the St. Louis Browns moved east to give Baltimore a major league team (which took over the Orioles name), Memorial was expanded with a second tier of seating, bringing it from a capacity of thirty-one thousand seats to roughly forty-eight thousand.

Although the expansion was ostensibly to make the field more suitable for major league baseball, it made Memorial look even more like a football stadium than it had previously, at least from the outside. A huge bowl set within an enclosure of reinforced concrete and reddish-tan brick, its most notable feature was a plaque running the full height of the building's façade to take note of the war veterans in whose honor the stadium was named. TIME WILL NOT DIM THE GLORY OF THEIR DEEDS reads

Memorial Stadium in Baltimore

the façade, larger than a billboard. Memorial Stadium was also the only major league ballpark to have none of its seating under any kind of roof, which further separated it from the tradition of ballpark grandstands.

Memorial functioned reasonably well for baseball despite its football-like appearance. Reportedly football fans in Baltimore believed the stadium's layout favored baseball, which further underscores the paradox of the multi-purpose stadium: it is never ideal for any sport, and the most devoted fans of one sport, frustrated by the facility's shortcomings, are likely to think that the design favors the needs of another sport over their own. And like many of the ballparks built in the 1950s, Memorial Stadium was in an outlying section of the city, relatively disconnected from the web of activities and transportation that came together in Baltimore's downtown—although here, too, it was unusual in that it was not alongside an interstate highway but in a residential neighborhood of small houses, and was not surrounded by acres of parking. Memorial was an anomaly: architecturally it was in every way a postwar, new-style stadium, but urbanistically its location gave it something of the flavor of an old-style neighborhood ballpark.

Unlike most postwar concrete mixed-use stadiums, Memorial Stadium in Baltimore was located in a residential area.

More characteristic of what was happening in the 1950s were Municipal Stadium in Kansas City and Metropolitan Stadium in Minneapolis–St. Paul, both expansions of minor league ballparks intended to make their cities competitive for major league baseball. The Kansas City stadium occupied the site of the city's venerable Muehlebach Field at Brooklyn Avenue and East Twenty-second Street; the old ballpark dated from 1923 and had housed both the Kansas City Blues minor league team and the Kansas City Monarchs of the Negro League, whose roster at various times included Hall of Famers Satchel Paige, Bullet Rogan, Hilton Smith, and, after he emerged from the Army in 1945, a shortstop named Jackie Robinson. It was at Kansas City Municipal that Branch Rickey, the general manager and co-owner of the Brooklyn Dodgers, saw Robinson play and signed him for the Dodgers.

Kansas City originally planned to expand by adding an upper deck. But the old stadium—called Ruppert Stadium after 1937, when Jacob Ruppert, the Yankees owner, bought the Kansas City Blues as a farm team, and then, after Ruppert's death in 1943, known as Blues Stadium—turned out to be too unstable to support new construction. Instead, it was demolished and replaced by a new two-decked ballpark seating just over thirty thousand that opened in 1955 as the new home of the Athletics, relocated from Philadelphia. The new stadium was constructed on the footprint of the original, however, which made it strikingly different from most other new ballparks. Kansas City Municipal's relatively small size and fairly straightforward, plain design—the field was a big rectangle, in effect a very large diamond with the infield diamond at one corner, and just a simple, low wall along most of right field and left center field—gave it an intimacy more reminiscent of early ballparks than postwar stadiums, despite the fact that the field was large. (Charlie Finley, who bought the Athletics in 1960, would move fences in toward home plate several times, most famously in an attempt to replicate the right field dimensions of Yankee Stadium.)

The upper deck, which curved gently around home plate, had supporting columns blocking some views, making the ballpark feel even more like a leftover from an earlier generation. Like so many ballparks in the 1950s, it was pressed into double duty for football, but Municipal Stadium was so intrinsically a baseball park that it only worked for football if the field was laid out along the first-base line, with a temporary grandstand erected opposite in left field. That meant that the Kansas City Chiefs had to start their season with a series of away games, since football could not begin until the baseball season was over and the stadium could be converted.

Municipal Stadium did not have a long life. Finley moved the Athletics to Oakland, California, in 1967, just a dozen years after former President Harry S. Truman had thrown out the first ball to open the new stadium. Two years later, Kansas City's expansion team, the Royals, arrived; they remained for three seasons, after which they moved to the new Truman Sports Complex, which opened in 1972.* Four years later, in 1976, Municipal Stadium was torn down and replaced with single-family houses. It had lasted for only twenty-one years.

If Kansas City built a bigger version of an old ballpark on the urban site of its early ballpark, Minneapolis went in another direction entirely in its quest to attract a major league team: it abandoned the city altogether and went to suburban Bloomington, midway between downtown Minneapolis and the center of its "twin" city, St. Paul. There, on 160 acres of farmland, the city erected Metropolitan Stadium, its incongruous name presumably a way of avoiding anything that referred specifically either to Minneapolis or St. Paul. When it opened in 1956, Metropolitan Stadium housed the Minneapolis Millers, a minor league team affiliated with the New York Giants, and there was hope that Horace Stoneham, who then owned the Giants and was considering a move out of New York, would see the Twin Cities as his team's destiny.

Once again Osborn Engineering was hired, along with architects Thorshov & Cerny, who produced a twenty-two-thousand-seat stadium that had relatively little character architecturally; it was a disjointed array of different sections, with a three-deck grandstand around home plate, an uncovered two-deck grandstand down the first-base line, and open bleachers down the third-base line. It did have an exterior composed of rectangular panels in various colors, giving the building something of the air of a 1950s Formica kitchen, but the stadium's most memorable feature was its siting in the midst of a vast sea of parking, a reminder that it was designed with the expectation that every one of its occupants would arrive by car.

* See Chapter 7.

It took some time to attract a major league team. Both Horace Stoneham and Calvin Griffith, owner of the Washington Senators, were impressed, if only because Metropolitan Stadium looked clean and new beside Stoneham's aging Polo Grounds and Griffith's Griffith Stadium, which looked no fresher. It was, Stoneham reportedly said, not only the best stadium the minor leagues had, it was better than almost every major league facility. Major league baseball's rules at the time gave the Giants first rights to a major league team in the area, and it was not unreasonable that local civic leaders thought the Giants were headed for Minnesota.

In the end, it would be Griffith's Senators who would relocate and become the Minnesota Twins, as Stoneham spurned both Minnesota and New York's offer to build a new stadium to replace the Polo Grounds and chose instead to decamp for San Francisco. Metropolitan Stadium was expanded to thirty thousand seats to mark the arrival of the Twins, who played their first game in April 1961, five years after the ballpark opened. It would accommodate noticeably better to baseball than to football, as the Minnesota Vikings would discover when they arrived to share the stadium and added a huge double-decked grandstand in left field parallel to where the gridiron was placed, making the stadium look even more like an assemblage of disjointed parts.

Metropolitan Stadium in Bloomington, Minn., a site that later became the Mall of America

Metropolitan Stadium had a longer life than Municipal Stadium in Kansas City, but not by much. The Twins left after the 1982 season for the Hubert Humphrey Metrodome in downtown Minneapolis, an indoor stadium that offered relief from Minnesota weather in exchange for giving up any semblance of a traditional ballpark. The Metrodome returned the Twins to a more urban venue, but as a fully enclosed stadium that offered not even a glimpse of the sky, let alone its surroundings, it was even more distant from early baseball parks than Metropolitan Stadium. As for the stadium on the former farmland in Bloomington, it lay empty for three years and was demolished in 1985, its land given over to a far more natural symbol of its suburban location. It became the site of the Mall of America, the largest shopping mall in the United States.

Horace Stoneham's flirtation with Minneapolis emerged from a long period of dissatisfaction with the Polo Grounds. Though it was never the greatest of its generation of ballparks, the unusual symmetry of the Polo Grounds' 1911 iteration, expanded in 1922, did give it a certain distinctive presence, with a semicircular grandstand embracing home plate at its center, and long, parallel rows of grandstands extending into the outfields. If it was often said to resemble a bathtub, it was a very grand bathtub indeed. But its horseshoe shape connected neither to the diamond itself nor to the history of idiosyncratically shaped ballparks, and it meant that many seats were at an awkward distance from the field of play. Foul lines were unusually short, and outfields were exceptionally deep. Ironically, with its extended parallel grandstands on opposite sides of the field, the Polo Grounds was the only one of its generation of ballparks that was better suited for football than baseball.

The Giants had lived with the design of the Polo Grounds for generations, however, and its curious configuration had been the venue of some of baseball's most memorable moments—among others, Willie Mays's famous catch in the opening game of the 1954 World Series against the Cleveland Indians and Bobby Thomson's game-winning home run against the Dodgers to give the Giants the National League pennant in 1951, a hit that had the luck of occurring in the first game to be broadcast nationwide, which led it to be remembered as "the shot heard 'round the world." But if the Polo Grounds was as established in baseball history as Ebbets Field or Yankee Stadium, it was older than both of them, and in no better condition. There was minimal parking, and its site high on Coogan's Bluff was in the northern reaches of Harlem, a part of the city that was not attractive to the Giants' fan base, much of which, like that of all the New York teams, had relocated to the suburbs. In 1956, the Giants attracted only 629,000 fans to the Polo Grounds, the worst attendance in the National League. The Giants, the mightiest franchise in New York before the rise of the Yankees, needed something drastic to revive their fortunes, and a new ballpark might be just the thing. Since the early 1950s, Robert Moses, New York's planning czar and its most active proponent of the bulldoze-and-rebuild philosophy of urban renewal common in that decade, had been eyeing the Polo Grounds as a site for public housing. Horace Stoneham, who was eager to move rather than refurbish the old ballpark, is not known to have objected.

But where? There were reports that the city of New York had offered to build a new ballpark for the Giants in midtown Manhattan, on the site west of Pennsylvania Station that had been considered by the Yankees decades earlier, but that project, if it was ever real at all, does not appear to have gone very far. Stoneham's flirtations with Minneapolis were well known, but they came to nothing. The city that seduced him was San Francisco, which in 1954 had joined the club of cities whose voters agreed to expend taxpayer funds to finance a baseball stadium in the hope of attracting a major league team. That year San Francisco passed a $5 million bond issue with the provision that the money would be spent only if a major league team agreed to come to the city within five years. Three of those five years would pass before Stoneham would make his decision to turn the New York Giants into the San Francisco Giants, and it would be another three years before the team would actually play in the stadium San Francisco built for it, which would become a story of delays, cost overruns, and ultimately embarrassments for the city.

There was, first, a fight over whether to build a new stadium downtown or in an outlying area. Ultimately fear of traffic congestion led to the decision to go to Candlestick Point, a peninsula overlooking San Francisco Bay south of the city, where a builder, Charles Harney, dangled before the city an undeveloped forty-one-acre parcel of land that he owned and sold to San Francisco for $2.7 million, more than twice the value it had been assessed for two years before. The city, desperate

Candlestick Park, on a point of land jutting into San Francisco Bay, which created unpleasantly windy conditions

to make up for lost time, gave Harney a no-bid contract to build the stadium himself, a deal that in 1958 prompted a grand jury investigation. Harney hired John Bolles, an architect who had never designed a stadium, and planned to name it for himself. This was the one aspect of the project on which the city, which was paying the bills, chose to challenge him. It decided to hold a naming contest. Candlestick Park was the overwhelming public choice.

Harney was probably lucky not to have his name attached to the stadium, since it was never a success. Bolles's modern, reinforced concrete stadium—and despite the word *park* in its name, everything about its design had more in common with the stadiums of the period than with the ballparks of an earlier age—cost closer to $15 million than the

$5 million appropriated in the bond issue, and despite the inflated cost turned out to be poorly built, with constant problems with structure and engineering, including a radiant heating system under the box seats that never worked because the pipes were incorrectly installed. It was the last ballpark built to have its upper deck supported by columns, meaning that some seats had compromised views of the field. Also, as with many postwar stadiums, its expansive layout had none of the intimacy of older baseball parks; while the original capacity—43,765—was not enormous, even the field seats felt distant from play, partly because of the excessively deep foul zones.

The biggest issue, however, was temperature. There were constant chilling winds in a site so open to the bay, which, despite a pre-construction test that reportedly showed no winds stronger than fourteen miles an hour, were frequent and often at much higher velocities than the test had shown. The portion of the site chosen for the ballpark was damp, foggy, and turned out to be especially susceptible to gusts of wind coming off the bay, which entered the stadium and then swirled around within its semicircular, double-decked concrete grandstand, giving Candlestick something of the effect of a wind tunnel in a barrel. Not for nothing was the stadium nicknamed "the cave of winds." (The initial wind test turned out to have been done in the morning, when winds off the bay are generally mild. City officials either did not know, or chose to ignore, the fact that San Francisco Bay winds generally increased as the day went on.)

The Giants moved to San Francisco in 1958 and played for two seasons at Seals Stadium, a handsome minor league ballpark with a vaguely Art Moderne air that had been built in 1931 in the Mission District, as they waited for the completion of Candlestick, which turned out to be behind schedule as well as over budget. It was finally finished in time for the 1960 season. As Michael Gershman would write, "It was a sad commentary on the first modern ballpark built with a franchise in place . . . it was built hurriedly, by novices, in the midst of civic recriminations, and in the wrong place."

The winds made the stadium so cold that the Giants played fewer night games than any major league team except the Chicago Cubs, who had the only field that lacked lights. After several years of suffering, the team's marketing officials tried to make the most of the situation by offering "Croix de Candlestick" pins to fans who stayed through the rare extra-inning night games, which showed a snow-capped version of the team's monogram and had the Latin motto *Veni, Vidi, Vixi* (slightly changed to "I came, I saw, I survived"). The wind and constant dampness also made it difficult to maintain the grass for play, and for a number of years Candlestick had artificial turf. In 1971, ostensibly to accommodate the arrival of the San Francisco 49ers football team but also in the hope that enclosing the stadium would reduce the winds, Candlestick was expanded to more than sixty thousand seats and its grandstands were extended around the open section facing the bay. The expanded stadium was awkward in shape—neither a circle nor an oval, it was an irregular geometric form that represented a compromise for football and made the stadium even less comfortable for baseball, since it guaranteed that baseball fans in the outfield were at maximum distance from the field of play. It was clear proof of the compromises inherent in multi-sports stadiums. True, the winds dropped somewhat, but the stadium remained chilly and damp, and the view of San Francisco Bay, which had been the one compensation for fans putting up with the stadium's discomfort, was gone.

As the arrival of intercity rail service had made the development of the leagues possible in the nineteenth century, it was the development of cross-country air travel, first in the form of turboprop planes and soon thereafter with fully jet-powered passenger airliners, that made it practical for major league baseball teams to even consider a California location, given the need to make frequent trips across the continent to hold to a tight schedule of games. Without nonstop air travel, it would have been unthinkable for a major league team to be based on the West Coast and maintain the same densely packed schedule as the rest of the league.

But if there were only a single team on the West Coast it would be an outlier, and in May 1957, by which time the Giants' move out of New York had become all but certain, the National League owners passed a resolution stating that they would approve a move only if at least one other team moved west also, so that other National League teams traveling to California could justify the cost of the trip by scheduling a series of games with each team. The National League's ruling, as much as any other factor, effectively tied the future of the two New York teams together, since at the time the Dodgers were the only other East Coast team seriously

considering a move. So either the Giants and the Dodgers would both relocate to California, or neither of them. In any event, when Stoneham announced in August 1957 that the Giants were moving to San Francisco, the destiny of the Brooklyn Dodgers remained far from clear. It was not impossible that Walter O'Malley might keep the Dodgers in New York, and if he did, the league's approval of Stoneham's move to San Francisco would almost surely be revoked under the terms of its May decree.

While Stoneham was the first to commit, then, it was O'Malley who held the cards. He had actually started all the talk about California years before, and had been unhappy with Ebbets since he first became co-owner of the Dodgers. A lawyer who saw baseball as a business, he had neither the legacy relationship to the Polo Grounds of Horace Stoneham, who inherited the Giants from his father, or the almost spiritual connection to Ebbets of his partner, the Dodgers president and general manager, Branch Rickey. O'Malley felt even more strongly than Stoneham that he was burdened with an old, deteriorating ballpark that had neither

The decline of the neighborhood around Ebbets Field was one of the reasons Walter O'Malley chose to abandon the famous ballpark.

modern conveniences—parking first among them—nor the space to add them. Ebbets Field, Jerald Podair has written, had "dirty bathrooms, narrow aisles, rusting pillars and a general down-at-the-heels raffishness that charmed only those who did not patronize it regularly."

O'Malley's view of Ebbets was one of many points of contention between him and Rickey, who also owned a share of the team. Rickey, who was the major force behind the team's historic decision to integrate major league baseball by signing Jackie Robinson to play for the Dodgers, was inclined to see Ebbets, however rundown, as a part of the team's legacy that should be improved, not replaced, but the future of the stadium was never Rickey's priority. O'Malley, for his part, had only owned a share of the team for two years when, in 1946, he began asking architects for advice about what he might do with Ebbets, well before Horace Stoneham began to look at alternatives for the Giants. According to Jerald Podair, that was the year that O'Malley first contacted the architect and engineer Emil Praeger—whom, years later, he would engage to design Dodger Stadium in Los Angeles—to ask his advice about "enlarging or replacing our present stadium." It was the beginning of a sixteen-year-long road that would connect O'Malley to two of the twentieth century's most celebrated designers, Norman Bel Geddes and Buckminster Fuller; to New York's planning and redevelopment czar, Robert Moses; and to the mayor of New York City, Robert Wagner, the governor, Averell Harriman, and numerous other public officials. It would involve struggles over two sites in downtown Brooklyn and one in Queens as well as an old stadium in Jersey City, and would finally end on the other side of the continent in Los Angeles with a whole new set of political, economic, and urban planning challenges.

O'Malley and Rickey did not have a smooth partnership, in part because both men wanted to be the boss. In 1950 Rickey convinced the real estate developer William Zeckendorf to bid $1 million for his share of the Dodgers, forcing O'Malley to come up with money to match it to gain full control of the team. By 1950, Rickey was gone and O'Malley became the team's president. Even though Rickey was the more experienced baseball executive and the man who, with Jackie Robinson, changed the modern history of baseball, the first years of O'Malley's tenure as president were years of glory for the Dodgers on the field, as the roster of iconic players Rickey had assembled, including Pee Wee Reese,

Duke Snider, Roy Campanella, and Carl Erskine, not to mention Jackie Robinson, won four pennants and, in their ultimate triumph, defeated the Yankees in the 1955 World Series. The Dodgers, always a beloved eccentricity in New York, solidified their position as the team of the working class, the idiosyncratic assemblage of likeable, ordinary guys who conquered the elite Yankees.

Off the field, however, things were in turmoil. The team's loyal fan base did not always translate into the highest profits, and O'Malley was convinced that Ebbets Field was an albatross, not an asset. With only thirty-two thousand seats, even a sold-out game yielded the team far less potential income than the Yankees or the Giants could earn in their ballparks. O'Malley closely watched the success of the former Boston team, the Braves, as they settled into their new, publicly owned stadium in Milwaukee, where they led the major leagues in attendance every year from 1953 to 1957. The Braves' total ticket sales their first year in Milwaukee were six times that of their last year in Boston.

O'Malley was willing to consider anything. He had been approached by civic leaders in Los Angeles in 1955 and 1956, but brushed them off both times, saying that he did not plan to move to the West Coast and

Jackie Robinson, with Dodgers president Branch Rickey

was intent on building a new stadium in Brooklyn. For a long time, he appears to have worked earnestly to bring that about. Even before his plans ran aground, however, he opened more serious discussions with Los Angeles, and made the decision in early 1957 to acquire a Los Angeles minor league team from the Chicago Cubs along with its ballpark, Wrigley Field in south Los Angeles, a small masterpiece from 1925 that had been designed by Zachary Taylor Davis, architect of Weeghman Park in Chicago, which would be given the same name, Wrigley Field, the following year. With a slender twelve-story office tower as its campanile, the Los Angeles Wrigley was arguably the most elegant of all minor league ballparks. It gave O'Malley a strong card to play in Los Angeles, even as he was continuing to push every lever he could find back East.

The year before, in 1956, desperate to make a public statement of some kind about his desire for change, O'Malley scheduled seven home games in Roosevelt Stadium in Jersey City, ostensibly an accommodation to the Dodgers' large body of fans from suburban New Jersey who traveled by automobile and found getting to Ebbets Field a nuisance, but also a public rebuke of his team's venerable home field and an implicit acknowledgment of his indifference to seriously trying to improve it. He would repeat the Jersey City stand in 1957.

Wrigley Field, Los Angeles, which was the most elegant of minor league ballparks

By then, O'Malley, obsessed with the desire for a new ballpark, was actively pursuing opportunities for the Dodgers on both coasts.

Yet for all that many Dodger fans, like those of the Giants and the Yankees, had decamped for the suburbs, Dodger fans as a group seemed, at least in the early 1950s, to be more content with Ebbets Field than the team's ownership was. For all the issues the old ballpark posed, it would never be the fans' frustration with Ebbets Field that would doom it. It would be Walter O'Malley's. And before O'Malley's determination to be free of Ebbets Field found its final resolution in Los Angeles it would lead to two of the most ambitious, if unworkable, unbuilt stadium designs of the twentieth century.

Norman Bel Geddes was one of the most admired designers in the United States in the 1940s, a man who straddled the worlds of architecture, planning, theater, and product design. His most celebrated work was the Futurama at the General Motors Pavilion in the 1939 New York World's Fair, an enticing vision of a city of handsome modern towers and open motorways filled with new cars that moved rapidly and smoothly across a sleek, glittering landscape. The automobile in the 1930s and '40s seemed to hold forth the promise of a new kind of city, beside which the grandstands of Ebbets and the old neighborhood of Flatbush in which they sat would seem not charmingly quaint but tired, inefficient, and obsolete. The Futurama was a highly seductive packaging of this new world of speeding cars and handsome towers. It is not surprising that O'Malley, whose view of baseball was shaped by his desire to attract larger crowds as well as a constant determination to modernize and update his business, would have thought that Bel Geddes might help him find a way out of what he considered to be the problem of Ebbets Field.

Whether or not O'Malley was serious when he asked Emil Praeger to think about improving Ebbets as well as replacing it, he made no such request of Bel Geddes when he approached him in 1948. He asked the designer to come up with a completely new stadium design, one that would aspire to the same postwar excitement that the Futurama promised. It would be on a different site, in downtown Brooklyn, where O'Malley had determined that the intersection of Atlantic and Flatbush Avenues, beside the Long Island Railroad station, would be ideal: at the crossroads of two of Brooklyn's main avenues, multiple subway lines, and a commuter railroad, not to mention within walking distance of several residential districts. Another bonus was that it was closer to Manhattan and New Jersey than Ebbets. It was hard to imagine a more convenient and well-connected site that could still claim a Brooklyn address.

There was one significant problem with the corner of Atlantic and Flatbush: O'Malley did not own it, and its centrality made it far more valuable than the land he had at Ebbets Field. To build there he needed help, and for that he turned to Robert Moses, who controlled New York's urban renewal program with an iron hand. Other cities were building municipal stadiums, O'Malley reasoned, and he was not even asking that New York build the Dodgers a new stadium, only that Moses acquire the land he wanted through Title I of the federal government's urban renewal act, which allowed condemnation of private property for beneficial public use. What more public use could there be, O'Malley argued, than a big new baseball stadium that everyone would enjoy?

If Moses would declare Atlantic and Flatbush an urban renewal area eligible for federal funding and would make the acquired land available to the Dodgers, O'Malley knew just what he wanted to build. Bel Geddes unveiled the design of O'Malley's dreams in 1949: a sprawling, swooping structure that would have been the first baseball park with a retractable roof, anticipating the SkyDome in Toronto by forty years. Bel Geddes, encouraged by O'Malley's desire to entertain ever-larger crowds, and working in tandem with Emil Praeger as engineer, envisioned a stadium with what amounted to an enormous amusement complex and shopping mall beneath the stands, with parking for five thousand cars. "It won't be just a ballpark, of course. It will have to be more of a community center, with shopping facilities, playgrounds for children, possibly a couple of movie houses," Bel Geddes said. O'Malley envisioned nothing less than a new center for Brooklyn's commercial, civic, and social life, in the form of "a perfect enclosure that would allow the Dodgers to control their park's surroundings," as Andrew Lang has written. "Where Ebbets Field was surrounded by a hodgepodge of tenements, factories and shops, the Dodgers would control and own this enclosed corporate community, allowing them to maintain an ideal setting for middle class suburban fans." Bel Geddes had in mind a stadium that could also double as a convention and exhibition center, and would even include winter ice skating, harking back to the days of Union Grounds and Washington Park.

It was undoubtedly spectacular, and a stunning advance in stadium design. It was also utterly indifferent to the practical needs of baseball as a game, not to mention to its traditions. Bel Geddes broke with almost everything that had defined the best early ballparks, particularly the sense of connection they had both to their immediate urban surroundings and to the sky. The Bel Geddes stadium's huge size—it would have seated fifty-five thousand for baseball, on top of all the space devoted to other amusements—as well as its inward focus put it at a complete remove from the active Brooklyn streets. If it had any spiritual ancestor among old ballparks, it would have been Chris Von der Ahe's Sportsman's Park in St. Louis, which Von der Ahe conceived of as an entertainment zone that had a baseball game at its center. But there was no physical resemblance to Sportsman's Park, which was an integral part of its St. Louis neighborhood, whereas the instincts behind the Bel Geddes design were more those of the urban shopping malls and entertainment complexes of a later generation, enormous structures that presented themselves as alternatives to the urban fabric rather than as parts of a city's connective tissue. The delicate balance between structure and nature that marked the great baseball parks was altogether absent here. The aspect of baseball's past that seems to have excited Bel Geddes and O'Malley the most was not its physical setting, but its potential to serve as popular entertainment. They set out to connect baseball to what they saw as the new forms of entertainment of the postwar age, and to house it in a place that emphasized a new view of urbanism in which connection to either sky or street meant little.

The design was, if nothing else, remarkably prophetic, foreshadowing much of what would happen in the 1960s and '70s, when baseball would take a long, frustrating detour into the realm of domed stadiums, vast, enclosed public objects that most fans traveled to in smaller, enclosed private objects on wheels. Bel Geddes's design acknowledged the changing world in another way, too: in a long presentation of a later version of the scheme in the September 27, 1952, issue of *Collier's* magazine, it was billed as "Baseball's Answer to TV," the presumption being that O'Malley's pleasure dome would be so enticing that it would eliminate the temptation for fans to stay at home and watch games on television.

The author of the *Collier's* feature, Tom Meany, described the new stadium as designed "on the rather novel theory that baseball fans are people. They have been planning a baseball park in which the customers will be comfortable," a not very subtle dig at the conditions of Ebbets Field. But Bel Geddes's notion of comfort in the 1950s was not unlike that decade's view that shoppers would be happier in covered malls than on the street. Yes, there would be parking and certain creature comforts, but these things would exact a huge price in the quality of urban life, a price that it would take decades to discover. Bel Geddes, like the designers of early shopping malls, thought standardization was a plus, and he pointed with pride to the fact that his field would have an identical home run distance in all directions. "He deplores the pop fly which becomes a four-bagger merely through the architectural fluke of the proximity of the stands at the foul line," Meany wrote. "At the Polo Grounds, for instance, a ball hit down the right-field foul line need travel only 258 feet and clear a 10½ foot wall to become a home run. In the same ball park, a ball hit 450 feet toward right or left-center can be caught for an out. In the new Dodger Stadium there will be a constant home run range of 380 feet over a 10-foot wall anywhere in the outfield between the foul lines." Bel Geddes believed that the idiosyncrasies that made ballparks distinctive and varied the game from place to place were not an asset but a liability, and he was proud that his design would eliminate them.

Unfortunately for O'Malley—but perhaps luckily for those who believed Brooklyn deserved something other than an early version of the Toronto SkyDome at its heart—Robert Moses had no interest in supporting his plan. It had nothing to do with any reluctance to replace Ebbets, which Moses, who famously had little patience with old and shabby structures anywhere in New York, would probably have been as happy to dispose of as O'Malley was. And it was certainly not a disagreement with Bel Geddes's vision of a city redesigned for the convenience of the automobile, since that was exactly what Moses, a builder of expressways and bridges who almost always prioritized cars over mass transit, did in many of his other projects. The problem was more that Moses, an autocrat to the core, favored those public works projects that he conceived of himself and could personally control, and he had relatively little interest in anything else. He had not originated the notion of a stadium for the Dodgers in downtown Brooklyn, nor would he have had any say in running it. The project would belong to O'Malley, a scrappy, Bronx-born Irish Catholic and a man whom Moses, who had been born of

Jewish parentage but who saw himself more as a patrician Anglo-Saxon Protestant, treated with disdain. Moses decreed that to use Title I urban renewal powers to help a professional baseball team would be an inappropriate use of public funds to benefit a private corporation. "A new ball field for the Dodgers cannot be dressed up as a Title I project," Moses wrote. That private enterprise regularly benefited from the Title I urban renewal program in the form of real estate developers who built urban renewal housing under its auspices was, apparently, of little relevance to Moses, who appeared mainly to be seeking an excuse to reject O'Malley's request.

Another reason for Moses's intransigence regarding Atlantic and Flatbush Avenues was that if there was to be a new baseball park in New York he had another site in mind for it, not in Brooklyn but in Flushing Meadows, Queens. It was the site of the 1939 World's Fair, which Moses had been in charge of building and where Norman Bel Geddes's Futurama had been displayed; in the 1950s, one of Moses's projects was to oversee the conversion of Flushing Meadows into a permanent city park. There was room for a stadium and all the parking the Dodgers could want there, Moses felt, and he would be willing to build it and lease it to the team. O'Malley visited the site as a courtesy to Moses. But he had not the slightest interest in it. To move the Brooklyn Dodgers to a stadium in Queens—and one that he could only rent, not own—was, to him, tantamount to leaving the city altogether. It would not matter, he said, if he took the Dodgers "five miles or 3,000 miles" away. If they were not in Brooklyn, they could be anywhere.

There were many other twists and turns in the long saga of the Dodgers' departure, including another version of the domed stadium, this one designed by the visionary engineer and futurist Buckminster Fuller in 1955, which Fuller produced in association with his class of graduate students at Princeton, and which was to have had one of Fuller's trademark geodesic domes spanning relatively conventional, circular grandstands. If Bel Geddes's design prefigured the lavish SkyDome that would be built for the Blue Jays in Toronto in 1989, Fuller's anticipated the circular, fixed-roof Astrodome that would open in Houston in 1965. By the time of the Fuller scheme it had dawned on the city and state governments of New York that Robert Moses's intransigence regarding O'Malley's site at Atlantic and Flatbush Avenues made the loss of the team a serious pos-

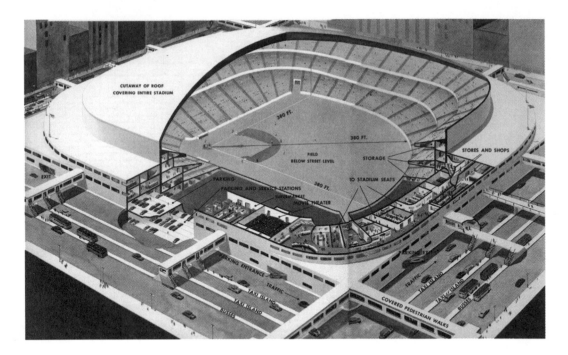

sibility. In a desperate attempt to get around Moses's bureaucratic grip on public construction funds, they set up the quasi-public Brooklyn Sports Center Authority in 1956. The authority was charged with issuing bonds to finance a large stadium that would have been part of a broader urban renewal project for the site.

But it all came to naught. O'Malley negotiated with the city and state through 1956 and 1957, even as he was also in serious conversations with political and business leaders in Los Angeles who were eager to have the Dodgers on the West Coast. O'Malley is widely thought to have decided to move the team by early 1957 and to have skillfully played New York's politicians for the rest of the year in order to get a better deal out of Los Angeles, although Jerald Podair has argued that the Dodgers' owner, for all that he saw baseball as a business, was not so cynical, and was genuinely undecided for much of that year, waiting for the best offer from either city. "As he faced the most important decision of his professional life and peered into the unknown, he simply did not know what to do," Podair has written. "Walter O'Malley knew what he wanted, but not how to get it."

What O'Malley really wanted was to reinvent the experience of the

Norman Bel Geddes planned for a domed stadium in downtown Brooklyn, which would have included shopping, a movie theater, and parking in a single huge structure.

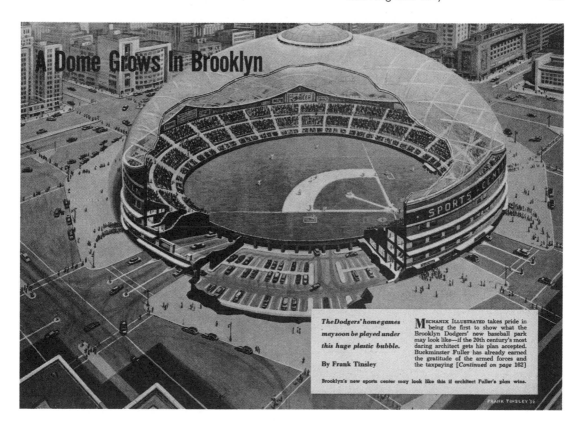

A Dome Grows In Brooklyn

The Dodgers' home games may soon be played under this huge plastic bubble.

By Frank Tinsley

MECHANIX ILLUSTRATED takes pride in being the first to show what the Brooklyn Dodgers' new baseball park may look like—if the 20th century's most daring architect gets his plan accepted. Buckminster Fuller has already earned the gratitude of the armed forces and the taxpaying [Continued on page 162]

Brooklyn's new sports center may look like this if architect Fuller's plan wins.

FRANK TINSLEY '56

ballpark, and he was prepared to do it on whichever coast he could find the financial support, and the freedom, that he needed. Los Angeles was not making it any easier for him than New York. O'Malley had agreed with the proposal of Los Angeles officials that he build the new Dodger Stadium in Chavez Ravine, a 350-acre site near downtown Los Angeles that the city offered him in exchange for Wrigley Field, south of downtown. It was what he had sought in Brooklyn—land for no charge—and though technically a trade and not a gift, it was by any measure a generous deal since Chavez Ravine was many times the size of the parcel O'Malley was giving up in exchange, and more favorably located. The city's contract with the Dodgers committed it to preparing the site, and to building access roads from nearby freeways, while O'Malley would build the stadium structure itself.

Chavez Ravine was not without its issues, however. The first problem was that it was not the virgin land that it appeared to be. It was

Buckminster Fuller, like Bel Geddes, led a design team that came up with a scheme for a large domed stadium in downtown Brooklyn, with parking underneath the field.

*Chavez Ravine
excavations to make
way for the new Dodger
Stadium in Los Angeles*

the longtime home to a neighborhood of Mexican immigrants, most of whom had been forcibly removed from their residences when the site was cleared in 1950 for a huge public housing project designed by the architect Richard Neutra that had never been built. In the minds of many Angelenos, the name Chavez Ravine still had the stigma of association with the destruction of a poor Latino community. Although the property was controlled by the city, several Mexican families still remained on it in defiance of city orders.

If O'Malley had expected that California would bring him relief from the relentless battleground of New York, then he was quickly disappointed. He arrived in Los Angeles late in October 1957 to find himself in the midst of a political firestorm over Chavez Ravine that was in some ways more intense than what Robert Moses had put him through in New York. An organization called the Citizens Committee to Save Chavez Ravine for the People objected to the contract the city had signed with the Dodgers, and filed suit to override it. While the City Council had approved the contract by a vote of 10 to 4, it was clear that a significant minority of the city's public officials, and plenty of its citizens, were not prepared to greet O'Malley with open arms, and he found himself swept up in a whole new wave of political turmoil that would lead to a public referendum in 1958 challenging the validity of the city's contract with the Dodgers. Even that was only the beginning: after voters narrowly approved the contract in the referendum, opponents took the city and the Dodgers to court, and won. The appellate process went all the way to the United States Supreme Court, which finally upheld the city's contract with the Dodgers in September 1959.

By that point, the team had already been playing in Los Angeles for two seasons, and had yet to break ground on its new stadium. O'Malley, rejecting Wrigley Field as too small for the team's temporary home—it had ten thousand fewer seats than Ebbets—tried and failed to negotiate a lease for the Rose Bowl in nearby Pasadena, and finally settled on the Los Angeles Coliseum, a vast oval constructed in the 1920s, enlarged for the 1932 Olympics, and far more suitable for football than baseball. The largest stadium ever to host major league baseball—with almost ninety-five thousand seats, it made Cleveland Municipal Stadium seem as intimate as Ebbets Field—it resisted all natural configurations for baseball. O'Malley himself came up with the plan the Dodgers used, which put the baseball diamond in one corner of the oval, yielding an exceptionally short left field, and an enormous right center field. Technically, a hit to left as little as 250 feet could be a home run, and a hit to right center as long as 440 feet could be caught as an out. To compensate for the short left field, the Dodgers erected a 40-foot screen atop the left field wall so that balls that were not hit high would bounce back and remain in play rather than be automatic home runs. But that tweak did nothing to make up for the fact that many of the seats in the Coliseum were so far from the diamond that their occupants could barely see the infield.

The Dodgers would play at the Coliseum for four seasons, and would win the World Series in their second, in 1959. That triumph could do only so much, however, to offset the daunting politics of building at Chavez Ravine. Not only were there the Latino families who remained on the land—O'Malley would end up buying them out at considerable cost—there were also planning issues, including disputes about road access to the Chavez Ravine site and about what other uses the city's zoning would permit there beside the stadium. Plans for other commercial structures, which would have given the new stadium at least a smattering of an urban context, were defeated by downtown merchants who feared that O'Malley's stadium would become the genesis of a commercial neighborhood that would compete with the city's downtown.

The result was that Dodger Stadium, by the time construction finally started in 1960, was an island in the midst of a sea of parking, from an urban design standpoint no more advanced than stadiums like Metropolitan, outside of Minneapolis. The urban context of Chavez Ravine was questionable, of course, since it was hilly and cut off from surrounding neighborhoods by its topography; an enormous amount of earth moving would be required to make it flat enough to accommodate the stadium and its parking lots. While the center of downtown Los Angeles was little more than a mile away and the city's skyline, modest as it was in the 1950s, could be seen from the site, downtown nevertheless seemed another world from Chavez Ravine, which felt all the more isolated because of the presence of three adjacent freeways that made the stadium site accessible from other parts of the city but also cut it off from its surroundings.

It was a site like no other in Los Angeles: accessible and secluded at the same time. It was, in a sense, a metaphor for the city itself, or at least for what the city aspired to, which was both movement and privacy. Los Angeles in the 1950s was redefining urban form, establishing a new kind of city for the twentieth century, where almost all architecture of note was residential, not public. The city was based around the needs of automobile travel, and it implicitly elevated the private realm over the public realm. It was easy to think that the most important public spaces in Los Angeles in this era were its freeways, which seemed to express the city's nature far more than its streets.

But if Los Angeles then did not have lively streets like Fifth Avenue in New York or Flatbush Avenue in Brooklyn, or many significant monumental public buildings, it did have one major piece of public architecture that would, at least conceptually, exert as much influence on Dodger Stadium as any previous ballpark. It was called Disneyland, and it had been completed just two years before, in 1955. It was, the architect Charles Moore has written, the one place in which southern Californians could enjoy the traditional urban idea of walking around together in a pleasant public space. "Disneyland must be regarded as the most impor-

tant single piece of construction in the West in the past several decades," Moore wrote. "The assumption inevitably made by people who have not yet been there—that it is some sort of physical extension of Mickey Mouse—is wildly inaccurate. Instead, single-handed, it is engaged in replacing many of those elements of the public realm that have vanished in the featureless private floating world of southern California, whose only edge is the ocean, and whose center is otherwise undiscoverable. Curiously, for a public place, Disneyland is not free. You buy tickets at the gate. But then, Versailles cost someone a great deal of money, too. Now, as then, you have to pay for the public life."

O'Malley's intentions paralleled Disney's. With Dodger Stadium, O'Malley sought to go beyond the funky baseball parks of old in the same way that Disney's park went beyond the tawdry amusement parks and carnival midways of old. O'Malley, like Walt Disney, wanted to create a public experience in the city of private experiences, to expand the notion of an attractive public realm in a city notoriously short on public space. Like Disneyland, of course, O'Malley's public space would not be truly public, and would require tickets at the gate. And like Disney, O'Malley was determined to justify what he was charging by making his place as bright and wholesome as possible, and relying heavily on the tools of entertainment.

Walter O'Malley, in the press box of his lavish new Dodger Stadium

Architect Emil Praeger's rendering of Dodger Stadium, 1959

What mattered most to O'Malley was that no one mistake Dodger Stadium for an old-style ballpark—especially the one he had been so determined to leave in Brooklyn. It would be big, open, shiny, and clean, the opposite of all the things he hated about Ebbets. If a sea of parking lots was the price one paid for this—well, what of it. An inability to accommodate to the automobile was one of the things that, in O'Malley's view, had done in Ebbets; this time there would be no similar mistake. One of O'Malley's most intriguing ideas on that front failed to win approval from the city, namely his notion that holders of the most expensive box seats might drive right up to the entrance to their boxes: the baseball park as part of the southern California drive-in experience. When Dodger Stadium was being planned, the notion that the automobile might choke Los Angeles rather than liberate it was not on anyone's radar, let alone Walter O'Malley's.

To turn his ideas into construction plans O'Malley went back to Emil Praeger, the New York–based engineer whom he had first approached in 1946 for advice about Ebbets Field, and who had partnered with Norman

Bel Geddes on his proto-SkyDome. This time O'Malley put aside both Norman Bel Geddes and Buckminster Fuller, associating them, it would seem, mainly with the notion of a domed stadium, which in Los Angeles' benign climate no longer seemed necessary, rather than seeing them as imaginative designers who might have come up with inventive plans for an open stadium. Despite his having worked with Bel Geddes and Fuller, there is no sign that O'Malley's own tastes were anywhere near the cutting edge, and probably he and Praeger were a more natural match.

In any event, Praeger gave O'Malley what he wanted: a baseball-only stadium with excellent views, both of the field and, from many seats, of the San Gabriel Mountains to the east. None of the fifty-six thousand seats was obstructed by a column, because there were none; the field was sunken, so that fans entered at a mid-level, minimizing the climb to even the highest seats; there were broad aisles, seats wider than the standard, and plenty of concession stands offering what, for the early 1960s, was a generous variety of food options. An extra-large scoreboard, its shape an extended hexagon, stood on legs behind the outfield bleachers, giving the

Dodger Stadium, with its hexagonal scoreboard and undulating roof, with downtown Los Angeles in the background

stadium, much of which was painted bright blue, a hint of 1960s verve.*
The concrete roofs over the upper decks were folded to resemble a series
of low triangles, an added expression of mid-century modern design.

What O'Malley sought was the relaxed ease he had seen at Disneyland, where he had sent Dodgers executives to observe what Charles
Moore described as "no raw edges [to] spoil the picture. . . . Everything is
as immaculate as in the musical comedy villages that Hollywood has provided for our viewing pleasure for the last three generations. . . . Everything works, the way it doesn't seem to anymore in the world outside." It
was the un-Ebbets, even unto the near lack of a façade, the result partly
of the decision to place the field below the entry level, making Dodger
Stadium appear to be far shorter than most stadiums, and partly due to
Praeger's own relative lack of interest in giving the building any kind of
external architectural identity. There was nothing to see from the street
because there were no streets; there was nothing to see from afar because
the topography of Chavez Ravine meant that you couldn't see the stadium from afar anyway. Everything would be about the experience once
you went through the gates.

And there, O'Malley wanted a benign experience that would attract
not only the men who had traditionally been the core fans of most teams,
but women and families. O'Malley, Podair has written, was driven by a
"desire to make Dodger Stadium a class-inclusive venue. Celebrities and
elites, folks and families, there would be a place for all of them in his new
ballpark . . . A sense of openness and possibility would drive attendance
at the new stadium."

Earlier postwar stadiums had made the leap from city streets to suburban parking lots, but none of them represented the degree of rethinking
the experience of being at the ballpark that Dodger Stadium did. It was
not a great work of architecture by any means, but it showed how much
ordinary architecture, well conceived, could contribute to the experience
of attending a baseball game. In that sense, for all its obvious differences
from the ballparks of the Fenway and Ebbets generation, it had something in common with them that a ballpark like Candlestick Park did

---

* A second scoreboard in the form of a rectangle was added in the 1980s, a gift from Mitsubishi to advertise its new "Diamond-Vision" technology. In a 2012 renovation the new
scoreboard was rebuilt to match the hexagon shape of the original.

not. It is where the spirit of the early ballparks met the age of the auto-mobile, and sought to make common cause with it.

Los Angeles, of course, is hardly a conventional suburban environment; the years since Dodger Stadium, now the third-oldest major league ballpark, was built have proven beyond any doubt that it is a major city of the world, for all its sprawling, difficult-to-define physical form. In the sixty years since the Dodgers came to Los Angeles, the city has evolved considerably, and many of its downtown neighborhoods, in serious decline when Dodger Stadium was built, are thriving. The infrastructure of public transportation is expanding, and older neighborhoods are gentrifying. In recent years Dodger Stadium itself has been restored and its public spaces expanded under the sensitive design leadership of Janet Marie Smith—who after working for the Red Sox became an executive of the Dodgers—and the architect Brenda Levin, who treated Praeger's mid-century modern design as a historic relic to be preserved and updated with respect, even affection.

Still, Dodger Stadium remains largely an island in the midst of the city's developing urbanism. The relative isolation of Chavez Ravine has discouraged attempts to connect the stadium to the city's growing mass transit infrastructure, although in 2018 the Boring Company, a tunnel-building company run by the tech entrepreneur Elon Musk, unveiled a plan for a 3.5-mile tunnel system it called the "Dugout Loop" to connect Dodger Stadium to a mass transit station in either Los Feliz, East Hollywood, or Rampart Village, which the team's management said it would support. There have been other transit proposals to ease traffic over the years, including aerial trams. But as of now, while the stadium's excellent recent restoration is a testament to the twenty-first century's rediscovery of mid-century modernism and Los Angeles' key role in it, Dodger Stadium, choked with cars on every game day, remains also a symbol of the twentieth century's willingness in matters of urban design to let the automobile have its way.

Still, the construction of Dodger Stadium, Jerald Podair has argued, helped give Los Angeles some of the focus, both physical and cultural, that it had lacked. It would turn out to be, he has written, "a unique civic unifier . . . a place of inclusion where Angelenos came together with a common purpose. . . . Dodger Stadium would ground a civic community whose members would disagree about many things, but not about the Dodgers." O'Malley's anti-Ebbets has a banal exterior, is impossibly frustrating to drive to, and sits within a sea of parking. And yet once you reach your seat, it is an idyllic site for baseball, made better still by its recent renovations. John Pastier was engaging in only mild hyperbole when he wrote that Dodger Stadium has come to be "regarded with near-universal reverence as one of the best ballparks ever."

Era of Concrete Doughnuts

B Y THE LATE 1950S, the notion of a stadium designed only for base-ball had begun to seem like an anachronism. Although some pure baseball parks would be built, most notably Dodger Stadium in 1962 and, just over a decade later, Royals Stadium in Kansas City in 1973, it would be almost the end of the century before the idea of separate facili-ties for football and baseball would come fully back into favor. The altera-tion of Metropolitan Stadium for the Minnesota Vikings and the design of Memorial Stadium in Baltimore marked the beginning of a period in which design decisions seemed to favor the rising public interest in professional football. While football teams in older cities often became the tenants of established baseball teams, as the New York Giants were of the Yankees, and even the Chicago Bears, for a time, were of the Cubs, football seemed to fit especially smoothly into the newer generation of suburban stadiums, whose huge parking lots offered a perfect venue for pre-game tailgate parties, which were never a part of the culture of base-ball, but for many fans were a key part of the experience of attending a professional football game.

Football was also a game that, more than baseball, was well suited to the increasingly important medium of television. Baseball had been tele-vised for years, but football seemed a more natural match for it. Football's

CLOCKWISE ON SPREAD, FROM ABOVE

Oakland Coliseum; Robert F. Kennedy Stadium, Washington, D.C.; Fulton County Stadium, Atlanta; Veterans Stadium, Philadelphia; Three Rivers Stadium, Pittsburgh; Busch Memorial Stadium, St. Louis

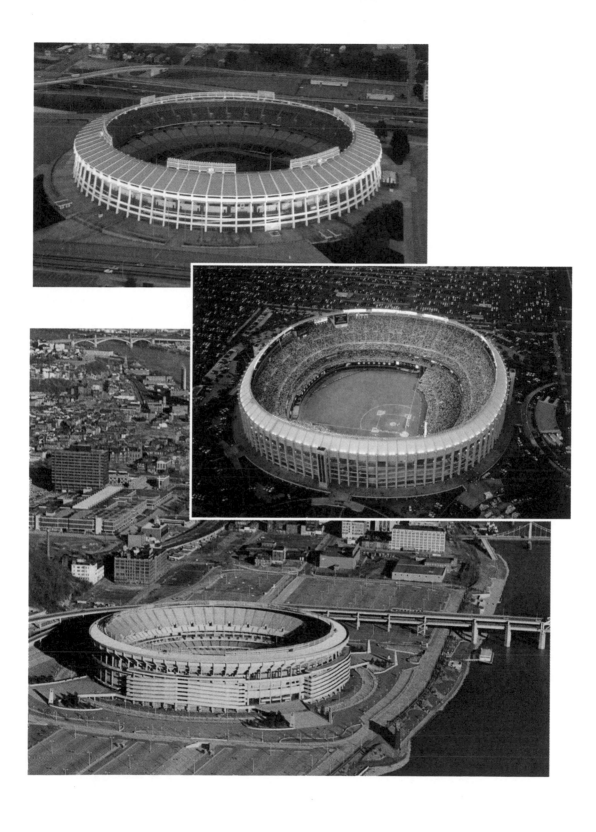

clock gave the game a constant sense of tension that baseball's graceful ebb and flow lacked. The precisely defined, contained football gridiron seemed to have even more intensity when seen through the lens of the television camera, unlike the distant outfield of baseball, populated by three widely spaced outfielders who spent most of their time standing, not moving, in quiet waiting for a possible hit into their territory.

It is no accident that the National Football League and television more or less grew up together, and that the combination of professional football and the broadcast networks could become a powerful force for change in stadium design, less by any formal diktat than by the economic strength of their growing audience. Not for several decades would the view that the needs of both football and baseball were better served by building them separate facilities again hold sway; in the 1960s, the rise of football led to more and more pressure to create large, bland stadiums that could accommodate the needs of televised professional football in combination with baseball. Baseball may have had the longer history, but the needs of football coexisted more comfortably with both the rise of suburbia and the economic power of television.

Football also pushed stadium designers toward larger facilities, and not only because football teams have only a few home games a year in which to sell tickets. Baseball is often best watched from seats that are close to the field of play, but the action on the football gridiron tends to be better seen from high above. Intimacy, a quality that was once important to baseball parks and would be again, counts for little in a football stadium, and can even be a liability. So it was not surprising that stadiums built for both baseball and football were almost without exception round and large—huge concrete doughnuts, surrounded by acres of parking lots. The eccentricity of early baseball parks was replaced by a kind of standardized design that eased the challenges of meeting the different needs of baseball and football in the same place. The simple form of a perfect circle was surely also a reaction against the eccentricity of the early ballparks, whose irregular shapes were determined by the pattern of surrounding streets and, on occasion, by the unwillingness of neighboring owners to part with their property. In an age of huge suburban stadiums, there was no urban context to provide such constraints— constraints that, however frustrating they were to the designers of early ballparks, yielded the idiosyncrasies that would do so much to make those places beloved, and to make the nature of play at least a little bit different in every ballpark.

Large, circular stadiums also accommodated well the gradual expansion of amenities both for fans and for players. The meager clubhouse areas that the older stadiums provided for players were no longer considered adequate in the postwar years, and they began to take up more and more space. And as players' salaries grew—moderately through the postwar years, and then dramatically after the reserve clause was ended in 1975 and players became free agents—the owners needed more and more cash to meet their inflated payrolls. If television contracts and souvenir sales helped, skyboxes, special luxury seating areas, and private dining rooms and clubs for fans, all of which took up space in the ballpark, brought plenty of money, too. It was as if the ballpark, once held tight by the corset of surrounding streets, had responded to the open space of the suburbs by indulging itself, expanding its program to grow ever larger.

A third reason the circular stadium became the standard is that the suburban ballparks of the postwar era were generally publicly financed, and the blunter priorities of public works projects, far less accommodating to circumstances, came to the fore. The notion of a multi-purpose stadium appealed to a bureaucratic sensibility, and the circle was the easiest way to make a dual-purpose stadium seem palatable. Yet a fourth factor was aesthetic: postwar modernist architects often demonstrated a preference for the directness of a pure geometric shape over the complexity of irregular geometries shaped by a building's architectural context, and stadiums became an exemplar of this trend, especially as they increasingly became freestanding objects with no real context other than a sea of parked cars. While the concrete doughnuts of the 1960s were hardly identical—there were often marked differences in the exterior, and the pattern of seating and the field dimensions still varied from stadium to stadium—by the end of the decade the differences from one ballpark to another seemed less important than the similarities. And once you were inside it, one pure circle felt pretty much the same as another, or so it seemed.

The first of the circular stadiums designed from the beginning to accommodate both baseball and football was District of Columbia Stadium (later RFK Stadium) in Washington, D.C., which opened in 1961. A structure with a banal concrete exterior, an undulating roofline, and a particularly awkward configuration for baseball, with a wall around the outfield and seats above it but none at field level, it opened, fittingly enough, without a baseball team. The stadium was never occupied by its first intended baseball tenant, the Washington Senators, who had been playing in the venerable Griffith Stadium, a welcoming if shabby eccentricity from 1911 notable primarily for the odd shape of its center field, the lines of which were defined by the property lines of some neighboring houses whose owners had refused to sell when the stadium was built. The Washington Redskins agreed early on to move to the new stadium, leaving Calvin Griffith, who inherited control of the Senators and Griffith Stadium from his uncle, Clark Griffith, in 1955, without the tenant whose rental income had helped to make the old ballpark economically viable. Griffith and the District of Columbia could not agree on lease terms for the Senators, and Griffith, like Horace Stoneham and Walter O'Malley, let it be known that he would not be unhappy to be courted by other cities. In 1960, before the new Washington stadium was even finished, Griffith decided to head to Minnesota and rename his team the Minnesota Twins. Left at the altar by its baseball bride, the District of Columbia Stadium in its first season housed only the Redskins. By the spring of 1961 an expansion baseball team arrived, taking over the abandoned name of the Senators; the new team would remain for only a decade before moving to Arlington, Texas, to become the Texas Rangers. It was not the case that the D.C. stadium itself drove teams away, but one could be forgiven for thinking so.

A moderately improved version of the concrete doughnut opened three years later in New York City to house another expansion team, the New York Mets, who in 1962 had brought National League baseball back to the city that had been abandoned by both the Dodgers and the Giants. The Mets played first in the ballpark the Giants had vacated, the Polo Grounds, there being, as Murray Kempton would write, "no place for them except this old shrine," Ebbets Field having been demolished and their new stadium as yet incomplete. The Mets "could not, even for one year as a tenant, let the Polo Grounds rest as the raddled, gray, pigeon-speckled old rookery its mourners had left," Kempton wrote, explaining why the Mets repainted the old ballpark—where they would spend two seasons, not one, owing to construction delays—in orange, blue, and green. Spiffing up the Polo Grounds merely covered in garishness what

remained of the Giants' aura, including the numbers that had indicated the distance to the foul poles, which disappeared from view. The paint job, which did little to help the fortunes of the Mets—they finished last in the league both years, and in 1962 were 60½ games behind the pennant-winning Giants—seemed merely to make the absence of the Giants from their longtime quarters all the more painful. Painted or not, the Polo Grounds could hardly be blamed for the Mets' poor debut, since the team did no better when it moved at the beginning of the 1964 season into Shea Stadium, where it finished last for the third year in a row.

Named for William Shea, the New York lawyer who played a major role in the effort to establish a new team in New York, it was in a sense Robert Moses's revenge on Walter O'Malley, since it was constructed on the same site in Flushing Meadows Park that Moses had offered O'Malley for the Dodgers and he had rejected. Or perhaps it was not Moses's revenge, but O'Malley's, since the site of the stadium, despite being in the nation's largest city, has almost no urban qualities, and was not nearly as appealing for baseball as Dodger Stadium. It was surrounded by parking lots, and within the flight pattern of nearby LaGuardia Airport, so the roar of jet planes taking off became part and parcel of attending a Mets baseball game. The Los Angeles skyline is visible from the grounds of Dodger Stadium, a mile away; the New York skyline is several miles from the site of Shea, and cannot be seen at all.

Shea was designed by Praeger-Kavanaugh-Waterbury, whose senior

A pamphlet for the dedication of Shea Stadium, April 16, 1964

partner, Emil Praeger, was the architect of Dodger Stadium in Los Angeles, but Praeger's design for Shea had little in common with Dodger Stadium. It was exceptionally high, with three steeply tiered decks rising over the field, and its exterior consisted largely of a series of concrete ramps decorated with panels of blue and orange, the team colors, that appeared from a distance to be floating over the concrete. (In a 1980 renovation, the panels were removed and portions of the exterior filled in with solid blue panels decorated with massive, abstract neon images of baseball players.)

Roger Angell, one of the greatest observers of both baseball's play and its physical surroundings, had Shea exactly right when he wrote in *The Summer Game* that the stadium "is built of reinforced concrete, and its banked seats, set almost entirely within the foul lines, sweep around in a lovely circle, offering everyone a splendid and unobstructed view of the action. Unobstructed and, I should add, too distant . . . this imposed geometry keeps the elevated fan forever distant from the doings within the contained square of the infield. All this is because Shea Stadium (and all the future big-city stadiums) must also be suitable for professional football . . . at the expense of the baseball fan, for the best ballparks—Ebbets Field, say, or Comiskey Park—have all been boxes." Angell concluded: "In the broad, sky-filled circle of the new stadium, the shouts, the clapping, the trumpet blasts, and the brave old cries of 'Let's Go, *Mets!*' climbed thinly into the air and vanished; the place seemed without echoes, angles, and reassurance. No longer snug in a shoebox, my companions and I were ants perched on the sloping lip of a vast, shiny soup plate, and we were lonelier than we liked."

Still, Shea Stadium had some positive elements, or at least some elements that were not as bad as they might have been, most notably the fact that its form was not a completely closed circle, as its grandstands did not extend all the way around the outfield, giving fans in the upper decks and field seats wide vistas and at least some of the sense of openness of an older ballpark. Even that aspect, however, represented no commitment to the traditions of baseball, since the stadium was designed for the eventual expansion of its grandstands if additional seats were desired, which would close the circle. Thus the ghost of Osborn's original enclosed design for Yankee Stadium hovered perpetually over Shea, although thankfully it never did descend to obliterate the stadium's most pleasing quality and place it in the ranks of such utterly unbaseball-like enclosed stadiums as the ones that would be built in Pittsburgh, St. Louis, and Atlanta. Shea did also possess one minor piece of wit, added in 1980, a pleasant spherical counterpoint to the dreary geometry of the generation of circular concrete stadiums: the enormous apple that would rise out of a huge hat beyond the outfield every time a Met hit a home run.

Two years after Shea Stadium, in 1966, came Busch Memorial Stadium in St. Louis, unlike Shea a fully closed circle. But also unlike Shea, Busch was built downtown, representing a welcome reversal of the suburban trend in location if not in design. And it had one pleasing architectural conceit. Edward Durell Stone, who served as consulting architect to Sverdrup & Parcel, ringed the top of the circle with ninety-six parabolic arches, giving Busch a distinctive profile intended to echo the vast parabolic arch of St. Louis's Jefferson National Expansion Memorial by

The enormous A, symbol of Angel Stadium, as the stadium neared completion in 1965

Eero Saarinen just a few blocks away. If it was a trite way to pay homage to the city's most famous modern landmark, its scalloped roofline did provide an amiable harmonic accompaniment to Busch's circular form, and it gave the stadium at least some visual distinction.

Atlanta opened its doughnut, Fulton County Stadium, the same year as Busch. Designed by Heery, Heery & Finch, a local architectural firm, it had neither the decorative appeal of Busch nor the openness of Shea; the best thing that can be said about it as a work of architecture was that its circular form made it instantly recognizable from the freeway to drivers heading toward downtown Atlanta. Also in 1966 came Angel Stadium of Anaheim, a relatively open, modern ballpark built on farmland not far from Disneyland in Orange County, California. In its original form it was notable mainly for the enormous letter *A,* as tall as a twenty-story building, that stood in left field and held the electronic scoreboard, which gave the ballpark its nickname, the Big A. (The *A,* today painted in red, was moved to the parking lot when the stadium was expanded and enclosed for football use in the 1970s; in the late 1990s the stadium was converted back to baseball-only use.) Two years later came the Oakland Coliseum, designed by Skidmore, Owings & Merrill, architects of some of the greatest postwar skyscrapers in the United States, but not, if Oakland is any indication, of its greatest stadiums. Oakland was conceived as a multi-sports complex, and its high point architecturally is the circular arena adjacent to the stadium, which is marked by diagonal columns and a cable-supported roof. Because the field of the stadium is sunk roughly twenty-nine feet below grade, the smaller arena is the more conspicuous structure from the freeway, which is just as well, since the arena is the better piece of architecture; the enormous round stadium is mainly a stark, open concrete structure containing a seating bowl. If Oakland offers the pleasant experience of entering what appears to be a low structure and having the immensity of the space within come as a surprise, as in so many sunken fields from the Yale Bowl onward, it is also, like every combination stadium, more comfortable for football and soccer than for baseball. Not only are the size and the distance of the upper-deck seats at odds with the tradition of the baseball grandstand, the circular shape in this instance yields huge foul territory, with field seats set far back from the baselines. Oakland was constructed, like so many of the stadiums of this period, without a baseball tenant; it was only in 1968, two years after it opened, that Charlie Finley succeeded in moving the Athletics from Kansas City to Oakland.

Three Rivers Stadium in Pittsburgh did not even have the relative understatement of the sunken Oakland Coliseum. The stadium was a heavy-handed concrete monolith of 1970 designed by Osborn Engineering, and its brutalist architecture was a double sadness: it showed, first, how far the mighty Osborn organization had slipped since its glory days of Fenway Park and Yankee Stadium; second, it marked a major step backward for Pittsburgh, where since 1909 baseball had been played at elegant Forbes Field, one of the many ballparks from the early years of the twentieth century that, like Fenway Park and Wrigley Field, would in all likelihood be cherished icons had they managed to survive into the twenty-first century. That it was closer to the heart of downtown Pittsburgh did little to mitigate its architectural weakness; Forbes Field, a short distance from downtown in Schenley Park, felt far more connected to the city than the closed-off concrete bunker of Three Rivers.

The 1970s brought only one exception to the general abandonment of baseball's traditions, and that was in Kansas City, which built a pair of adjacent stadiums, called the Truman Sports Complex, for its baseball and football teams. From the home plate side, Royals Stadium, designed by Charles Deaton along with the firm of Kivett & Myers, looked not unlike many of the concrete doughnuts, but the grandstands descended in a graceful slope as they moved toward the outfield, which was entirely open to a vista of the surroundings. In keeping with the times, the view was mainly of suburban sprawl, but it was punctuated in the foreground by a twelve-story-high scoreboard topped with a crown and by the stadium's most unusual feature, a 322-foot-wide waterfall and fountain display in right center field, taking the space that otherwise would have been occupied by bleachers.

In the age of the single, mixed-use stadium, the two-stadium Truman Sports Complex in Kansas City broke the mold, with plans, at one point, for a retractable roof that would slide back and forth over the two facilities.

Royals Stadium and its companion football stadium, Arrowhead, were originally conceived by Deaton as sharing a roof that would roll back and forth between them, covering either stadium as needed. Deaton's bold idea proved too costly, but it nevertheless started his associates on the paired stadium; the success of the plan set the local firm of Kivett & Myers on the road to becoming the Osborn Engineering of a new era, the primary architects of choice for large-scale stadium design. In 1978, five years after the Royals Stadium was finished, Kivett & Myers merged with another local architectural firm, HNTB, and continued to develop a specialty in the design of sports facilities; in 1983, several of its partners broke away and joined the large, St. Louis–based firm Hellmuth, Obata & Kassabaum (HOK) to establish a department of sports facility design, which they continued to base in Kansas City. Many years later, the sports division would become independent and change its name from HOK Sport to Populous and would grow into an international presence, but its headquarters would remain in Kansas City. By happenstance Kansas City became, for all intents and purposes, the nation's center of sports architecture, and from the last quarter-century of the twentieth century onward, many of the architectural designs for sports facilities all over the world would emerge from this medium-sized midwestern city that otherwise had no claim as an architectural center.

Unfortunately, despite the effect it would have on architectural practice, as well as its open feeling and good intentions as a baseball-only park, Royals Stadium—renamed Kauffman Stadium in 1993 in honor of Ewing M. Kauffman, the team's owner—shared one of the least appealing elements of the other ballparks of its time, which was a symmetrical outfield of predictable dimensions. Circular stadiums built on huge suburban parcels of land were not, in the first place, a natural fit with the wedge-shaped baseball field. No matter who was designing them, they were an invitation to standardization. It is no exaggeration to say that the aspect of the legacy of old ballparks that the postwar years really destroyed was not elegance—of which there was precious little to start with—but idiosyncrasy. They all looked, and felt, the same.

"Ballparks with no idiosyncrasies are poor ballparks," Philip Lowry has written. "When every fence is 10 feet tall, every foul line is 330 feet, every power alley is 370 feet, and every center field fence is 400 feet, [baseball's] subtleties are minimized once the beauty of the game is scarred." "I stand at the plate in Philadelphia," said the Pirates' Richie Hebner, referring to Veterans Stadium of 1971, "and I honestly don't know whether I'm in Pittsburgh, Cincinnati, St. Louis or Philly." And so it was, whether in the first stadium the Texas Rangers occupied in Arlington, a suburban location midway between Dallas and Fort Worth that originally had the appropriate name of Turnpike Stadium; or Veterans Stadium in South Philadelphia, an elongated circle of concrete that opened in 1971 and that, despite having the architectural pedigree of a design by the respected firm of Hugh Stubbins, had all the charm of a highway underpass; or Riverfront Stadium in Cincinnati, another fully enclosed circle of concrete that opened in 1970. As with the concrete doughnuts of St. Louis and Pittsburgh, Riverfront had the virtue of bringing baseball to a central downtown location, but at the price of a standardized cookie-cutter design that cut off any connection to the city.

Then again, at least you could see the sky from these ballparks. Even that was impossible in the structure that was, if nothing else, the most memorable of this generation of stadiums: the Houston Astrodome,

where the roofed dreams that Norman Bel Geddes and Buckminster Fuller had for the Dodgers were finally realized. The architects of the Astrodome, which was finished in time for the 1965 baseball season, were from the Houston firm of Wilson, Morris, Crain and Anderson, but the real mover behind the Astrodome was Roy Hofheinz, a flamboyant entrepreneur, former judge, and former mayor of Houston who had received a commitment for a major league expansion team if he could house it in a domed stadium to protect fans from Houston's extreme summer heat and humidity. For a city whose growth was shaped by the ability to bring air conditioning almost everywhere—and one with no connection to the urban traditions of baseball—the notion of an air-conditioned baseball park seemed less a violation of custom than a natural extension of modern technology. Houstonians did almost everything indoors. Why not baseball?

The Astrodome, Houston, Texas

In the 1960s and 1970s Houston was experiencing explosive growth, driven largely by its role as the center of the nation's oil and gas business.

The combination of its new wealth, its absence of a long history, and its comfort with the Texas culture of bigness made it the perfect place for the nation's first domed stadium. Hofheinz chose a site on the south side of Houston near the 610 freeway, a place where there was no urban fabric to speak of. It could not have been more different from the site Walter O'Malley had sought at the intersection of Atlantic and Flatbush in Brooklyn, where a huge domed stadium would have been out of scale and ill-suited to its dense urban surroundings. On Hofheinz's site, there was no neighborhood context for a scale-less building like this to violate. Houston, famed for disdaining the very notion of zoning laws, was a city that embraced sprawl, celebrated the extravagant use of energy, and had little patience for restraint of any kind. The Astrodome—its ceiling 208 feet high, and 710 feet across—was its cathedral.

The building—and it is hard not to call it a building rather than a stadium—is at once gargantuan and banal. The low dome of the clear plastic roof gives it a profile unlike any other ballpark of its era, but the

At Houston's Astrodome, Judge Roy Hofheinz could view the action from his private apartment.

exterior is otherwise a windowless masonry façade with a whiff of mid-century modernist trim insufficient to make it look like anything more than a cylindrical version of a government building of the same era. For all that it was built for the Houston Astros (who were called the Colt .45s for their first three seasons, played in temporary quarters), at the Astrodome, even more than with most of the multi-purpose stadiums of the age, the particular needs of baseball seemed an afterthought.

The domed stadium was shared by the Houston Oilers football team and the Houston Livestock Show and Rodeo almost from the beginning; even the Houston Rockets of the National Basketball Association played there for a period in the 1970s, and the famous "Battle of the Sexes" between tennis stars Billie Jean King and Bobby Riggs took place there in 1973, as did Muhammad Ali's fight in 1966 against Cleveland Williams for the heavyweight championship. Every large baseball park has been used from time to time for other kinds of events, including concerts, but the Astrodome felt from the beginning more like a multi-purpose arena blown up to the scale of a stadium.

Workmen zipper up the Astroturf carpet

What made it memorable, of course, was the inside, the huge room in which the Astros played, a room that, however much it may have transgressed the traditions of baseball, unquestionably had a presence, even if it could best be described as that of a basketball arena that had grown too big for itself. Not the least of Hofheinz's innovations was his decision to offer high-paying customers the chance to sit high above the crowd, in glass-enclosed skyboxes, where they could socialize with their own private guests. It recalled, however inadvertently, the early years of baseball's preference for economic segregation. Hofheinz gave himself the biggest skybox of all, a huge, private apartment tucked into the upper reaches of the Astrodome.

If Walter O'Malley wanted Dodger Stadium to feel like a clean, fresh, up-to-date version of a baseball park, Hofheinz, mindful of the presence of the NASA Space Center in Houston, seems to have been driven more by a desire to express an overall futuristic quality, whether or not it had much to do with baseball. "It reminds me of what my first ride would be like in a flying saucer," Mickey Mantle reportedly said when the Yankees arrived to play the Astros, and it is hard not to imagine Hofheinz thinking that Mantle had gotten it just right.

The architects, for their part, seem to have wanted to have the room possess at least some of the qualities of the outdoors, which is why the roof was made of 4,596 Lucite panels to maximize the presence of sunlight, and the field was planted, at first, with natural grass. Neither of these things worked as planned. The clear plastic focused the sun's rays and caused glare, sometimes making it difficult for the players on the field to see fly balls; the fix that was tried, covering many of the panels with a thin coat of translucent off-white paint, reduced the glare but caused the grass to die. The dead grass on the field was briefly painted green, and by the Astros' second season it was replaced with an artificial turf manufactured by Monsanto, making the Astrodome the first place in which major league baseball was not played on natural grass. The management dubbed the new creation Astroturf, and it soon became a synonym for any kind of artificial grass.

Such was the mood in the 1960s, at least in Houston, that the failure of the grass was generally not seen to emerge out of some deeper flaw in the idea behind the Astrodome. Technology would solve the problem with the field, just as it had allowed the engineering that made the Astrodome buildable, and the air-conditioning that made it habitable. The disillusionment of the late 1960s had not yet set in, at least not fully, and for Houston it was still a time in which American power, and American technology, could solve all things, an age in which bigger was often perceived as better. Baseball would come to Houston, but on Houston's terms, and it hardly mattered that the Astrodome was, as Casey Stengel put it, "the kind of building where from the outside you can't tell where first base is."

The attention garnered by the Astrodome all but guaranteed that it would be followed by other domed stadiums, but its shortcomings as a baseball park did not go unnoticed, and most of the domed stadiums built after it were used exclusively for football. Only three other cities, Seattle, Minneapolis, and St. Petersburg, constructed multi-purpose domed stadiums for the use of their major league baseball teams or, in the case of St. Petersburg, in the hope of luring a team. Seattle's Kingdome, opened in 1977, was designed by the local firm of Naramore Bain Brady and Johanson, working with Osborn Engineering, Praeger-Kavanaugh-Waterbury, and Skilling Engineering, an all-star team that somehow managed to produce a structure so banal that it made the Astrodome seem vibrant and fresh. It was a harsh object of gray concrete that had none of the Astrodome's verve and all of its problems. The Kingdome's impact on its city was far more negative than the Astrodome's effect on Houston, since it was constructed not amid a laissez-faire landscape of sprawl, but on the edge of Seattle's dense, lively downtown, beside which it sat with a deadly heavy-handedness.

More determinedly different from the Astrodome was the Metrodome in Minneapolis, later renamed the Hubert Humphrey Metrodome, which had an air-supported fabric roof, whose white color often made it difficult for fielders to see fly balls. Designed by Skidmore, Owings & Merrill and opened in 1982, by which time the Astrodome was seventeen years old, the Metrodome replaced Metropolitan Stadium in suburban Bloomington, and gave major league baseball a welcome presence in downtown Minneapolis. But there was nothing urban about its design. Paradoxically, Metropolitan Stadium, with its quintessentially suburban site, had more of the urban qualities of openness and connection than the closed-off Metrodome, which became famous both for the level of noise inside it and for the way in which balls would bounce off its hard, artificial turf surface. The most memorable visual feature of the dome's interior came as a result of its double-duty as a football stadium: a twenty-three-foot-high

section of seats for football use that during baseball season was retracted and covered with canvas, which fans nicknamed "the Hefty Bag."

The Suncoast Dome in St. Petersburg, later named Tropicana Field, was a latecomer, designed by HOK Sport and not completed until 1990. Although it has been used for other sports, it is the one dome that was designed with particular attention to baseball, with an asymmetrical out-field and, after a renovation intended to further enhance its appropriate-ness for baseball, a large entry vestibule modeled after the rotunda at Ebbets Field. Tropicana is an anomaly: a stadium that possesses some qualities of a traditional ballpark, but gathered under the architectural element most antithetical to the traditional ballpark, a fixed roof.

St. Petersburg had hoped that its stadium would attract the Chicago White Sox, whose old Comiskey Park was badly deteriorated and seemed ripe for replacement, or the Seattle Mariners or the San Francisco Giants, both of which were thought, at least briefly, to be considering a move in the late 1980s. None of these teams came, and it was only when an expansion franchise was granted to the Tampa Bay area in 1995 that the

The fabric ceiling of Minneapolis's Metrodome

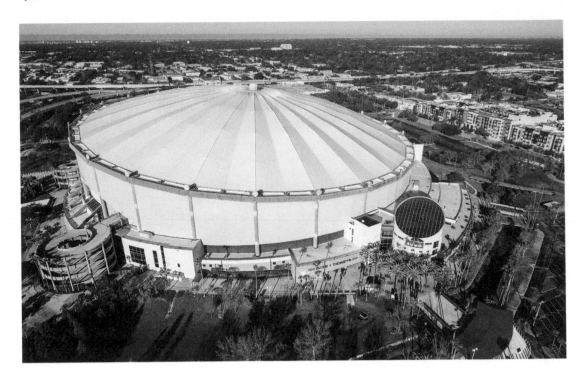

stadium had a baseball occupant. The Devil Rays began play in 1998, by which time their dome had been waiting for eight years.

The embarrassingly long wait for a tenant was a wound that time would have healed quickly if Tropicana Field had turned out to be a great success as a baseball venue, but it was exactly the opposite: by the time it was finished, the idea of a fixed dome had fallen out of favor. It was one thing to have the option of protection from rain or extremes of temperature; it was quite another to force baseball inside under all weather conditions, all the time, as Tropicana Field, like the Astrodome and the Metrodome, did. The Astrodome was twenty-five years old by the time the St. Petersburg stadium was completed, and from its first days Tropicana—or Suncoast as it was first known—was a relic from another era.* It was becoming increasingly clear that the answer, for

Tampa Bay's Tropicana Field, the last domed ballpark still in use

* In 2018, the Rays (the Devil Rays previously) announced plans to move to a new stadium in Tampa with the unusual configuration of a fixed roof but open sides. The announcement primarily acknowledged the team's continued desire to replace Tropicana Field and was a way of reassuring the Tampa–St. Petersburg region that the team was not intending to move. The team's owner, Stuart Sternberg, abandoned the plan after only six months, and as of now the Rays continue to play at Tropicana.

baseball teams that felt the need for some sort of weather protection, lay in a roof that, like a convertible top, could be opened and closed at will.

Architects had been experimenting with the notion of a retractable roof that would allow a stadium to move easily back and forth between open-air play in good weather and indoor play in inclement weather since Norman Bel Geddes proposed the concept to Walter O'Malley in the late 1940s. Although Bel Geddes as a designer was known as an enthusiastic celebrant of technology, there is no evidence that he or any engineer had ever fully worked out a structural system to enable a roof to retract. When the time came to try it would prove difficult.

The first serious attempt to construct such a flexible stadium came in Montreal, decades after Bel Geddes made his sketches for Brooklyn, where it was planned to serve both as a home for the new Montreal Expos major league team and as the stadium for the 1976 Olympic Games. The French architect Roger Taillibert produced the design, which could not be faulted on visual terms: it was striking, with a slanting tower and swooping forms that seemed almost to prefigure the work of Zaha

Olympic Stadium, in Montreal, with its tower and its fabric roof, which was later removed

Hadid. But Olympic Stadium turned out to be both a functional and a financial disaster, with huge cost overruns and a roof system that never worked smoothly, and often did not work at all. Taillibert's stadium was a low, graceful circle, bearing far more resemblance to Mickey Mantle's flying saucer than the Astrodome ever did. The roof system Taillibert designed for Montreal called for an orange covering made of Kevlar, a synthetic fiber, connected by twenty-six steel cables to an inclined tower, which was 550 feet high—as tall as a skyscraper—and which would fold in on itself as the cables tightened. Not only was this elaborate mechanical system not up and running in time for the 1976 Olympics, it would take another dozen years, until 1988, before the tower was finished and the roof could be attached to it. Between 1976 and 1988 the stadium was used in an incomplete state, without a roof.

Once the roof was ready, it proved less than optimal. It could not operate in high winds, and when it did function it took forty-five minutes to open. Taillibert's roof system proved so frustrating to maintain that it was soon left in the closed position, where it remained until 1998, when it was removed altogether and the team played in the open air. In 1999, it was replaced with a fixed roof as part of a renovation that also made the stadium suitable for football. The slanted tower to which the roof had been attached had an observation deck, reachable by a funicular that ran along its exterior, which continued to operate after the original roof was removed. The slanted tower at least gave Montreal the distinction of having the only baseball stadium in the major leagues with its own cable car ride and observation tower.

That Olympic Stadium turned out to be a major act of architectural folly did not prevent further attempts to create a workable retractable roof, however, and in 1989, the year after the Montreal roof had its first awkward trial, a stadium with an entirely different kind of retractable roof was completed not far away, in Toronto. Named the SkyDome, it became the new home of the Toronto Blue Jays. (The name was later changed to the Rogers Centre.) Not only was the Toronto roof different from Montreal's in design, it was different in outcome: this one worked, with only minor hiccups. The architect was a Canadian, Roderick Robbie, who had never before designed a stadium. (Taillibert had, which says something about the virtues of experience.) Along with the engineer Michael Allen and the Toronto architecture firm NORR Partner-

ship, Robbie designed a roof system consisting of three massive, vaulted movable roof panels, each weighing more than 1,800 tons, and a fourth fixed panel. When the roof retracts, two of the panels slide on tracks to one end of the stadium, opening up the middle of the roof to the sky, after which a rounded panel at the far end rotates all the way around the stadium and disappears beneath the fixed panel, the panels clustered together to form a great arch at the northern end of the structure. Robbie's real achievement was in designing the pattern of roof panels to glide around each other and fold together into a tight, small slot under the arch so as to open virtually the entire stadium to the sky. He said that

An interior view of the SkyDome (now known as the Rogers Centre) in Toronto

as its sections moved, the roof reminded him of "a great big lobster—all those plates sliding around each other."

Indeed, to see the roof in Toronto move is to watch something that seems at one moment like a great machine, at another like a living object, stretching and flexing, as the building undergoes its smooth, silent metamorphosis from an indoor stadium to an outdoor one. It is startling to see, since parts of buildings aren't supposed to open up as smartly as the roof of a convertible, transforming from one kind of building to another before your very eyes.

But if the elegantly retracting roof of the SkyDome offered triumphant proof that the dream of Montreal—that the same stadium could offer baseball played in the open air and under a roof—was achievable, it came at a price. The SkyDome is huge, and beside the lyrical if dysfunctional stadium in Montreal, its conventional, fairly bland exterior looks more like an overblown arena or a convention center. Its designers tried to contribute to the traditions of baseball stadiums as both venues of entertainment and places of urban connection by including, among other things, an eleven-story, 350-room hotel set into its superstructure, with 70 rooms having windows looking directly onto the field. A five-hundred-seat restaurant overlooks center field, and there is a miniature golf course. But however much all of this urban activity may try to allude to the early ballparks, what it really evokes is Norman Bel Geddes's scheme for the Dodgers, designed four decades earlier: a huge urban mega-structure, as cut off from the city as a shopping mall, a substitute for the organic activity of the city more than a natural part of it. Roderick Robbie managed to build Norman Bel Geddes's dream.

Outside its doors, the vibrancy of downtown Toronto awaits, and this alone sets this stadium apart from the suburban concrete doughnuts set amid oceans of parking. The architects tried to make the most of a key downtown site by including walkways connecting the stadium to the nearby convention center, to Union Station, and to the CN Tower next door, Toronto's tallest structure. With the mammoth downtown stadium beside it, the tower, which once stood alone as an awkward needle in the skyline, took on a new meaning: it became a kind of campanile to the stadium, and together they created an architectural dialogue at vast scale, justifying each other's hugeness, and giving each other a visual counterpoint. The tower became better for the stadium, and the stadium's vastness became easier to take because of the tower. Their combination made for a whole that was greater than the sum of its parts, and because of it the SkyDome became more valid as a piece of architecture and urban design than a gigantic enclosed stadium in the midst of a densely built city would otherwise be. But whatever its merits, it was still uncomfortably huge and awkward as a place to play baseball. Roderick Robbie's architectural and technological achievement did not give the postwar era something that could properly be called a baseball park. That would have to wait until the next decade.

8

Camden Yards: Baseball Returns

THE COMPLETION of the SkyDome in Toronto in 1989 seemed to end the 1980s on a note of extravagance and overreach as the trend toward the grandiose, enclosed stadium that had begun with the Astrodome two decades earlier reached its climax. There would be other retractable-roof ballparks to follow, but none would have quite the impact of the SkyDome, which for its time was both technologically advanced and visually bold. Yet for all that baseball stadiums at the end of the 1980s seemed in thrall to the massive and the futuristic, the true legacy of that decade would turn out to be something else altogether. As Rod Robbie was working on his retractable dome in Toronto, the architects of HOK Sport, the firm based in Kansas City,* received a commission to design a medium-sized ballpark in downtown Buffalo, New York, a city that hoped, as many had before it, that the act of construction would be sufficient to attract a major league team.

It did not, but the ballpark that Buffalo built, named Pilot Field (and now called Sahlen Field) would have a different kind of impact. It was an anomaly for the 1980s: modest in scale, with just under twenty thousand

* See Chapter 7, page 182.

seats, it sat comfortably within the downtown grid of streets, just like the ballparks of an earlier era. In fact, from the outside it looked almost like a scaled-down version of Wrigley Field or Tiger Stadium, with a certain easy casualness to its design. It was understated, and it looked at home in the city. Pilot Field, which opened in 1988, the year before the SkyDome, was everything the SkyDome was not: simple, unpretentious, unroofed, and woven into the urban fabric of the city that surrounded it.*

Pilot Field's exterior was not entirely plain. The architects had decorated it with a few arches containing a pattern that imitated traditional ironwork, and there were what might be called primitive versions of classical columns and pediments. It looked like a kind of modest, low-budget riff on a traditional ballpark, which is pretty much what it was, and it provided the first hint that ballparks might be influenced by a larger

Sahlen Field (formerly Pilot Field) in Buffalo, New York, marks a return to traditional ballpark architecture in an urban setting.

* The Buffalo Bisons, a minor league team affiliated with the Toronto Blue Jays, have played in the field since its completion. It is now the largest minor league field in regular use.

trend that had been going on in architecture for some years, the rise of what came to be known as postmodernism. Frustrated by the limits of conventional modern architecture, which seemed to be trapped between austerity on the one hand and harsh heaviness on the other, and aware that neither glass boxes nor concrete bunkers were generally very popular with the public, architects were increasingly seeking ways to make buildings richer, warmer, and more complex. If people perceived contemporary buildings as feeling like blunt instruments, well then, architects would show that they were listening, and were ready to give them an alternative.

More often than not, their route to that alternative would involve turning back toward the past, the very thing that modern architecture had made a fetish of rejecting. Architects began actively looking at traditional buildings and trying to find ways to integrate historical elements into new buildings. Some architects mimicked older buildings directly while others tried to evolve more abstract, up-to-date versions of traditional elements; either way, the result was a tide of architecture in the 1980s that looked different from the buildings of the previous several decades.

It was inevitable that this trend would somehow reach the realm of baseball. Ballparks are rarely on the cutting edge of architecture, but as structures from the Victorian grandstand of South End Grounds in Boston to the classical grandstand of the Palace of the Fans to the façades of Shibe Park and Ebbets Field had shown, where other architecture went, ballpark architecture would soon enough follow. The concrete stadiums of the 1960s and '70s were in part a reflection of the brutalist style taken up by so many other buildings of that era. And so it was with the return to historical style that began in the 1980s with that decade's postmodernism. It seemed to tiptoe quietly into the realm of ballpark design via a small ballpark in a city barely on the radar of baseball, and within a few years it would grow to yield an entire generation of what would come to be called "retro" ballparks, becoming so much the mode of the age that by the end of the 1990s, places like the SkyDome would seem not advanced, but almost old-fashioned.

One of the most important early achievements of this period of ballpark design was never built, but its story tells as much about both architecture and baseball as many parks that were. It was called Armour Field, and was planned for the South Side of Chicago as a replacement for

Comiskey Park, the home of the Chicago White Sox. Comiskey, which opened in 1910, had been one of the earliest of the ballparks of the great age of steel and concrete from the early twentieth century; by the mid-1980s, it was in poor condition and needed serious renovation. As the managements of the Dodgers and the Giants had done thirty years earlier with Ebbets Field and the Polo Grounds, the owner of the White Sox, Jerry Reinsdorf, used the challenges of Comiskey to render the team's future on the South Side of Chicago uncertain. Like Walter O'Malley before him, what motivated Reinsdorf most was his determination to get rid of an old ballpark. Where he built a new one was secondary.

Actually, the White Sox had flirted with moving for years. In 1968, two years after Milwaukee lost the Braves to Atlanta, Bud Selig, then known mainly as a Milwaukee businessman, made a deal to buy the team from its owners at the time, Arthur Allyn, Jr., and John Allyn, and move it north to Wisconsin. The American League blocked the sale. When Selig later bought the Seattle Pilots and moved them to Milwaukee to become the Brewers, there was momentary interest in turning the Chicago White Sox into the Seattle White Sox to fill the gap left by the departing Pilots, but nothing came of it. Far more serious was the desire of Reinsdorf, who led an investor group that bought the team in 1981, to follow much of the White Sox fan base to the suburbs and build a domed stadium in Addison, some thirty miles northwest of Comiskey, in 1986. The Addison scheme, designed by HOK Sport, was later changed to an open ballpark, presumably to save money, and fell apart when it was narrowly defeated in a local referendum.

What finally got Reinsdorf a new ballpark was the active courting of the White Sox by Tampa–St. Petersburg as the tenant for its new domed stadium. The possibility that the White Sox might end up in Florida led state politicians, determined that Illinois not suffer the fate of New York when it lost the Giants and the Dodgers, to give the team an even better version of the deal that Walter O'Malley had sought in Brooklyn. The state set up a sports facilities authority to help build a ballpark on the condition that the team stay on its home turf, and gave it the power of eminent domain as well as the right to issue $120 million worth of bonds, later raised to $150 million. The sports authority was merely an enabling vehicle, however; the White Sox were given nearly unchecked authority over the planning process.

After years of dancing with multiple suitors, the White Sox remained where they had always been, on the South Side of Chicago, and their decision to stay, so far as Chicago authorities were concerned, meant they could have pretty much whatever kind of stadium they wanted. The White Sox organization was empowered to reject any consideration of renovating its old park, which, while it never inspired the deep affection of Wrigley Field, was by any measure a significant historic structure. Comiskey Park was, after all, four years older than Wrigley, and with Shibe Park in Philadelphia gone (it was demolished in 1976), it was the oldest survivor of what was coming increasingly to be considered the golden age of baseball park design. Comiskey was architect Zachary Taylor Davis's first ballpark design, and when new it was nicknamed the "Baseball Palace of the World," so it was not surprising that it became the object of an earnest local preservation effort called SOS, for Save Our Sox. The group produced a leaflet in 1987 with a text that read, "Should all of Chicago . . . be in the style of the Loop and sub urban expressway corridor buildings? . . . Or is there a place for Comiskey Park, with its tubular railings and wooden seats and overhangs like the balconies of the long-lost neighborhoods of our youth?"

Save Our Sox never gained significant traction, however, in part because the sports authority's policy of deference to the team's wishes seemed to be shared by the city's historic preservation officials, who never gave the preservation effort serious consideration. Reinsdorf's management had its way on nearly every design decision for the new structure that it favored over restoration, beginning with the team's wish to locate what was then referred to as New Comiskey immediately to the south of the original Comiskey. The team's preferred site required the removal of roughly seventy-eight houses in a neighborhood called South Armour Square, most of which were occupied by African American families, and which the state and the city were prepared to condemn for the sake of getting the ballpark built.

The notion of demolishing houses in a predominantly black neighborhood to help the White Sox did not sit well with many Chicagoans, one of whom, a baseball-loving architect named Philip Bess, had another idea for how the White Sox could get a new stadium built. Bess, who had set up a practice in Chicago a few years before, was sympathetic to the changing sensibilities of his profession in the 1970s and 1980s, and was particularly interested in traditional urbanism. He wondered if he could somehow combine what the White Sox needed from a modern ballpark—revenue-generating skyboxes, lounges and dining areas, seats with unobstructed views, and plenty of circulation space for ease of movement and access—with the tight connection to the urban fabric of an earlier generation of ballparks. Convinced that his concerns had implications beyond the South Side of Chicago, he managed to get the support of both the Society for American Baseball Research and the National Endowment for the Arts, which underwrote his design for Armour Field, an alternative proposal for the White Sox that Bess developed at more or less the same time that the official, sanctioned design of New Comiskey Park was being prepared by the prolific architects of HOK Sport.

The two designs could not be more different, and together they demonstrate the extent to which ballpark design was on the cusp of major change in the late 1980s. While New Comiskey Park—later renamed U.S. Cellular Field, and then, under a different corporate naming rights deal, Guaranteed Rate Field—is a baseball-only park and eschews the circular shape of the 1960s and '70s stadiums, despite those virtues it is really the last of the twentieth century's concrete behemoths. Its overall design bears a distant resemblance to the Royals stadium, but without the graceful curves of the Kansas City grandstand. The design of New Comiskey's enormous, wide, and steep upper deck, which was set far back out of a desire to avoid the deep upper-deck overhang that led to so many obstructed-view seats at the old Comiskey, meant that a vast number of seats were at a great distance from the field. It was a poor trade-off for getting rid of the columns that had supported old Comiskey's upper deck. The critic John Pastier observed that the seats in the first row of the upper deck in the new park are farther from the field than the seats in the last row of the old one.

The new Comiskey that HOK produced may have been built right next to the old Comiskey on Chicago's South Side, but it was in every other way a suburban stadium. By some measures it was worse, since it was a suburban stadium placed inside the city, and building it required the destruction of several blocks of original urban fabric, the very dense city blocks of South Armour Square that had crowded close to the original Comiskey Park and given it a sense of being integrated into its sur-

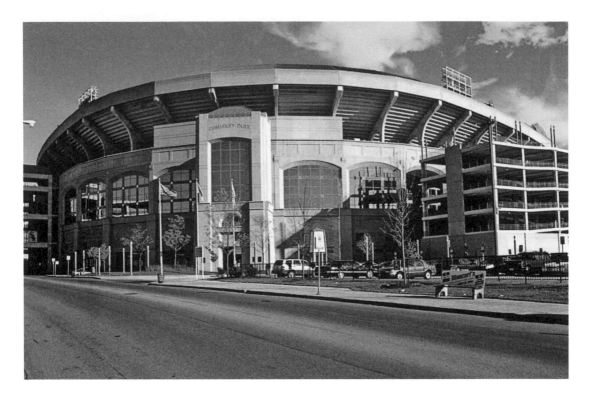

roundings. To make the New Comiskey Park, HOK took an urban site and turned it into a suburban one.

Philip Bess had a very different notion in his Armour Field plan. He wanted to place the ballpark just to the north of old Comiskey, preserving the houses of South Armour Square residents, instead of to the south. A small neighborhood park, Armour Square Park, would have been sacrificed, but the lost park space could have been recaptured on the site of the old Comiskey, which Bess envisioned as "a new public park and an historic landmark, fronting directly upon the entrance to the new ballpark." Bess's design was both tighter and lower than the new Comiskey, although he was able to work in skyboxes, clubs and dining facilities, and other elements of the expanded program of the postwar ballpark. Bess viewed the challenge of ballpark design as an intricate puzzle, starting with an overall shape into which the architect needed to fit complex parts, and then joining it to its surroundings to make a coherent whole. He set aside nine acres surrounding Armour Field for new mixed-use development including retail, offices, and studios. His plan would have

Guaranteed Rate Field (formerly New Comiskey Park), in Chicago

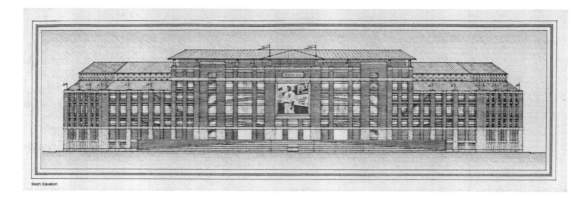

added almost five hundred units of rental or condominium housing in addition to preserving the houses in South Armour Square that were to be destroyed to make way for the ballpark on the site the White Sox preferred. Bess showed not only that the ballpark could be successfully integrated into the existing context, but that it was possible to construct new urban fabric that would weave the ballpark even more tightly into the cityscape. In Bess's plan, some of the new structures were placed directly to the north of the field, giving their occupants views into the field over the center field bleachers, recalling the quirky rooftop galleries of buildings adjacent to many of the early ballparks.

Armour Field itself was to have a curving exterior façade, and in the manner of early ballparks it looked from afar like a building, not like a concrete stadium. The main entrance called to mind Shibe Park or Yankee Stadium more than any recent ballpark, if only in the way it aspired to the formal grandeur of a classical civic building, although it did contain a billboard-sized video screen, a welcome reminder that Bess knew the difference between designing a modern ballpark with traditional elements and designing a structure that sought only to mimic the buildings of the past. He was, however, determined to avoid one of the worst pitfalls of the postwar concrete doughnut, the exterior concrete circulation towers, and placed all circulation within the overall volume of the building.

In response to the symmetry of the site—though somewhat incongruous for a building so determined to recall the idiosyncrasy of older ballparks—Bess designed the field to be symmetrical. The overall footprint, however, was considerably smaller than that of New Comiskey

Philip Bess's rendering of the façade of Armour Field, for the Chicago White Sox, which was never built

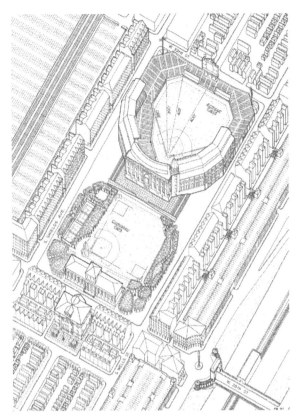

Park, whose very expansiveness has turned out to be one of its main shortcomings. Bess did manage to give Armour some unusual field dimensions: 283 feet to the foul lines, 421 feet to the deepest corners at left and right center field, and 400 feet to the middle of center field. "The playing field's short foul lines and deep power alleys would make for short home runs and long fly-outs, increase the number of triples and inside-the-park home runs, and place a premium on speed in the outfield," he wrote. "It would reward players and teams smart or talented enough to adjust their skills to their surroundings. . . . The predictably unpredictable environment that follows from genuinely urban site constraints is what distinguishes traditional urban ballparks from modern suburban stadiums."

Armour Field was the first attempt at the scale of a major league ballpark to respond to the financially lucrative program of contemporary baseball—lots of fan-friendly facilities, lots of support facilities for the players, and generous amounts of special, high-priced luxury seats and skyboxes—with a design that would restore baseball's intimate connection with the urban fabric. It is impossible to know how well it would have succeeded had the White Sox been interested in building it instead of the design that they did commission, and decades later, Bess was still disappointed that the Illinois Sports Facilities Authority seemed uninterested in his belief that developing the surrounding blocks as commercial real estate would not only improve the ballpark environment but would throw off substantial income that would help to underwrite the ballpark itself.

Armour Field, set within Chicago's South Side neighborhood, would have had new housing along either side.

"We presented it to the ISFA, and it was politely received but that was it," he said. "It was politically naïve." The White Sox had made their decision, and by the time Bess was allowed his courtesy presentation before the sports authority the team was already working with the architects of HOK Sport who, back then, appeared to have little interest in any of the ideas for an urbanistically sensitive, traditional ballpark with modern amenities that Philip Bess was promoting. In the 1980s, with more domed stadiums and concrete doughnuts still to come, the idea of a modern ballpark that was tightly woven into the city blocks around it seemed too hard to fathom, certainly for a team whose first choice had been to build a new stadium thirty miles away, next to an expressway in suburban Addison. In the end, the White Sox got their suburban ballpark. They just put it on the South Side of Chicago.

All of that would change when another major league team, whose management had a very different notion than the White Sox of what it wanted its ballpark to be, would decide that it, too, needed a new place in which to play baseball. The team was the Baltimore Orioles, and it would build Oriole Park at Camden Yards, which opened in 1992 and began a new chapter of ballpark design as surely as the Grand Pavilion of South End Grounds in Boston and Shibe Park in Philadelphia had in their time. Camden Yards would be the most influential ballpark since Yankee Stadium, and its story, like that of every notable ballpark, is a complex saga of sports mixed with architecture, politics, and money.

There had been talk in Baltimore since the 1960s of a new ballpark to replace Memorial Stadium, which housed both the football Colts and the baseball Orioles. If Memorial housed baseball more comfortably than many multi-use stadiums it was still far from ideal, and one of its quirkiest aspects, the fact that it was a suburban-style concrete hulk located in a low-rise residential neighborhood, did not endear it to suburban fans searching for parking. When William Donald Schaefer, an unconventional politician who was nothing if not passionate about his city, became mayor in 1971, he floated the idea of new sports facilities on a downtown site occupied by the Baltimore & Ohio Railroad's old Camden railyards.

But the plans did not get serious until the mid-1980s, when city and state officials, upset over the sudden departure of the Baltimore Colts football team to Indianapolis in 1984, feared that they might lose their baseball team as well if they did not give the Orioles a better place to play than Memorial Stadium. In 1987, by which time Schaefer had become governor, the state created an entity called the Maryland Sta-

The interior of Oriole Park at Camden Yards in Baltimore, incorporating the B&O warehouse—in a way that echoes the integration of the Moore & White Co. Paper Machinery building into Philadelphia's Baker Bowl

dium Authority to oversee and finance what was initially conceived of as a multi-purpose stadium, and the authority hired HOK Sport, the ubiquitous firm of stadium architects from Kansas City, to prepare some preliminary plans and to investigate potential sites, including one in suburban Lansdowne. The authority did not begin with any intention of creating a new urban paradigm for baseball in downtown Baltimore; indeed, its tentative beginnings suggested that the more likely outcome of its efforts would be yet another suburban mega-multi-sport palace, perhaps even with a dome, a replication of the mistakes of the previous generation of stadiums.

That it turned out to be quite the opposite—a baseball-only park in the center of downtown Baltimore that redefined what the baseball park would be and how people would experience it—was the result of an extraordinary confluence of factors, not to mention an unusual cast of characters from the worlds of architecture, politics, and finance, none of whom could have created Camden Yards without the others. It would take a striking reversal of course from a major architectural firm, a changeover in the state administration, and new ownership and management for the Orioles—not to mention a fair amount of luck—to see the plan to completion.

In 1979, five years before the traumatic departure of the Baltimore Colts, Edward Bennett Williams, the celebrated Washington lawyer, bought the Orioles. Williams purchased the team with the expectation that he might move it to Washington, which had been without a major league team since 1971, when the Washington Senators, established a decade earlier after the previous Senators team left to become the Minnesota Twins, moved to Texas and became the Texas Rangers. Williams never announced a plan to move the Orioles to the capital, but his refusal to commit to more than short-term leases at Memorial Stadium sent a clear signal that he was considering other options, including a possible suburban ballpark midway between Baltimore and Washington. To Schaefer, then the mayor, keeping the team in the state of Maryland was not enough; he wanted the Orioles in Baltimore, and he made it his business to charm, cajole, and romance Williams in the hope of convincing him that the team needed to remain within the city.

The sudden loss of the Colts gave the project a political urgency, and also gave Williams the upper hand. Neither Williams nor his chief lieutenant, a lawyer named Larry Lucchino who became the Orioles' chief executive after Williams bought the team, had any interest in a multipurpose stadium. Lucchino pushed hard to have the new Maryland Stadium Authority build a baseball-only park. A native of Pittsburgh, he had seen the lyrical Forbes Field replaced by the multi-use monolith of Three Rivers Stadium, a downgrade that he felt had forever shaped his view of baseball parks. "I said to [Williams] what do the Red Sox, Tigers, Yankees, Dodgers and Cubs have in common? They all play in baseball-only parks," Lucchino said. "He said 'we're in a battle over one stadium, and you want to build two?' But the most successful teams all played in baseball-only facilities." Now Governor Schaefer, realizing that there was little benefit in offending the baseball team he still had, the Orioles, to satisfy a football team he did not yet have, agreed to abandon all thoughts of a shared stadium, and left the question of where some future football

Larry Lucchino, an advocate of traditional ballparks who was the public face of the Orioles management during the years Camden Yards was designed and built

team would play to another day. The new park would be at Camden Yards in downtown Baltimore, and it would be for baseball only.

It was Lucchino, too, who negotiated the team's contract in 1988 with the stadium authority, which not only gave the Orioles favorable financial terms—this was becoming increasingly common in an age in which public entities built and owned ballparks—it required that the team have "design concurrence," a deftly chosen pair of words that meant that while the stadium authority would hire the architect, pay design fees, and would technically be the architect's client, the team would effectively control the design by having veto power over any element that it disapproved of. Lucchino and Williams's goal was to get the ballpark they wanted, and to have the Maryland Stadium Authority pay for it.

Lucchino had high architectural ambitions. He began one planning meeting by distributing brochures for the Yugo, the small Eastern European car that was briefly imported into the United States and quickly became a symbol of banality. "We don't drive Yugos and we're not going to play in a Yugo ballpark," he said. Lucchino's target, as much as the Maryland Stadium Authority, was a plan floated by Peter Ueberroth, who had become commissioner of baseball in 1984, to have major league baseball endorse a basic, standardized stadium design by the construction firm Bechtel that could be replicated in any city. Nothing would be less suitable to Baltimore, Lucchino thought, and he wanted to have nothing to do with the commissioner's idea.

Lucchino had no more patience with HOK Sport, regarding its architects both as lacking in imagination and as primarily loyal to the stadium authority, which had retained the firm to do its initial studies. In the hope of setting the project in a different direction he invited several prominent architects and urban designers to make presentations to the team, including William Pedersen of Kohn Pedersen Fox, a New York–based firm known primarily for its commercial towers; Alexander Cooper, the architect and urban planner who had designed the master plan for Battery Park City in New York; Ayers Saint Gross, probably the most design-savvy Baltimore-based firm; the eminent modernist national firm Skidmore, Owings & Merrill; and the firm of Philip Johnson and John Burgee, whose recent postmodern tower for AT&T was probably the most talked-about skyscraper of the decade. Only Skidmore, the architect of the Oakland Coliseum complex, had any experience in ballpark design, but to Lucchino, that in itself was probably enough to disqualify the firm. He was one of the few baseball executives

who understood how mediocre most baseball parks finished in the previous two decades had been, and he saw no advantage to hiring an architect who had designed so much as a single one of them. HOK, even less to its credit, had done most of them.

Nothing came of Lucchino's elaborate parade of architects. The stadium authority hired HOK Sport, as it had probably intended to do all along. Design concurrence gave the Orioles management the right to say yes or no to specific design ideas, but not to choose the architect. It was a major defeat for Lucchino, but 1988 would bring an even more serious challenge when Edward Bennett Williams, who had been battling cancer for years, died, and his widow put the team up for sale. With a signed contract between the stadium authority and the Orioles the Camden Yards stadium project was unlikely to be abandoned, but a new owner could well have very different ideas about what it should be. And it was hard to know at that point what HOK Sport would come up with. The firm had recently designed the pleasing and modest Pilot Field in

Eli Jacobs, Orioles owner, had a passion for architecture and urbanism, and he insisted through the design process that Camden Yards be different from other postwar ballparks.

Buffalo, widely respected as the first postwar example of a baseball park successfully integrated into the urban fabric of an older city, but its portfolio leaned heavily toward the sort of enormous and unwieldy concrete stadiums that Lucchino was determined to avoid.

If Larry Lucchino provided the initial push to send the design of Camden Yards in the right direction, his efforts would probably have dissipated had it not been for two people who joined the project after the death of Edward Bennett Williams: Eli Jacobs, a New York investor who bought the Orioles in 1989, retaining Lucchino as the team's president; and Janet Marie Smith, an architect whom Lucchino decided to hire after she wrote him a letter offering her services as someone who might be able to help get the Orioles' new ballpark built. They made an unlikely trio: Lucchino, a lawyer turned baseball executive who as the public face of Orioles management increasingly had to focus on navigating the complex political waters of Maryland; Jacobs, a private, New York–based financier with a long-standing interest in public policy, security, and Republican politics, who intensely disliked the public spotlight that Lucchino appeared to revel in; and Smith, a Mississippi-born architect who had worked on the staff of the Battery Park City Authority in New York, helping to execute Alexander Cooper's widely admired urban design plan for this new community in Lower Manhattan.

But they all had one thing in common, besides liking baseball. They all loved old-fashioned, dense, walkable cities, and the traditional baseball parks that were often a part of them. Jacobs had grown up in Boston, and Fenway Park was his baseline for what a baseball park should be; moreover, as a student at Yale he acquired a lifelong interest in architecture and urban design. Unlike most private equity investors, Jacobs could talk knowledgeably about the differences between Frank Lloyd Wright and Louis Kahn, not to mention between Fenway Park and Ebbets Field,

*Janet Marie Smith,
at Camden Yards in
Baltimore*

and talking about architecture was, for him, both a form of relaxation and intellectual exercise. In conversation he and Lucchino were both inclined to make references to Jane Jacobs, whose 1961 book, *The Death and Life of Great American Cities,* did more than any other work to shift thinking away from postwar notions of automobile-oriented urban renewal, and toward a greater respect for the pedestrian-oriented urban fabric of older cities. Larry Lucchino, Eli Jacobs, and Janet Marie Smith spoke Jane Jacobs's language at a time when almost no one else in baseball would have known who she was, or cared anything about her ideas.

Smith, who became the team's vice president in charge of stadium design and construction, was hired almost by accident. Lucchino was not looking for an in-house architect, and he found her resume when he was signing a pile of routine rejection letters to job-seekers. "I said 'I'm drowning in this project, maybe we should at least interview her,'" he recalled, and he invited her to Baltimore. "When she came in, I said 'Let's start with your telling me which league has the designated hitter.' She said 'I'm offended by that question.'" It was clear that Smith knew baseball, and it soon became equally clear that her view of what a baseball park should look like paralleled Lucchino's. He hired her, and she became the person who determined what the Orioles wanted, conveyed it to the architects, and represented the team as the public face of design. Smith "carried out all the details—she deserves a lot of the credit," Eli Jacobs said. "She is the real heroine." Larry Lucchino described Smith as "the best free agent acquisition we made that year."

If Jacobs, Lucchino, and Smith shared a desire to give the Orioles a baseball park that broke away from the concrete doughnuts of the time, their view was not, initially, shared by either their architects, HOK Sport, or the public stadium authority that was the legal entity charged with actually getting the ballpark built. When HOK presented the first version of the design, Jacobs recalled, it looked far more like the stadiums of the previous decade than the sort of thing that he had in mind. He told Joe Spear, the HOK partner in charge of the project, that the design—which he would later be quoted as saying "looked like a spaceship"—was absolutely unacceptable. "HOK said to me, here's your new ballpark, and I looked at it and said we can't accept this design," Jacobs said. "When we bought the Orioles I did not understand that we had veto rights, but by then I knew this clause was in the contract." Jacobs's rejection was so blunt that it concerned Lucchino, who later said that he didn't like the design either—"I tore it apart, it was nothing like what we wanted." But Lucchino was worried that the team would be attacked in the local press for getting into a spat with its architect before construction had even begun, and that the delicate balance of power between the team, the architect, and the stadium authority would fall apart if the team were perceived as obstinate and difficult. A negotiator by nature, Lucchino seemed inclined to trust that the Orioles could improve things working behind the scenes with the architects; Jacobs was adamant that the team send HOK a stronger message of disapproval. He would not moderate his view, but to smooth things over, he turned back to the architects. "I said 'I'm confident that working together we will create something we can be proud of.'" And then he left for New York.

The design progressed, in stages, pressured from a distance by Eli Jacobs and on a daily basis by Janet Marie Smith. The most important early decision, which had been the subject of debate well before HOK revealed its original design, involved the Baltimore & Ohio Railroad's brick warehouse, as long as a train and eight stories high, at the edge of the site. Lucchino wanted to tear it down, but a number of others involved in the project thought it was worth keeping as a backdrop to the outfield. The warehouse, they reasoned, would not only frame and visually enclose a portion of the outfield, it could give the park a sense of connection to Baltimore's architectural history and enhance the tie between ballpark and city. "I had a feeling it would define the entire campus by enclosing the space without making it feel suffocating, and would frame the view of the skyline of Baltimore," Jacobs said. And it would certainly serve the larger goal of making the Baltimore ballpark distinctive and not generic: a brick warehouse just beyond the outfield was the sort of thing one expected to see in photographs of the ballparks of the previous century, whose designers took it for granted that the playing fields and the grandstands would have to fit around what already existed. That the immediate surroundings were different on every site in every city meant that the field of play was different, too, and those differences were a key part of baseball's identity. The warehouse was less an obstacle than a gift, a way of making Baltimore's ballpark unique.

The decision about the B&O warehouse was probably the biggest

issue early on in the design, but it receded quickly once the stadium authority and the architects at HOK decided to go along with the notion of retaining it, rejecting a compromise plan—to cut the building in two and save half of it—that would have satisfied no one. Lucchino, nothing if not a savvy dealmaker, knew to give way to the majority view. As the design moved forward, the decision to save the warehouse and integrate it into the complex seemed, in fact, to set the tone for many of the decisions that followed, since the ballpark became increasingly referential to the past as it inched away from HOK's original scheme, which bore a curious resemblance to the design for New Comiskey Park, the concrete stadium that the firm was providing at roughly the same time for the Chicago White Sox.* Round exterior towers containing ramps, which

* See Chapter 7. New Comiskey Park was finished in 1991, a year before Oriole Park at Camden Yards, but the parks were begun at approximately the same time. Eli Jacobs has said that he thinks the design the Orioles rejected was quickly reworked by HOK Sport and offered to the White Sox.

The brick and cast stone façade of Oriole Park at Camden Yards

Janet Marie Smith considered a particularly unpleasant hallmark of the concrete doughnut generation of stadiums, were banished, and circulation integrated into the main structure, which was sheathed primarily in red brick, a material that had not been common in major league baseball parks for at least a generation.

The façade was made more building-like and less stadium-like with a series of wide arches, alluding to traditional architecture without imitating it directly, and further linking the ballpark to the adjacent warehouse. The upper decks were set back from the façade, so that the building would not appear too massive as you approached it, and the cast-iron gates were labeled not with numbers but with the names of the streets that they opened onto, making them both easier to remember and further branding them into Baltimore's cityscape.

And inside the seating areas, the visible structural members supporting the grandstands were made of steel instead of concrete, another deliberate return to a design element common to a much earlier generation of ballparks. Exposed steel called to mind Wrigley Field or Fenway Park; concrete structural supports suggested places like Veterans Stadium in Philadelphia or Memorial Stadium down the road—the associations Jacobs, Lucchino, and Smith were determined to avoid.

The design of the seating areas and their relationship to the field was another basic challenge. Jacobs, Lucchino, and Smith all favored a seating capacity of less than Memorial Stadium's 53,371 seats, and they wanted the seating areas set asymmetrically around the field to further distinguish the new park from the oversized concrete doughnuts of the previous generation. Each row of green slatted seats was decorated by a replica of the logo of Baltimore's first baseball team from the 1890s, a tiny detail that probably did as much as the steel trusses to tell fans that this ballpark was designed to look back at baseball's history. The field was relatively tight as well as asymmetrical, and welcoming to power hitters with a 400-foot distance in dead center, 410 feet in left center, 333 feet in left, and only 318 feet in right field. The final design would call for 48,876 seats (reduced to 45,971 in a 2011 renovation), but more important than the number of seats was the goal of giving seats clear sightlines to the field, and assuring that as many seats as possible would have a sense of intimate connection to the infield, not to mention good views of the downtown skyline to the left of the warehouse over the bleachers.

The skyline views were a way of further emphasizing the sense of place, reminding fans that they were in Baltimore and nowhere else. Enhancing a sense of connection to the field, however, was more directly tied to the game itself. The round form of the mid-century concrete doughnut stadiums encouraged wide arcs of field seating behind large foul areas, which had the effect of pushing even prime field seats far from the baselines. By the same token, another common trait of mid-century concrete stadiums, the worthy desire to avoid having supporting columns that obstructed views, came at the price of pushing the upper decks far back, putting their seats at a far greater distance from the field than they would have been in an older ballpark. Architects often tried to compensate for this by making the upper decks exceptionally steep, thus pulling the highest rows somewhat closer to the field, but this configuration still left the highest seats at a considerable distance from the playing field,

Eutaw Street is closed to traffic on game days and becomes a public promenade.

and added the awkwardness of uncomfortably steep, even dangerous, steps.

For Baltimore, then, the foul territory was smaller to allow the field seats to be closer to the field, and the side walls were straight, not curving, to bring seats closer in. The upper decks, too, were closer to the field than they were in most recent stadiums. Eli Jacobs thought it was all a matter of mathematics. He thought that no upper deck should be raked at more than a 37-degree angle, and his instincts made him a quick study. During the contentious meeting when he first saw the initial designs that HOK had prepared for Baltimore, one of the things he told the architects was that the decks were too steep. Long afterward, an official of the Maryland Stadium Authority recalled the meeting: "Jacobs walked in and after ten seconds he said he didn't like it. He said it as if he'd been studying it for three months. . . . He said 'The upper deck is too steep.' I said to myself, 'How the hell does he know that?' We knew it was too steep. But with a model that small, you can't tell. But he could."

The stadium was positioned so that the B&O warehouse—which was used for team offices, support space, and a private club—was just beyond the right center field bleachers. Eutaw Street, between the warehouse and the bleachers, was retained, and closed to traffic during game days, when it turned into a lively urban promenade. The grandstands stopped short of the warehouse in right field, but on the other side made a sharp turn to enclose left field, enhancing the asymmetry. The low right field wall had some advertising signs, the kind of gesture that elsewhere might have seemed cravenly commercial, but here came off more like another charming reference to baseball's past. (It was the first time a ballpark had advertising on a wall inside the field of play since Connie Mack Stadium, the former Shibe Park, which closed in 1970.) Indeed, if the overall architecture could be faulted at all, it would be for having reversed aesthetic direction so completely from the plans HOK Sport started with that it left few indications that it was designed at the end of the twentieth century.

The most important sign that this was a modern stadium—and the aspect of the Baltimore ballpark that would do as much to set the tone for the ballparks to follow as its "retro" aesthetic—was the plethora of luxury boxes, dining facilities, and souvenir shops it contained, not to mention its generous amounts of public circulation space, features like a children's playground, and the extensive club rooms and locker rooms provided for both the Orioles and visiting teams. All of the ballparks of the first generation, whatever their other virtues, were cramped, with mean public facilities, awkward circulation spaces, and almost no amenities for either fans or players. The concrete stadiums of the second generation were only slightly better, and generally offered only marginal improvements in amenities in exchange for the total abdication of any charm, leaving neither fans nor players any better off.

So Baltimore's new ballpark was not truly a return to the past at all: if it had been, it would have been far smaller, and would probably have had a third as many restrooms, scant eating options, cramped corridors, and minimal accommodations for luxury seating. The Camden Yards ballpark may have looked like an old-fashioned ballpark, but that was merely its external garb; underneath, it was very much the product of modern baseball, a corporate business whose team owners were increasingly seeking ways to maximize revenue far beyond the sale of basic tickets. To accommodate its expanded program, the Baltimore ballpark spread out in a way that classic, more tightly vertical ballparks like Ebbets Field and Shibe Park did not. Not the least of the accomplishments of its design was the success with which the architects managed to integrate the far more expansive functional demands of the modern baseball park with the look and feel of a more traditional one. Its overall design was, in a way, a triumph of balance.

Another aspect represented a triumph of balance as well, or at least a triumph of compromise—the name of the ballpark, which, happily, was never sold to a corporate sponsor but intended to evoke the team itself. Governor Schaefer, who had enabled the park's construction through the Maryland Stadium Authority, wanted to call it Camden Yards in tribute to the old neighborhood. Eli Jacobs, eager to keep the name of the team he owned front and center, wanted to call it Oriole Park, in tribute to an early ballpark used by the team's minor league ancestor. Jacobs, who never had the easy relationship with the governor that Edward Williams had, found himself in a deadlock with Schaefer, and their disagreement played out in the press. Finally they met for breakfast, and Jacobs suggested "Oriole Park at Camden Yards," which became the official name. From the opening day on April 6, 1992, however, almost everyone called the park what Schaefer had expected them to, which was Camden Yards.

. . .

Opening Day was jubilant: not only did the Orioles defeat the Cleveland Indians in a 2–0 shutout before a sellout crowd, the new ballpark was recognized from the beginning as the start of a new era in baseball. *The Washington Post* called it "an irregularly shaped, all-green masterpiece of a stadium" and said that opening day "lived up to the years of anticipation." In a major feature in *Sports Illustrated* written by Tim Kurkjian, then a senior writer, the magazine called Camden Yards "a real ballpark built into a real downtown of a real city." Kurkjian continued: "The splendor of Oriole Park is in its character and in its details. It is built of brick and steel, not of concrete like the flying saucers that landed in too many major league cities starting about 25 years ago. Sunlight pours in not only from above but, as at Wrigley, through openings between the upper and lower decks as well. The park combines elements from the best ballparks of the early 1900s—Fenway, Wrigley, Ebbets Field, Shibe Park, Crosley Field, Forbes Field—with the high-tech amenities of the 1990s." *The New York Times* did not even wait until the ballpark opened. While it was still under construction the paper described it as "a design that enriches baseball, the city and the region, all at once, and makes every sprawling concrete dome sitting in a sea of parked cars look bloated, fat and tired. . . . Baltimore is not the first city to understand the virtues of urban design, but it is the first one to prove that they need not be incompatible with the pleasures of professional sports."

Architecture critics, frequently skeptical of projects that appear to have been designed to evoke the past rather than point to the future, seemed to put these concerns aside when it came to Camden Yards. There were no sneering comparisons to Disneyland in critics' descriptions of this piece of architectural nostalgia, in part, surely, because the critics figured out that this time, at least, looking toward the past actually was the future. The Orioles and their architects, wrote Edward Gunts, the architecture critic of the *Baltimore Sun,* "have created a seminal building that will influence the way major-league sports facilities are designed from now on. It holds more lessons for combining sports and cities than the past five decades' worth of cookie-cutter stadiums that were passed off as people places. And Baltimore will be remembered as the city where they broke the mold."

President George H. W. Bush threw out the first ball, and watched the game with Eli Jacobs in the owner's box, along with Dick Cheney, then the secretary of defense, and members of the Bush family. George Will, the conservative columnist who, at Jacobs's request, joined the board of directors of the Orioles, said, "No fan who goes to this park will find a place that's better, with the possible exception of Fenway and, maybe, Wrigley." Later, Will would elevate his praise for Camden Yards beyond the realm of architecture, and write that the Baltimore ballpark had changed the nature of baseball. "The three most important things that have happened in baseball since the Second World War," Will wrote in *A Nice Little Place on the North Side,* a riff on baseball in the guise of a tribute to Wrigley Field on its hundredth birthday, "were Jackie Robinson taking the field in 1947, free agency arriving in 1975, and Oriole Park at Camden Yards opening in 1992."

Like a team that wins the World Series and then breaks up, the makers of Oriole Park at Camden Yards scattered not long after the park was finished. Eli Jacobs had said he wanted to build a park that people would treat as a destination, and would want to visit whether or not they were committed fans of the Orioles. That effort succeeded so well that a year after Camden Yards opened, the team was worth $173 million, more than $100 million more than Jacobs had paid for it four years earlier. That was fortunate since many of Jacobs's other ventures were not doing as well in the early 1990s, and to satisfy his bankers he sold the team. The new owners, a group of Baltimore investors led by Peter Angelos, replaced both Larry Lucchino and Janet Marie Smith. Unlike Jacobs, who never returned to major league baseball, both Lucchino and Smith used the acclaim of Camden Yards as a springboard to their future careers. Lucchino moved on to run the San Diego Padres and to oversee the construction of Petco Park, another widely acclaimed urban ballpark, and then was brought to Boston as chief executive of the Boston Red Sox. There he helped to scuttle a plan to replace Fenway Park, and hired Janet Marie Smith to oversee its renovation and restoration. Smith would later join the Los Angeles Dodgers, where she directed a renovation of Dodger Stadium that, like her work at Fenway Park, riffed on the original architectural themes while adding new and profitable amenities that were intended to have a greater effect on the team's bottom line than on the physical appearance of the stadium, which she and the architect

Ornamental details at Camden Yards

in charge, Brenda Levin, and landscape architect Mia Lehrer worked hard to maintain. The tenacity and sharp eye for detail that had served Smith well in Baltimore proved equally adept in Boston and Los Angeles, where she supervised projects that managed to be at once historic restorations and reinventions. Smith never went back to the general practice of architecture and urban planning; she would spend the rest of her career in baseball, serving as a consultant to multiple teams and spreading a gospel that she would summarize with a line from Larry Lucchino, who liked to describe Camden Yards as "an old-fashioned ballpark with modern amenities." Smith became the Johnny Appleseed of Lucchino's vision.

HOK Sport, which later broke away from its parent firm, Hellmuth, Obata & Kassabaum, and renamed itself Populous, perhaps profited the most of all from the success of Camden Yards. Joe Spear and Earl Santee, two of the firm's founding partners, became ardent champions of the genre that even before the completion of Camden Yards was becoming known as retro ballpark design, and they promoted it with the zeal of converts. HOK Sport skillfully used the acclaim of the Baltimore ballpark to position itself as the go-to architects for this new-yet-old style of baseball park, and before long HOK had cornered the market for retro ballparks as fully as it had once dominated in the world of round concrete monoliths. It was conveniently forgotten that

HOK Sport had first come to Baltimore with a very different notion of what Camden Yards might be—and that if Eli Jacobs, Larry Lucchino, the Maryland Stadium Authority, and Janet Marie Smith had not challenged it, Camden Yards would not have changed baseball history as it did.

9

After Baltimore: Looking Back
or Looking Forward?

THE 1990S would bear out George Will's observation that the opening of Oriole Park at Camden Yards in 1992 was one of the three most influential events in the post–World War II history of baseball, bringing about an architectural sea change so vast that no future ballpark could be designed without reference to it. After Camden Yards, the heavy, circular concrete stadiums of the fifties, sixties, and seventies, never admired by either players or fans, seemed suddenly obsolete. Other major league teams saw what the Baltimore Orioles had and wanted something similar, hoping that the aura of Camden Yards could be replicated in their city. Even an organization like the Boston Red Sox, which possessed in Fenway Park a truly beloved ballpark that had been one of Camden Yards' models, began to consider building anew once Baltimore had shown them that a new ballpark did not always mean tossing aside everything fans and players valued in favor of a circle of concrete amid a sea of parked automobiles. In one fell swoop, Baltimore had slain the multi-purpose dragon, the huge stadium that was made for both baseball and football and served neither adequately. In the post–Camden Yards era, Dodger Stadium in Los Angeles and the Royals Stadium in Kansas City, the only baseball-only facilities built since World War II, seemed prescient, no longer outliers. By contrast, New Comiskey Park in Chi-

cago, the last of the concrete hulks, had opened in 1991, and already felt
outdated; only the fact that it, too, had been built exclusively for baseball
kept it from looking like a complete dinosaur. But after Camden Yards its
architecture still made it seem like a relic from another age.

With startling suddenness, expectations had changed. Camden Yards
was the new paradigm, setting baseball architecture on a different track:
building in the city; celebrating local qualities through both a ballpark's
specific architecture and the connections it established with its surroundings; leaving room for idiosyncrasy and design quirks. Baltimore's success
set off a wave of new ballpark construction that would last through the
nineties and well into the following decade, and while the ballparks of
the nineties varied considerably in quality as well as in the particulars
of their designs, it is fair to say every one of them showed the influence
of the seminal design for Camden Yards by the architects of HOK Sport.

The term *retro ballpark* entered the language after Camden Yards, and
while it was memorable and an accurate summary of the motivating
concept behind the Baltimore ballpark, it was also, by most measures,
a gross oversimplification. It suggested that looking backward was all
that architects were doing in the design of these new ballparks, and it
ignored the fact that, whatever their appearance, all of these ballparks

*Joe Spear, a senior
design partner at
Populous, in the firm's
main office in Kansas
City. Behind him is
an early version of
the firm's design for
the Miami Marlins
ballpark.*

of the nineties, like Camden Yards itself, had a wealth of facilities for both fans and players that older ballparks lacked—facilities that would give most of them a far larger footprint than the traditional ballparks they sought to emulate. And if the presence of architectural details that recalled traditional brick buildings gave Camden Yards much of its visual definition, so did the size and layout of the seating bowl, the visibility of the Baltimore skyline, and the asymmetry of the field—all elements that did not depend on old-fashioned ironwork gates and traditional lamp-posts and brick arches, however appealing they might be.

Joe Spear and the architects of HOK Sport understood that of the first two ballparks they finished at the beginning of the decade, the comfort-able and inviting Camden Yards won hands down in the court of public opinion over the concrete hulk of New Comiskey Park. But Spear, proud as he was of the final product of Camden Yards, was eager to show that the quality of the Baltimore ballpark went far deeper than its veneer of historical detail, and that there were other lessons to be learned from its success. The real message of Camden Yards, he thought, was that a ballpark design should be specific to its city and, within that city, to its site—that you do not build the same thing everywhere.

"I had four or five developers approach me after Camden Yards offer-ing to buy the plans for a million dollars," he said, "but the last thing I would ever want to do is the same thing twice. I wanted the freedom to do something different."

He would have his chance in the first major ballpark HOK Sport would complete after Camden Yards, in Cleveland, where Richard and David Jacobs, who then owned the Cleveland Indians, made it clear that their priority was to have the Indians' new field somehow express the feel-ing of Cleveland as a city. The origins of the project go back well before the opening of Camden Yards, and before the Jacobs brothers, who had made a fortune in real estate development, had bought the team. The Indians were still playing in Cleveland Municipal Stadium, a massive, round prewar coliseum built in the 1930s and standing alone on the lake-front, the precursor of an entire generation of isolated, postwar concrete doughnuts built by cities rather than by team owners, and intended for both baseball and football.* In the mid-1980s, Cleveland held a referen-

* See Chapter 5 for a detailed discussion of Cleveland Municipal Stadium.

dum to consider replacing the old stadium with a new domed field to be funded through higher city property taxes, and while it may have been the notion of a property tax increase that offended citizens more than the idea of a domed stadium, the referendum went down in defeat, and took the notion of a mixed-use stadium down with it.

When the Jacobs brothers bought the team, they were unwilling to give up on the idea of replacing the old Municipal Stadium. "But in a city that had already rejected public funding of a new stadium, it would take masterful manipulation to persuade the populace to fund such a project," wrote Neil deMause and Joanna Cagan. The Jacobs brothers were prepared to put some money into the project, but not to fund it themselves, and the county responded with a plan to pay for a new down-town ballpark and a separate basketball arena for the Cleveland Cavaliers with a new tax on alcohol and tobacco sales, putting the proposal before voters in a 1990 referendum. Convinced by an advertising campaign that proclaimed "No property tax; no sales tax; no income tax; no tax abate-ment," as well as by a not-so-thinly-veiled threat by Fay Vincent, the commissioner of baseball, to allow the Indians to leave Cleveland if the voters did not give them a new ballpark, the voters narrowly approved the new tax and the project it would fund.

The baseball park would go in the economically depressed area near the city's central business district that had once held Cleveland's Central Market, an open-air produce market, the same place that was to have been the site of the failed domed stadium. It was a part of downtown that was close to the central business district, but had been largely untouched by the redevelopment that had brought new office towers to Cleveland and turned the heart of its downtown into a symbol of the potential of troubled, rust-belt manufacturing cities to reinvent themselves by cater-ing to the needs of a service economy. The area had continued to decline as the domed stadium was being debated, since the uncertainty about what would happen all but ruled out private investment there. Daniel Rosensweig referred to it as a neighborhood that "had come to embody the collateral damage of urban renewal and suburban flight—a part of town so neglected that even some stores catering to the urban poor fled from it to distant neighborhoods."

To suggest a new beginning, the old market area was renamed Gate-way, and the Gateway Economic Development Corporation was set up to manage what was christened the Central Market Gateway Project. By then, Camden Yards was well under way and the notion of a new age in baseball park design was just visible on the horizon. Even with Baltimore's ballpark not yet complete, it was clear that Cleveland had no wish to end up with something like New Comiskey Park in Chicago. The Gateway corporation hired Sasaki Associates, a prominent urban design and landscape architecture firm based in Watertown, Massachusetts, to create a master plan for the project and design its outdoor public spaces; along with HOK Sport, Sasaki positioned the ballpark on the larger project site both to maximize city views and to assure optimal orientation for sun. As to the design of the ballpark itself, Gateway, encouraged by the Jacobs brothers, preferred a ballpark that was integrated into the downtown the city's enormous old stadium had spurned, and urged that its design be in some way distinctive to Cleveland. If "retro" could be taken to mean an asymmetrical, baseball-only park with a moderate seating capacity similar to that of Camden Yards, the same tight foul lines, and an open vista to downtown, Cleveland was willing to follow the trend. But if it meant sprinkling the ballpark with old-fashioned historical details, those would be left behind in Baltimore.

Joe Spear, to whom formal architectural concepts were inseparable from his struggle to fulfill the wishes of his clients—an attitude that allowed him to rationalize the awkward design of New Comiskey Park in Chicago, but also led him to accommodate quickly to the higher ambitions in Baltimore—was pleased by the expectation that the architecture of the ballpark in Cleveland reflect the image of the city. Spear arrived at an open meeting held to get public input at the beginning of the design process armed with a set of pictures of what he considered iconic Cleveland structures: Terminal Tower, facing Public Square in the center of the city; steel mills and smokestacks representing the city's industrial heritage; and the metal truss bridges over the Cuyahoga River. He had not yet designed the ballpark, he told the audience, but he wanted those pictures to inspire him, and he wanted the final result to fit into the city they represented.

"We were looking for something symbolic of Cleveland," Spear said, "and I knew it would be okay when somebody said we know we will like this because it will be all about Cleveland."

The decision to place the domed stadium, and later the new ballpark and arena, in the Gateway meant that the city was looking at the area not so much as a neighborhood to be renewed as one to be replaced. Cleveland had come to see "the future of this portion of downtown as, in part, a kind of theme park for an increasingly homogeneous crowd," as Rosensweig put it. Cleveland has always been a working-class city, and the new ballpark—which was initially named Jacobs Field after the brothers purchased naming rights, and later became Progressive Field, for the insurance company that made a subsequent deal for naming rights— would have plenty of bleacher seats for fans who did not have a lot of money to spend. But like all new ballparks of the post–Camden Yards era, it would also be chockablock with luxury boxes and private dining clubs, putting the economic divide that had always been present in base-ball into ever higher relief.

Indeed, if there would turn out to be any notable weakness of Spear's design for Progressive Field, it was that it gave an unusual degree of prominence to luxury suites. Instead of being slipped unobtrusively between main seating levels, they were designed as three levels of glass-enclosed boxes, which had the unfortunate effect of pushing the upper deck higher, and all of its seats farther from the field. To bring the upper-deck seats slightly closer to the field the architects gave the deck a steep 33-degree rake, an unpleasant design element that did little to make up for what was still a substantial distance. ("It feels as if you are watching a ballgame from the moon," the *Chicago Tribune* would comment.) And it could do nothing to offset the way that the three levels of boxes collectively dominated the view from the bleachers back toward the grand-stand. Progressive Field even included the dubious innovation of a few extra glass-enclosed field boxes tucked into the edge of the field level, dugouts for high-paying customers.

The plethora of private, glass-enclosed boxes facing the diamond unfortunately undercut the larger design goal of tying the ballpark in to the life of the city, which Spear's design otherwise admirably succeeded in doing. Progressive Field replicated many of the best features of Camden Yards, including an asymmetrical field and a close connection to the city's street pattern, and it even surpassed Camden Yards in terms of the open views it offered to the city's skyline. Cleveland's iconic Terminal Tower was visible from much of the ballpark, as Spear had first hoped, and the light stanchions, if they looked vaguely like toothbrushes, nevertheless did seem loosely to recall the image of the city's smokestacks. The exterior, which was defined by steel trusses that even more closely echoed the bridges over the Cuyahoga River, gave it a crispness and sharpness very different from the brick arches of Camden Yards. If the long, brick

Progressive Field,
integrated into the
urban fabric of
Cleveland

Baltimore & Ohio warehouse had set some of the tone for the exterior of Camden Yards, the steel bridges of Cleveland influenced Progressive Field.

That said, Spear went only so far in evoking the city's industrial infrastructure, aware that fans' desire to see the ballpark as a Cleveland-centric design did not make them likely to be enticed by the harshest aspects of the city's look. Black steel trusses on the bridges became white steel trusses in the ballpark, and the allusions to smokestacks were far from literal. The overall effect of the exterior was of a kind of benign, almost cheerful industrial look, more defined by open steelwork than by a formal façade, and enhanced by large, brightly colored signs announcing the ballpark's name and including the Indians logo. As a piece of architecture, Progressive Field is more openly playful than Camden Yards. If nothing else, its lighthearted use of vaguely industrial motifs is an apt

symbol of the evolution of the city from a place of industrial production to a place of leisure and recreation.

At the same time, however, Progressive is woven even more tightly into its city's streetscape than Camden. In what might be considered its most overt and determined act of retro design, the overall shape of the grandstand structure makes a 90-degree turn in right field, echoing the pattern of the intersection of Carnegie Avenue and East Ninth Street. In an interview with *The Washington Post,* Bob DeBiasio, a longtime Indians executive, explained the shape by saying, "We had to build this facility within the boundaries of three main streets in the city. The ballpark fits into the natural boundaries of the urban area. It fits into the cityscape." All true, and yet, as with almost every new ballpark, Progressive Field is set back from the neighboring streets, not built right up to them as, say, Ebbets Field was. There is plenty of open space around it, much of it landscaped by Sasaki into public squares, and the structure is far

Glass-enclosed skyboxes and special facilities at Progressive Field in Cleveland undercut its gritty feel.

enough away from the corner of Carnegie and East Ninth so that there is even room for a tight parking area tucked into the corner. The shape of the ballpark structure is actually something of a conceit: it symbolically echoes the layout of the streets and the turn of the corner, but it isn't really determined by them.

At its opening, Jacobs Field was every bit as big a hit as Camden Yards had been. When Cleveland played its first game on April 4, 1994, with President Bill Clinton in attendance, Richard Justice of *The Washington Post* wrote that "after 61 years at baseball's worst address, a cavernous old stadium that was dark and cold and utterly depressing, the Indians now have a home that can stand beside any of the game's other showcases." He saw the ballpark as an essay in retro design—"Jacobs Field has the cozy feel of Wrigley Field, the urban backdrop of Camden Yards and the nooks and crannies of Fenway Park," he wrote—but his point was to declare that the opening of the ballpark meant "the rebirth of baseball in Cleveland and, in a sense, the rebirth of Cleveland. Once a deserted shell of a city, Cleveland has had two luxury hotels open in the past year and eight restaurants spring up within a five-minute walk of Jacobs Field."

Blair Kamin, the architecture critic of the *Chicago Tribune,* was as enthusiastic as Justice—he called Jacobs Field "an architectural and urban design home run"—but he saw it less as a continuation of the architectural ideas of Camden Yards than as a considerable advance over them. Jacobs, Kamin wrote, "is no exercise in historicism, refusing to indulge in the dripping-with-sentiment nostalgia that has washed over baseball architecture since the 1992 opening of Oriole Park at Camden Yards." It possessed "a certain Tinker Toy matter-of-factness about it, a workmanlike building for a working industrial landscape." Jacobs Field proves, Kamin concluded, "that architecture can go forward even as it stirs the memory." Kamin was also quick to point out what he considered the superiority of Jacobs not only over Camden Yards, but over his own city's New Comiskey Park. "Now, the joke's on Chicago," he wrote, observing that while Chicago's and Cleveland's new ballparks were designed by the same architects, HOK had a far more exciting site in Cleveland, not to mention a more enlightened client, than it had had in Chicago.

The success of Jacobs/Progressive Field was clear from the beginning. But it was underscored by what followed a game against the Baltimore Orioles in June 1995, at which all of the ballpark's roughly forty-three thousand seats were sold out—not astonishing in itself, since the park had often been filled since its opening the previous year. But after that night the team would continue to sell every single seat in Jacobs Field until the beginning of the 2001 season, a streak of 455 consecutive sold-out games, a record in baseball up to that point. Even Oriole Park at Camden Yards would not achieve anything to equal Jacobs Field's six-year streak of sellouts, the clearest evidence there could be of how fully Cleveland embraced its new ballpark.*

If Joe Spear, the architect at HOK Sport, wanted to show in Cleveland that he was not fully encumbered by the traditional elements of Camden Yards and that he could make a retro ballpark that looked modern, another architect, David Schwarz, had no such worries when he designed the new home of the Texas Rangers, The Ballpark in Arlington, which opened just a week after Jacobs Field. Schwarz, whose Washington, D.C.–based practice, David M. Schwarz Architectural Services, has been devoted almost exclusively to traditional buildings, got the job because the Rangers wanted to go even further than Camden Yards in looking backward. And the team was not troubled by the fact that Schwarz had never designed a ballpark. "I wanted an architect who would look upon this as a once-in-a-lifetime chance, because that's what it was going to be for me," Tom Schieffer, the president of the team, told *The New York Times.* Schwarz was happy to oblige, and worked hard to design a classic urban ballpark. He faced an unusual challenge, however, since Arlington, a banal suburban community midway between Dallas and Fort Worth, has no urban context to speak of, and an architectural tradition of neither urban grit nor urban elegance, but mainly of suburban sprawl.

The result was a ballpark as stage set, an elaborate concoction of red brick and stone, with four pyramid-topped corner towers and a rhythm of repeating arches, an urban palazzo in search of an urban setting. The outer walls are decorated with sculpted Texas longhorns and lone stars and a frieze of Texas history in bas-relief, not to mention rooftop lamps

---

* The Cleveland sellout streak more than doubled the previous run of 203 sellouts by the Colorado Rockies. The team held a special ceremony on April 22, 2001, at which it officially "retired" the number 455, and placed a jersey with the number 455 and the name "The Fans" on display beside the jerseys of Cleveland greats such as Bob Feller, Larry Doby, and Bob Lemon.

in the form of huge baseballs. It is handsome, even sumptuous, in its way, but more than a little bizarre amid surroundings of parking lots, amusement parks (Arlington is also home to Six Flags Over Texas), hotels, and a convention center. John Pastier, the writer and critic who has been a longtime advocate of traditional baseball park design, found the discordance between Arlington's faux-urban design and its complete absence of an urban setting disconcerting; he wrote that it "may be the most peculiar stadium ever designed. The ballpark's neo-Romanesque veneer seems oddly irrelevant to its open site in a postwar suburb."

David Dillon, the architecture critic of the *Dallas Morning News,* would agree that the ballpark was a "stage set, its brick towers evoking everything from the campanile at St. Mark's to the Ponte Vecchio," although his tone was more of bemusement than offense, and he praised David Schwarz, the landscape architects Newman Jackson Bieberstein, and the Rangers for breaking up the fifteen thousand parking spaces into separate, landscaped "rooms" containing between fifty and two hundred cars surrounded by trees. That the Ballpark in Arlington was a suburban stadium that broke away from the model of the baseball park as a mountainous island standing amid a vast, open sea of asphalt and thousands of parked cars was probably, in the end, the design's most unequivocal success. It was, after all, a model that had begun in the mid-1950s with Metropolitan Stadium in Minnesota and had become standard not only

for the bland concrete doughnuts like Veterans Stadium in Philadelphia and Shea Stadium in New York, but also otherwise better ballparks like Kansas City's, whose architectural qualities are compromised by the unbroken vistas of parked cars surrounding it. At Arlington, at least, there were grassy berms, cedars, and honey locusts, and a mix of formal axial vistas and curving walkways. If David Schwarz could not have an actual city with urban activity, he seemed quite intent on creating a different kind of urban image by surrounding the structure with a park in the manner of a Beaux Arts vision of urban grandeur, in this case as much

A decorative lone star at Globe Life Park in Arlington

of a fantasy as the decorations on the façade of the ballpark, though with the worthy goal of minimizing the visual impact of the thing that made the location viable in the first place, the automobile.

Schwarz's eclectic taste continued inside the ballpark, where he used details that attempted to recall classic ballparks of the past: a roof truss inspired by the original Yankee Stadium; a three-story veranda, called a "home run porch," whose name if not its essence paid homage to Tiger Stadium; a right field shape loosely calling to Fenway; and a few nooks and crannies that were meant to suggest Ebbets. Like the park itself, the details were friendly, well-meaning, and a bit thin, even sentimental. More problematic was the decision to enclose the park on all sides, creating a tall, closed-off seating bowl with an upper deck far from the field, and the so-called home run porch set in center field, cutting off any view outside the ballpark.

It was understandable as a way of blocking the strong winds that affected this part of Texas, but it undercut the effect of all of Schwarz's architectural allusions to baseball's past, since it removed one of the most important characteristics of traditional ballparks, a sense of connection to the world beyond the field, which historically was always visible over the bleachers. The outfield was never truly infinite, but in a classic ballpark you could enjoy a moment of fantasy that it extended forever. There is no such pleasure in a ballpark built up fully on all sides. Even though the outfield enclosure claimed descent from a similarly named section of Tiger Stadium, it was a somewhat disingenuous connection, since the so-called home run porch in Arlington was in distant center field, unlike the close-in right field deck in Detroit that was named because it was an easy shot for home runs. Closing off the outfield was an instance in which the Ballpark in Arlington was less paying homage to the past than it was throwing off its retro garb and making common cause with the round concrete doughnuts of the postwar era.*

---

* It is important to note here that Tiger Stadium, alone among the great classic ballparks, actually was enclosed on all four sides, or at least was after an ambitious expansion by owner Walter Briggs that was completed in 1938, with an upper deck that extended all the way around the ballpark, giving center field what were, in effect, two levels of bleachers. The grandstand roof at Tiger Stadium did not extend over the upper deck of the bleachers, however, leaving a sense of at least some openness in the center. By contrast, the so-called home run porch in center field at Arlington is almost as high as the grandstands on either side and is topped by signage, so the result is a much greater sense of total enclosure of the field.

. . .

For all the urban planning sophistication that its axial approach vistas and discreet handling of parked cars represented, the Ballpark in Arlington, next door to a theme park, could feel almost like a theme park itself. You could say that the ballpark—which later became Ameriquest Field in Arlington, and then, when a naming rights deal was abruptly terminated, Rangers Ballpark in Arlington, and since 2014 has been Globe Life Park in Arlington—took the traditional side of Camden Yards as its inspiration, and exaggerated it.

One traditional aspect of Schwarz's design that was not popular was the absence of a roof, given the intense Texas sun. In 2017 the Rangers began construction next door on a replacement park with a retractable roof, designed by the architectural firm HKS, which will be called Globe Life Field and is scheduled to open in 2020. It will seat somewhat fewer people than Globe Life Park, but owing to its enormous roof structure it will be a larger building. HKS has used a mix of red brick and reflective glass, very loosely echoing Schwarz's traditional arches, but without any of his care in detailing; the renderings suggest a building somewhere between bombastic and sleek. The new ballpark will be adjacent to an entertainment zone called Texas Live, which will, in effect, make the new ballpark far more of a theme park environment than Schwarz's was. Indeed, the combination of Globe Life Field and Texas Live will be a union of the ideas of the ballpark and the theme park—a corporate environment far from both Dallas and Fort Worth that attempts to mimic their urban energy and visual diversity.

Although Schwarz's ballpark will have an exceptionally short life—it will be little more than a quarter century old when it is replaced—it remains a notable moment in baseball, if only because it was one of the first two ballparks to be completed after Camden Yards, and the one that embraced the idea of traditional design more wholeheartedly than any ballpark since. In this sense Arlington was the opposite of Cleveland, where Joe Spear played down the retro aspect and sought to create a modern design that would have just as much appeal as Baltimore. Cleveland and Arlington were the first two children of Camden Yards, but they each developed from a different part of their parent's DNA.

HOK and Spear would have the chance to achieve more of a genetic balance, so to speak, in the firm's next project, Coors Field in Denver, which opened in 1995, a year after Jacobs Field and the Ballpark in Arlington. Like Camden Yards, Coors is built of red brick, and it is full of traditional elements. No one would mistake it for a work of modern architecture. But the design is less self-conscious than Arlington, more intentionally generic and less determined to flaunt historical references. If Schwarz was making a stage-set palazzo in Texas, Spear in Denver got much closer to a nineteenth-century vernacular building, to the ordinary commercial architecture that filled the downtowns of cities like Denver in what Lewis Mumford called "the brown decades" of the late nineteenth century.

Like Jacobs/Progressive Field in Cleveland, Coors Field is deeply embedded in a real urban core: in this case the Lower Downtown, or LoDo, section of Denver, a historic district filled with nineteenth-century buildings of brick and stone that was once the city's Skid Row and by the late 1980s was evolving into a neighborhood of restaurants, bars, hotels, and commercial and residential lofts. The decision to place Coors Field in a former Union Pacific railyard at the edge of LoDo was made in the hope that the ballpark would connect to the district and reinforce it without putting any of its historic architecture in jeopardy.

The area was gentrifying slowly but steadily before Coors Field was built—twenty-three blocks of it had been declared a historic district in 1988, with protections placed on much of its older architecture—and one of the main challenges in creating the ballpark was to assure that it would neither physically nor economically overwhelm the healthy neighborhood it was joining. It would be by far the biggest thing in LoDo and on game days it would bring enormous crowds, and the ballpark needed somehow to fit smoothly into its surroundings. HOK responded with a ballpark whose exterior was far more building-like than the one in Cleveland, and which from some angles seemed to echo the original portion of the façade of Fenway Park, not so much in its specific details—although that, too, is of red brick—but rather in the way that it could almost be mistaken for just a building, something other than a ballpark.

It was a very different design problem from the one HOK had faced in the troubled urban neighborhood in Cleveland that was earmarked for Jacobs Field—just as it could not have been more different from the archetypally non-urban site that was designated for the Ballpark in Arlington. In both of these places, the problem was to generate some degree of urban activity. In Denver, the problem was not to engulf the urban regeneration that was flourishing on its own. This was the first ballpark whose architecture might reasonably be described as contextual. It had to fit in, in a way that even the classic ballparks did not.

Denver Mayor Federico Peña was convinced that the LoDo site, despite its challenges, could work, and in the late 1980s as the revival of LoDo was gaining momentum he selected it over competing locations for the ballpark, including a huge parcel of land on the outskirts of the city occupied by the old Denver airport, which was soon to close. At that point Denver did not even have a major league team—it would not get the Rockies until major league baseball's owners awarded the city an expansion franchise in 1991—and Peña's determination to build a downtown ballpark was more than a gamble on a particular site; it was a bet not unlike the ones made long before by Minnesota, San Francisco, and Tampa–St. Petersburg, which invested in new ballparks not to serve an existing team but in the hope of attracting a new one. But those were all on sites far from city centers. None of those cities was willing to build a speculative ballpark in the heart of downtown, the way Peña was, on an unusual site that gave Denver the potential of synergy with the city's most up-and-coming neighborhood, but that also posed multiple risks. If the city did not win a major league team, the ballpark would be a conspicuous sign of failure in the heart of downtown. But equally troubling was the possibility of success: that a team would come to Denver and bring so much crowding and traffic with it that LoDo would be crushed by the very structure that was supposed to help it.

Peña turned out to be right. Since the ballpark opened, property values in LoDo and around Coors Field have grown three times faster than the average for Denver, according to the city assessor's records quoted in a *Denver Post* study of the impact of the ballpark on the city, and LoDo became more, not less, desirable as an urban entertainment district. The ballpark site, while reachable by public transportation and light rail at nearby Union Station, was also near an interstate highway, making it more convenient for suburbanites than some urban sites, but also less desirable for the other kinds of uses that were filling up LoDo. (To

The brick façade of Coors Field was intended to blend in with Denver's LoDo, its revitalized downtown historic and nightlife area.

encourage fans to use public transportation or to walk from nearby sections of downtown, there was minimal parking.)

Most important, the large scale of the ballpark made a logical transition between the pedestrian scale of LoDo and the larger scale of the freeways and the mountains beyond. HOK's design, produced by Earl Santee, seemed to acknowledge this with its brick façades facing the city, and its high grandstands looking outward, with those on the first-base side having a distant view toward the Rockies. The field level was set twenty-one feet below the grade of the main entrance at the intersection of Blake and Twentieth Streets, which allowed the façades to be not much higher than most of the nearby buildings that had inspired them, underscoring the visual connection to LoDo's historic fabric rather than to the whole of downtown. Coors is the only recent downtown ballpark that faces away from its city's skyline.

Constructing a ballpark in Denver also brought another challenge, unique to this city. Denver is 5,280 feet above sea level—the precise point at which the ballpark meets the city's official altitude coincides with the twentieth row of the upper deck, which is marked by purple instead of green seats—and baseballs fly farther in its thinner atmosphere. That made Coors a hitter's park from the beginning. Even though its field dimensions are intentionally large (415 feet to center field, 347 feet to left field, and 350 to right), they are not large enough to make up for a roughly 9 percent increase in the distance a hit ball will travel in Coors's thinner air.*

Coors Field was followed by an ordinary ballpark in Atlanta, Turner Field, that opened in 1997. Its most notable feature had less to do with its appearance than with its unusual history; it was constructed originally for the 1996 Olympics, held in Atlanta, and contained eighty-five thousand seats arrayed around a running track. By the late 1990s few people held to the illusion that the way to make an enormous track-and-field stadium work for baseball was simply to chop off one end and take away half of its seating capacity, so the original design had been cleverly configured to ensure that it could be converted into something relatively close in appearance to a baseball park of the post–Camden Yards era, complete with brick entry arches. But the design had little character, and was every bit as banal, in its way, as the round, concrete Fulton County Stadium across the street that the Braves had occupied since 1966—indeed, the rhythmic, angled concrete pillars of Fulton County gave it a more striking visual profile from the nearby expressway than Turner had. Turner Field stood as a cautionary tale, a reminder that a baseball-only stadium that aspired to the heights of Camden Yards could still end up being as blandly generic as the concrete doughnuts of the generation that had come before.

Far more important to the evolution of the ballpark were two stadiums that closed out the decade: Chase Field, in Phoenix, and T-Mobile

---

* There is also less air pressure, which means that curveballs pitched at Coors don't break as much as they would elsewhere. Fastballs, on the other hand, are faster. For a detailed explanation of the way in which Denver's high altitude affects the game, see Robert K. Adair's *The Physics of Baseball*.

Park, in Seattle, known until 2018 as Safeco Field and renamed for a new corporate sponsor after a twenty-year naming-rights deal expired. These two were the first ballparks in the post–Camden Yards era to have retractable roofs, and they represented an attempt to combine the ideas behind Camden Yards—baseball-only, intimate, idiosyncratic, distinctive to its city—with the bravado and the technology of the Toronto SkyDome.

It was, in a sense, an impossible goal, since the two are inherently contradictory. A roof, even a retractable one, makes a space an indoor space, and baseball is a game played outdoors. And even the most technologically sophisticated retractable roof, if it is to cover the huge area of a baseball field, requires a massive superstructure, as well as an elaborate mechanical infrastructure, all of which goes against the grain of architecture intended to recall the simpler, earlier age of baseball.

In Phoenix, the Arizona Diamondbacks, a team created in a 1995 expansion of the National League (they began play in 1998), felt they had no choice: like Roy Hofheinz when he built the Astrodome in 1965, they feared not rain but heat. The Arizona climate was drier than Houston's, to be sure, but it was even hotter and sunnier, and there was little chance of inducing fans to come to games if they had to sit in 100-degree heat. Ellerbe Becket, the architects hired for what was initially called Bank One Ballpark and later, after a merger with JPMorgan Chase, became Chase Field, produced a design that the website Ballparks of Baseball would describe as "shaped like a massive airport hangar" on the exterior—and even that description flatters it—but that made attempts to accommodate baseball within. Not the least of them was the decision to use natural rather than artificial turf, which meant that the roof would remain open for much of the non-playing time, and would close as the start of a game approached. Given the Phoenix climate, the roof would rarely be left open through the course of a game except early and late in the season, when the odds of scorching weather lessened.* It was the opposite of Toronto, where the challenge was cold and rain, not hot sun, and the roof is often open at the height of the season, and closed in the chilly weather of spring and fall.

---

* The team's policy is to post information as to whether the roof will be open or closed on its website, so that fans will know in advance whether they will be watching a game in either an air-conditioned or a natural environment.

Phoenix's retractable roof, which required nine million pounds of structural steel, is made up of multiple sections mounted on large tracks that bridge over the field from right to left; when closed, these sections form a low arc. The tracks are always visible, but when the roof is open they are minimally intrusive, and even suggest the steel trusses in older ballparks, elevated to a monumental scale. The best design decision Ellerbe Becket made, and the one that connects Chase Field most successfully to the traditions of baseball, was to put roughly 80 percent of the seats between the foul poles, and to have no upper decks in the outfield. Although there is a huge digital scoreboard underneath one of the roof tracks that bridges across the structure beyond center field, the area to the left and right of the scoreboard contains advertising panels that can be pivoted, like doors, opening the ballpark to the view outside. When the roof is retracted and the side panels pivoted open Chase Field has a reasonable degree of connection with the city as well as with the sky. And even when the roof and the side panels are closed, there are windowed sections that bring some natural light into the ballpark.

Chase Field also has a swimming pool and hot tub just beyond the right field fence, where fans can buy tickets to swim as they watch the

Chase Field, in Phoenix, the first retractable-roof ballpark in the United States, has been described as resembling "a massive airport hangar."

game from the outfield—and, on occasion, catch home run balls hit into the water.* The pool is at once a uniquely Phoenix gesture—few other baseball cities are consistently hot enough to make such an idea attractive to fans—and a connection to the early days of baseball, to the world of Chris Von der Ahe and beer gardens in the outfield. Baseball has always provided associated entertainments; Phoenix simply came up with a new one.

The neighborhood of Chase Field is a banal mix of warehouses, an arena, garages, and a convention center, with little of the energy of a conventional downtown. The surroundings were quite different in Seattle, the next city to attempt to resolve the conflict between baseball and a retractable roof. T-Mobile Park, which replaced Seattle's widely hated Kingdome, was designed by the local architectural firm NBBJ and opened in 1999 at the edge of the Pioneer Square neighborhood at the

The advertising panels to the left and right of the scoreboard at Phoenix's Chase Field can pivot open, connecting the ballpark to the surrounding city

* Mark Grace of the Chicago Cubs was the first player to hit a ball into the swimming pool in May 1998, a month after the ballpark opened.

southern end of downtown, a site that qualified as genuinely urban. But that advantage made the architectural challenge all the greater. It was one thing to insert a hangar-sized structure into the characterless area of Phoenix around Chase Field, and quite another to add one to Pioneer Square's old streetscape, a neighborhood of older buildings that had much in common with Denver's LoDo. Coors Field fit easily into the LoDo streetscape, in large part because it was relatively low and had neither a roof nor a set of tracks on top of it. Seattle was attempting the same feat of surgically implanting a ballpark into a historic district, but with a much bigger structure.

The result was not nearly as unobtrusive as Coors Field; indeed, T-Mobile Park is not unobtrusive at all. But it is a far handsomer structure than Chase, and its exterior is crafted, far more than that of Chase, as a celebration of the industrial aspect of its mechanical roof structure. The south side of the ballpark, facing away from Pioneer Square, is made up of green-painted open steel trusses that support the tracks on which the roof structure moves back and forth; the other side of the building has a

A swimming pool in the outfield, at Chase Field, a modern-day reminder of the tavern in St. Louis's old Sportsman's Park's outfield

Safeco Field (now T-Mobile Park) in Seattle, with its open steel trusses that support the tracks for the roof structure

more conventional brick façade, an acknowledgment of the buildings of Pioneer Square and the rest of Seattle to which it relates. Unlike Chase Field, T-Mobile appears, particularly from the west, to resemble a building, and while that is not unusual for open ballparks of the post–Camden Yards era, it is strikingly different from both Chase Field and the Rogers Centre SkyDome, the two most important retractable-roof ballparks that preceded it. At T-Mobile, NBBJ managed to create a roofed ballpark that comes closer to looking and feeling like an open one.

The major reason for this stems from the decision not to enclose the ballpark completely, a departure from the design of its two predecessors. Seattle does not have a roof of multiple sections that shuts tight, but an enormous, arcing one-piece structure that slides over the field along two tracks, high enough above the grandstand level so that there is open space left between it and the top row of seats. It is more of a canopy or an umbrella than a true roof. If Chase Field is a garage, T-Mobile Park is a carport.

This means that fans are never truly indoors, even when the roof is over the ballpark, perhaps a disadvantage in extreme temperatures but a welcome assertion of the idea that, even with protection from rain, baseball remains an outdoor game. T-Mobile Park also has generous views of the nearby downtown Seattle skyline. When the roof is not in use, it is parked over a space on the east side of the ballpark. The rolling roof system is essentially the same as the one conceived a generation earlier by Charles Deaton for the Royals Stadium–Arrowhead Stadium complex in Kansas City,* which was to have a shared roof that would have slid back and forth between the two buildings.

T-Mobile comes far closer to replicating the experience of a traditional ballpark than Chase Field, and it proved that the presence of a retractable roof, while it certainly enlarged the size of the ballpark structure, did not

*See Chapter 7 for a fuller discussion of the Kansas City stadiums.

Fans at T-Mobile Park (originally Safeco Field) in Seattle are never truly indoors.

have to result in a massive object that lacks either human scale or sensitivity to its context. Seattle has at least some of both.

The two retractable-roof ballparks that followed it, Minute Maid Park in Houston, which opened in 2000, and Miller Park in Milwaukee, which opened in 2001, made similar attempts to relate to their surroundings and to demonstrate that their designs were not entirely indifferent to the history of baseball. They succeeded in varying degrees, and each has elements that set it apart from the early retractable-roof ballparks. Houston is the more contextual of the two—it incorporates the city's old Union Station, a historic building by Warren & Wetmore, architects of Grand Central Terminal in New York, that had been abandoned since the 1970s, as well as an antique steam locomotive that chugs along an aqueduct-like wall in left field. The train station serves as a pleasing lobby and main entrance to the ballpark, which was the first baseball park with a retractable roof to be designed by the prolific Kansas City firm HOK Sport.

While the integration of Union Station was an important act of preservation for a city that has paid relatively little attention to its architectural past, the station is hardly Houston's equivalent of the long B&O warehouse at Camden Yards, which is large enough to dominate the vista from many seats in the Baltimore ballpark. In Houston, the old Union Station is more of a quaint artifact, and it almost disappears beside the immense pile of Minute Maid Park, a large, rectangular building of brick and light-colored steelwork whose enormous bulk suggests that it is scaled to relate as much to Houston's skyscrapers as anything else.

Still, Minute Maid Park—originally called Enron Field after the city's high-flying energy company, which collapsed in scandal the year after the ballpark opened—fits more comfortably into the urban fabric than its predecessor, the Astrodome, ever did. The decision of the Houston Astros to abandon the Astrodome, one of the most historically important, if problematic, structures in baseball,* was not only a rejection of the idea of putting baseball indoors under a dome—a concept that the Astrodome had pioneered—it was also a rejection of the notion that a large sports facility was best located close to a freeway far away from downtown. With Minute Maid Park, Houston was turning away from

---

* See Chapter 7 for a fuller discussion of the Astrodome.

the anti-urban legacy of the Astrodome and, in its way, trying to adapt the more downtown-oriented legacy of Camden Yards.

It almost did not happen. Houston's inclination to celebrate sprawl—it is the only large city in the United States to have no zoning laws—came close to derailing the notion of a downtown ballpark. In 1996 Harris County judge Robert Eckels initiated an alternative plan to build a new ballpark adjacent to the Astrodome, telling the *Houston Chronicle,* "They keep telling me about these miracles in other cities, but it doesn't work in Houston. . . . If we are going to put this stadium some place, let's stick with a proven place."

It was Enron, based downtown and willing to support a downtown ballpark, which it later backed up with a $100 million commitment for naming rights, that helped to turn the tide, along with Houston's version of what was increasingly becoming the standard operating procedure for cities building new sports facilities. Harris County held a referendum to create a new sports authority that would be entitled to raise money to finance the new ballpark, in this case through new taxes on rental cars, parking, and hotels. As in quite a number of cities where some form of public financing is put to voters, the electorate was sharply divided. Anti-tax forces from the right often find common cause with opponents on the left who are inclined to view public support for expensive new sports facilities as public funding for private business, dismissing it as a form of corporate welfare for wealthy team owners. Not surprisingly, the strongest base of support for public financing often comes from the business and corporate community. In Houston, the referendum passed by a narrow margin of 51 percent to 49 percent.

The ballpark's ties to the business community would, of course, quickly come to haunt it when Enron went bankrupt only a year after its CEO, Kenneth Lay, threw out the first pitch at Enron Field in April 2000. Enron quickly became a national symbol of financial fraud, and the Astros wanted the company's name off their field. Enron resisted— the disgraced company's association with the baseball park was perhaps its only remaining tie to respectability—and the Astros initiated a legal proceeding. It took several months of negotiation before Enron finally agreed to give up its rights to the name of the ballpark in exchange for a $2.1 million payment from the team, surely the only time in the age of corporate naming that a professional sports team has had to pay ransom

to a company to take its name off its field. The ballpark became Astros Field, but only briefly. Within a few months, another $100 million corporate deal, this one with the Minute Maid subsidiary of Coca-Cola, gave the park its current name.

Minute Maid Park is not as handsome as T-Mobile, as innovative as Camden Yards, or as elegantly integrated into its surroundings as Coors Field. Its roof is gargantuan, and nothing about the design does much to hide that fact. And for all its virtues as a downtown ballpark, it is not as unified a work of design as its suburban predecessor, the Astrodome. But Minute Maid's architecture has a straightforwardness that sets it apart from the retractable-roof ballpark that opened a year after it, Miller Park in Milwaukee, which is more ambitious, even monumental in its aspirations, but which comes off as more than a little bombastic. Milwaukee, unlike Houston, did not see the construction of a new ballpark as an opportunity to move baseball downtown. Miller Park occupies a site adjacent to the old County Stadium, which it replaced, a good distance outside of the city center. It was designed by a consortium of architects including HKS, a Dallas-based firm with an expertise in enclosed foot-

ball stadiums; NBBJ, the architects of Safeco/T-Mobile; and the Milwaukee firm Eppstein Uhen Architects.

While the Houston ballpark incorporated an old train station, Milwaukee actually looks more like a train station, at least from the home plate front, with a brick façade of high arched windows and a clock tower. The ballpark's most unusual feature, however, is not its Disney-esque attempts at Beaux-Arts architecture but its shape, roughly a quarter arc, like a huge folding fan. The roof, in effect, is a huge folding fan itself, made up of sections that retract to both right and left fields, and close by moving toward the center. The design breaks in a refreshing way from the enormous box epitomized by Chase Field, which comes off looking more like a football stadium than a baseball park. At Miller Park, the fan shape of the structure feels in every way defined by baseball.

The problem with Miller Park, as with most baseball parks with retractable roofs, is that the architecture of its grandstands is at odds with the architecture of its roof. The traditional-style façades are all but overwhelmed by the enormous soaring arcs of steel and glass that are set above them and that contain the sections of the roof. While the great

Minute Maid's gargantuan roof, with Union Station just visible to the center left of the photograph

train stations of the nineteenth century also combined huge, curving arcs of glass with traditional architecture, their glass sections were train sheds behind traditional station buildings. Miller Park looks as if someone had put a nineteenth-century train shed on top of a nineteenth-century train station, and the result is both top-heavy and discordant.

There have been other issues with Miller Park's roof. The mechanical system for moving the unusual fan-shaped configuration, designed by Mitsubishi Heavy Industries of America, caused persistent problems, and had to be replaced with a different system after only five years of operation. Even more problematic was the relationship of the roof structure to the ballpark's orientation: with the roof open during many day games, home plate and the batter's box were in shadow while the pitcher's mound was in full sunlight, creating a safety concern for batters, whose view of the pitcher was blocked by glare. There was no solution other than to put the pitcher's mound in shadow as well, and the only way to do that was to keep one-half of the roof closed to create a larger shadow, significantly compromising the point of having an operable roof.

In Milwaukee, Miller Park's roof, like a folding fan, opens in both directions.

In the end, every retractable roof, from the unfolding lobster sections of the SkyDome/Rogers Centre in Toronto to the rolling canopy of T-Mobile to the Miller Park fan, involves a substantial compromise with the traditions of baseball. It's an understandable trade-off in an age when people expect to control the environment and not have their actions limited by the weather, and when major league baseball has spread far and wide into climates less welcoming to a summer game than the one where baseball began. The best of this generation of retractable-roof ballparks, surely, is T-Mobile Park, but that is because it looks the least like a roofed ballpark, and because it is always partially open to the elements, even when the roof is closed. And visually, T-Mobile's roof structure is the least overbearing. The reality of the ballparks in Toronto, Phoenix, Houston, and Milwaukee is that the roof always looms large, even when it is open to the sky.

10

Lessons Forgotten, Lessons Learned

THE COMPLETION of a sequence of ballparks with retractable roofs—Phoenix's Chase Field, Seattle's T-Mobile Park, Houston's Minute Maid Park, and Milwaukee's Miller Park—within a tight period of four consecutive years beginning in 1998 could make it seem as if the retractable roof had become baseball's intractable force, a fact of life in ballpark design going forward. It would turn out to be just the opposite, a relatively brief wave that would not shift the direction of ballpark architecture at all, and would only appear in one major new ballpark built after these four, Marlins Park in Miami, which would not be finished until 2012. Otherwise, the first decade of the twenty-first century continued more as the mid-1990s had been, with a series of open ballparks that showed the clear and continued influence of Camden Yards.

Two of them opened on the same day, April 11, 2000: Pacific Bell Park, later SBC Park, from 2006 to 2018 called AT&T Park, and now known as Oracle Park, in San Francisco; and Comerica Park in Detroit. The San Francisco Giants lost to the Dodgers 6–5 in their opening game; the Tigers were victorious in their stadium debut, defeating the Seattle Mariners 5–2. The Detroit game was played before 39,168 spectators on a cold, snowy afternoon that could well have led the team's management to wonder why they, too, had not opted for a retractable roof. The San

Francisco and Detroit ballparks were similar in many ways. They both had commercial names, thanks to the naming rights deals that were a sad reminder of the extent to which professional sports had become about money as much as athleticism; both were firmly in the retro style, with traditional architecture and lavish public space; both were downtown and successfully integrated into their surroundings, and both were designed by Joe Spear of HOK Sport, the firm whose hegemony over the field of ballpark design seemed only to increase.

But their backstories were very different. Oracle Park was an act of welcome liberation, freeing its fans from a ballpark that was one of the most notable failures of the concrete doughnut era, if one of its most strikingly sited: Candlestick Park, set beside San Francisco Bay far south of the heart of the city and famed mainly for its chilly winds. Candlestick was widely disliked, and its replacement yearned for.

Detroit was another matter entirely. Tiger Stadium, which had opened in 1912, was in active use until 1999, and had never been replaced by a concrete doughnut ballpark. Through the 1990s Tiger Stadium, along with Wrigley Field and Fenway Park, was part of a trio of early-twentieth-century ballparks still occupied by major league teams, and it was during that decade that both the Chicago Cubs and the Boston Red Sox began to see the advanced age of their ballparks not as a liability but as an asset that could be marketed. In the age of retro, Wrigley and Fenway could position themselves as offering authenticity, and would increasingly try to do so. Detroit, however, made a different decision, and became the only city in the major leagues to keep an early-twentieth-century ballpark through mid-century, when so many teams tore down their old ballparks to erect concrete stadiums, only to abandon it decades later, by which time old-style ballparks had become the fashion. Detroit chose to go from authentically old to less authentically retro, and skipped the period in between. Why it did so, and did not preserve and restore Tiger Stadium as Chicago did with Wrigley Field and Boston with Fenway Park, is partly a story of owners, politics, architecture, and historic preservation, but most of all a story of two different cities, and how baseball unfolded within them.

San Francisco first, since it is a less ambiguous tale, or at least one with a less ambiguous ending. It begins, unlike the Detroit story, with a ballpark so unsuccessful that it put the future of the team's continued presence in San Francisco into question. The Giants received overtures

AT&T Park, on San Francisco Bay, a welcome change from the much-derided Candlestick Park, and one of the best integrated into the urban fabric anywhere in the United States

from many cities to move beginning back in the 1970s; there were also proposals to enclose Candlestick Park with a dome, which went nowhere, as did referendums in both 1987 and 1989 to construct a new ballpark in San Francisco as well as separate proposals to build a new home for the Giants in suburban locations in San Jose and Santa Clara. They were all defeated by the voters. After that, Tampa–St. Petersburg, a metropolitan region that was probably the source of more unrequited baseball love than anyplace else—despite having an already complete domed stadium to offer, it failed to woo both the Chicago White Sox and the Seattle Mariners—decided to turn its attentions to San Francisco. Bob Lurie, who owned the Giants, agreed in the summer of 1992 to move the team to Florida. But the National League owners refused to approve the move, and by November the deal was off.

The team's future in San Francisco was saved by Peter Magowan, the president of Safeway, who led an investor group that purchased the Giants from Lurie in 1993 and pledged to keep it not just in California, but in San Francisco proper. Quickly, the climate surrounding the notion of a new ballpark changed. Magowan agreed that the Giants would pay for the construction of a ballpark containing roughly forty-two thousand seats if it could be on a waterfront site in the area south of downtown San Francisco known as China Basin, and the plans moved forward for what would become one of the most widely admired ballparks of the post–Camden Yards generation, and surely the one most gracefully integrated into an urban setting since Coors Field in Denver.

In the end, the ballpark required a fair amount of public money anyway, as most team-funded ballparks tend to do, for expenses separate from the brick-and-mortar construction costs of the stadium itself—in this case to relocate a Port of San Francisco maintenance yard, as well as to cover the cost of tax-increment financing, a common funding tactic for public projects under which the added taxes generated by a new project are set aside to service construction bonds rather than put directly into the city's coffers, effectively a bookkeeping device that indirectly turns what should be public funds into a form of subsidy. But to the citizens of San Francisco, who had rejected earlier proposals that would have left them to shoulder most of the costs of the ballpark, these costs were trivial. What they saw was that they would be free of Candlestick Park, they would keep their team, and it would cost them relatively little.

What mattered in the long run was that the new ballpark turned out to be one of the best in baseball, with a spectacular waterfront site that, while hardly tropical, was far less windy than Candlestick had been. HOK Sport gave the park a pleasantly traditional exterior of red brick with not one but two clock towers and a statue of Willy Mays out front. The ballpark avoids both cloyingly cute historical details and overtly modern ones, and it has an exceptionally well-considered relationship to its immediate surroundings.

Those surroundings were themselves in a state of rapid change; the neighborhood south of Market Street was in the midst of a period of growth and development that had turned it from a warehouse district into a mix of new condominium buildings, cultural facilities, and tech-oriented businesses, and the ballpark was positioned to take advantage of that. In the 1980s the area had been a derelict backwater of San Francisco; within a few years of the construction of the ballpark, it would be possible to stay at a Four Seasons or St. Regis hotel on Third Street south of Market Street and walk through the neighborhood to see a baseball

Kayakers in the water, hoping for "splash hit" home run balls, which are tallied on an electronic sign on the right-field wall of Oracle (formerly AT&T) Park

game. A new campus for the medical school of the University of California at San Francisco was across the channel just beyond the ballpark, a new streetcar ran past the ballpark, and other mass transit was not far away.

From within the ballpark there were open views over right field to the water, a section of the bay called China Basin but known to fans as McCovey Cove after the Giants' famed power hitter and first baseman Willie McCovey. Barry Bonds was the first Giant to hit a home run into the water; over the course of his career he would eventually hit thirty-five of what the team dubbed "splash hits." Not the least of the pleasures of the park is the electronic sign on the right field wall that keeps count of the number of balls hit into the water; as of April 2018, there had been seventy-seven.

Oracle Park did not replicate the intimate urban conditions of the earliest ballparks, but it fit as smoothly into its new, gentrified urban neighborhood as Ebbets Field had fit into its quarter of Brooklyn. The exterior, facing an urban street, is part of that street, but once inside,

urban density falls away and fans experience not only the brilliant green of the field, but the expanse of water just beyond. And, perhaps indicating that Walter O'Malley's anxiety over providing enough parking had come full circle, at least so far as San Francisco was concerned, Oracle Park was designed with relatively limited parking, and fans came by foot and public transit. Oracle Park, like Coors Field, showed that under the right conditions, a twenty-first-century ballpark could be as fully integrated into urban life as any early ballpark had been, and that the traditions of baseball had not been fully engulfed in the maw of suburbia.

Detroit is not San Francisco, and Tiger Stadium was not Candlestick Park. The park at the corner of Michigan and Trumbull—a corner where professional baseball had been played since 1896—although far from the most elegant of early baseball parks, was among the most admired.* John Pastier, who traced the ballpark's evolution in a long and masterful essay, "Longevity and Adaptability: Tiger Stadium's Evolution, Architecture, Functionality, Structure and Urban Context," observed that its configuration placed most fans closer to the field than at even the famously intimate Wrigley Field, and lamented that the more rough-hewn quality of

A trolley brings fans to Oracle (formerly AT&T) Park in San Francisco.

* See Chapter 4 for an extended discussion of Tiger Stadium.

Tiger Stadium meant that this aspect was never adequately appreciated. "In the popular mind, Wrigley's abundant charm equates to intimacy, while a park that had much more of that elusive and precious quality never came close to matching Wrigley's status as the stuff of sentimental and cult-like legend," Pastier wrote of Tiger Stadium. It also had the virtue, as Pastier pointed out, of being located closer to the center of its city's downtown than any other ballpark of its era. "It is a common misconception that the old parks were located downtown, but strictly speaking, none of the first steel-and-concrete generation structures were, with the possible exception of Detroit's," Pastier wrote. The intersection of Michigan and Trumbull was just a mile from the heart of downtown, neatly located on the edge of the residential area known as Corktown, so it was at once a neighborhood ballpark and central to the rest of the city.

By the early 1990s, San Francisco was riding the wave of Silicon Valley prosperity, and on its way to challenging New York's status as the most expensive city in the United States. Detroit was in a state of profound political and economic decline that would lead to its bankruptcy in 2013. Much of San Francisco's wealth was concentrated in expensive urban neighborhoods; almost all of the wealth in the Detroit area was in a sub-urban ring, and the city itself was seen as the place left for those who had nowhere else to go. The Corktown neighborhood around the stadium, the city's oldest settled quarter, had some pleasant blocks of small frame houses, but many were badly deteriorated, and the neighborhood did not yet have even a glimmer of the renewal it would experience decades later; Corktown's most famous landmark after Tiger Stadium was the magnificent Michigan Central Station, designed by Warren & Wetmore and Reed & Stem, which since its closing in 1988 had become perhaps the city's most conspicuous symbol of desolation.*

The Detroit Tigers had been owned since 1983 by Tom Monaghan, the founder of the Domino's Pizza chain (and an architecture fan who had a collection of Frank Lloyd Wright furniture and artifacts). Monaghan said upon buying the team that he planned to keep it at Tiger Stadium, which the previous owner, John Fetzer, had transferred to the city of Detroit in 1977 in exchange for its support of bonds to cover the cost of an extensive

---

* In 2018 the Ford Motor Company purchased the derelict building and announced plans to renovate it as the center of a new Corktown campus for research and development.

modernization he undertook in the final years of his ownership; when it took over the stadium, the city gave the Tigers a thirty-year lease on the property with an option to renew for another thirty years. With a renovation, a new lease, and a supportive owner—not to mention the ballpark's designation as a state of Michigan Historic Site in 1975—it did not seem out of line in the late 1980s to think that Tiger Stadium, having escaped the fate of replacement by a mid-century concrete hulk that affected so many early twentieth-century ballparks, was all but certain to join Wrigley and Fenway as a permanent fixture of major league baseball.

At the same time, however, "steady drumbeats of discontent with the ballpark had been emanating from politicians and club owners," Pastier wrote, and it was soon apparent that Monaghan's feelings were more ambivalent than he had let on, or that he had been less than candid. He may at one point have asked the British architect James Stirling to give him some conceptual ideas for a new ballpark,* and in 1990 he asked Bo Schembechler, the celebrated, newly retired University of Michigan football coach, to become the team's president. When Schembechler, presumably speaking for Monaghan, told the Economic Club of Detroit that "it's unfair for you to think that you can shackle us to a rusted girder in Tiger Stadium and expect us to compete and win, because it's not going to happen," it was clear that Monaghan was not committed to retaining Tiger Stadium, and that he, like so many owners, was finding it hard to resist the allure of the income that could be had from a new ballpark with large numbers of luxury boxes and private suites, club sections, dining amenities, event spaces, and merchandise shops.

Soon the lines in Detroit were drawn. Mayor Coleman Young claimed that Tiger Stadium was "falling down," an odd assertion given that the ballpark had recently been modernized, but one that would come up time and time again. Young became so fixated on the notion that the stadium was structurally unsound that after Lev Zetlin, one of the most prominent structural engineers in the United States, visited the stadium at the request of a local publication, pronounced it structurally sound,

---

* Pastier reported this in his essay in the book *Tiger Stadium,* but it is not confirmed by other sources.

and said that with proper maintenance it could last "indefinitely," the mayor said Zetlin "doesn't know what the hell he's talking about."

The more likely reason that both city officials and the team management were so eager to replace Tiger Stadium was not its physical condition, but the team's financial one, since the Tigers organization was reportedly losing more than a million dollars a year, and Monaghan, like almost every owner, saw a new ballpark as holding forth the potential of an endless fount of new income for him in exchange for minimal investment. The city's taxpayers would foot most of the bill, as was generally the case, which makes the mayor's interest in the project somewhat harder to understand, given Detroit's lack of resources and its dwindling tax base. But Young had very little new construction to show for his time in Detroit, and he would not be the first mayor to believe that the money he spent on a highly visible ballpark would distract from the money he was not appropriating for less visible schools, libraries, and social services.

The National Trust for Historic Preservation, realizing that the ballpark was seriously at risk, placed it on its list of America's Eleven Most Endangered Historic Places in both 1991 and 1992. And then, in 1992, facing other financial pressures and eager to avoid a threatened takeover of the money-losing team by the American League, Monaghan abruptly sold the Tigers to a rival in the pizza business, Mike Ilitch of Little Caesars Pizza. Unlike Monaghan, Ilitch had located his business in downtown Detroit and renovated some of its older buildings, including the landmark Fox Theatre. He seemed more seriously committed to the city than Monaghan, who was based in Ann Arbor, had been, and he said he would not make a decision about the question of a new ballpark until he had owned the team for a year. It was at least a brief reprieve.

In the meantime, however, Ilitch made some changes to Tiger Stadium, including adding a food court that a former team executive said "looked like an amusement park." Whatever else can be said about it, the addition of the food court made clear that retaining the historic feel of Tiger Stadium was not, for Ilitch, a priority, and far from satisfying his interest in wringing more income out of the ballpark, it seemed only to whet his appetite for more. In the end, he was no more able to resist the siren song of a new ballpark than Monaghan had been. Ilitch told the city that he would contribute $175 million toward a new ballpark if Detroit paid to acquire new land for the ballpark and build infrastructure around it. His offer set off another round of public debate and political battles from preservation groups seeking to preserve Tiger Stadium, this time extending as far as lawsuits.

Once Ilitch owned the team, the stakes seemed higher, since he, unlike Monaghan, had the resources to do as he pleased, and the potential loss of Tiger Stadium provoked what was surely the most difficult preservation battle ever involving a historic baseball park, including Ebbets Field. Ebbets may have inspired even greater passion than Tiger Stadium, but it did not become the subject of a similar preservation struggle, largely because in the late 1950s, when the Dodgers left Brooklyn, the historic preservation movement was in its infancy. The notion that any historic building, let alone a ballpark, could represent something of compelling social and aesthetic value was still little understood. But that would begin to change not long after the Dodgers left Brooklyn. In 1963, when Pennsylvania Station in Manhattan was torn down, all the latent anger New Yorkers felt about losing their landmarks burst forth, leading in 1965 to the establishment of the New York City Landmarks Preservation Commission, which asserted the city's right to save historic structures for the public's benefit.

By the time Tiger Stadium was endangered a generation later, preservation had become a major political force, not just in New York but in cities around the United States, and it had changed the political climate. As Frank Rashid, one of the founders of the Tiger Stadium Fan Club, the amicably named organization that spearheaded the preservation fight, would write, "We took heart from the writings and activism of people like Jane Jacobs who had successfully confronted powerful interests in New York and prevented freeways from cutting through its dense and lively neighborhoods. . . . We also found encouragement in local examples [like] Detroit's Orchestra Hall, celebrated for its superb acoustics and saved by a band of concerned citizens at the last minute from the wrecking ball."

What was unclear was how much any of this would matter in a controversy over sports facilities, the histories of which often follow very different trajectories. Despite creating a strong economic rationale for saving Tiger Stadium, and the commissioning of not one but two different renovation plans that showed that the Tigers' desire for enhanced income streams could be realized through a respectful renovation of the existing structure,* Ilitch was determined to have the kind of new ballpark that so many American cities were getting in the post–Camden Yards era. Public officials, including Michigan senator Carl Levin, indicated sympathies for saving the old ballpark, whose future remained uncertain when Coleman Young retired as mayor in 1994. Young's replacement, Dennis Archer, started out claiming to be agnostic on the matter of a new stadium, but after he took office he became one of its most ardent proponents, and it was during his tenure that the Detroit City Council rescinded a ballot initiative, put forth by the Tiger Stadium Fan Club, to require that any public financing of a new ballpark receive public approval. The city's establishment—its politicians, real estate developers, construction companies, building and trade unions, and corporations—cast their lot with Archer and the Tigers, and decided that Detroit needed a new ballpark, and that Tiger Stadium was expendable.

Not the least of the curiosities of the Tiger Stadium controversy was the fact that, as Frank Rashid wrote, "most of those arguing in favor of keeping Tiger Stadium were white, and most of the city officials arguing in favor of replacing it were black."

While Detroit was a heavily African American city, the fan base of the Tigers had not evolved to reflect the city's population. Some of this is undoubtedly due to the Tigers' own difficult history of racial relations: when Walter Briggs owned the team, he refused to sign any African American players, and the team did not integrate until 1958, six years after Briggs's death, and eleven years after Jackie Robinson was signed by the Brooklyn Dodgers. For many African Americans in Detroit, Tiger Stadium—or Briggs Stadium, as it was known until 1961—was a symbol of racial exclusion. They saw the preservation effort not as an attempt to honor one of baseball's greatest early venues but rather as a misdirected effort to perpetuate a site they associated more with humiliation than local pride.

---

* The more modest plan, known as the Cochrane Plan, was estimated to cost $26.1 million and would have "addressed most of the Tigers' stated needs, provided modern amenities for fans, removed some of the view-obstructing upper deck posts, and preserved the most important features of Tiger Stadium," according to Frank Rashid in the book *Tiger Stadium*. A more elaborate renovation plan by Gunnar Birkerts, a prominent Detroit-based modern architect, would have cost $85 million and involved more significant changes to the appearance of the old ballpark.

And Tiger Stadium was never beautiful. It never had the panache of Shibe Park, the whimsy of Ebbets Field, or the smoothness of Forbes Field. It was a funky combination of sections that evolved over many years to become one of the best places in which to view a baseball game, and it was full of history—not only did Tiger Stadium host the celebrated play of Ty Cobb and Hank Greenberg and Al Kaline, it was where Lou Gehrig took himself out of the lineup in May 1939, breaking his streak of 2,130 games, and it was the first ballpark ever to record ten thousand home runs. But it was never, even to its most ardent fans, a place of refinement, and it had little unity to its design. Its strengths, in Al Kaline's words, lay "not in its dazzling architecture or creature comforts, but in its character and charm."

The Tigers played their last game at Tiger Stadium on September 27, 1999. They beat the Kansas City Royals, and Robert Fick ended the game with a grand slam that was the park's 11,111th home run, after which came farewell ceremonies, including the digging up of home plate, which was moved to the new ballpark under construction in the center of downtown Detroit.

A long campaign to save Detroit's Tiger Stadium failed, and it was demolished in 2002.

Comerica Park in Detroit, embodying the tradition of integrating amusements and baseball, including a merry-go-round and a Ferris wheel

Mike Ilitch got his new ballpark, paid for largely by city funds, and while it was owned by the city of Detroit, the $66 million for naming rights from the Comerica financial services company was paid to the Tigers, not to the city. The Tigers, which like almost every major league team negotiated a hard deal with a municipal landlord fearful that the team might depart, also won the rights to income from parking, which it had never had at Tiger Stadium; Ilitch was able to use this future income as collateral for a loan against his share of construction costs, meaning that he laid out relatively little of his own cash. In the years following the opening of Comerica Park in 2000, the value of the Tigers multiplied many times over, and Ilitch's wealth rose to a reported $3.4 billion, making him the fourth wealthiest owner in major league baseball. He "would take all profits from the stadium, while the city would incur all the risk," Frank Rashid wrote. It was a situation by no means unique to Detroit. But the city's difficult financial circumstances, and the fact that Tiger Stadium was sacrificed on the altar of the city's deal with the Tigers, made it all the harder to justify.

Comerica Park, such as it is, turned out decently. It was designed by Joe Spear of HOK Sport, and it has many of the qualities that were becoming increasingly familiar in new ballparks by 2000: traditional architectural details including lots of red brick, an expansive view of the downtown skyline, and numerous luxury boxes, although this time neatly slipped in between the upper and lower decks and not dominating the vista. The central downtown location makes access easy, and there are multiple entertainment elements associated with the ballpark, including a carousel and a Ferris wheel with cars shaped like baseballs. Indeed, if there is anything that distinguishes Comerica from other ballparks of the first decade of the century, it is in the extent to which it seems designed as a family entertainment park in which baseball plays a major, but by no means exclusive, role. In *Sports Illustrated* Tim Newcomb observed, "Comerica Park has all the amusement park–like features you (wouldn't) expect from a ballpark, with a view of downtown Detroit on the side. Oh, yeah, they play baseball there, too."

Comerica Park's carnival-like qualities would turn out to prefigure a trend toward seeing baseball less as an end in itself than as the centerpiece of a broader entertainment zone. Of course, for years before the construction of Comerica Park, cities themselves were coming to function much more as places of leisure and entertainment than as places of work; as urban manufacturing increasingly gave way to the urban service economy, cities have flourished as places of culture, shopping, amusement, and entertainment, and the line between the city and the theme park has blurred considerably. Detroit, with a manufacturing economy that went into perhaps the steepest decline of any major U.S. city, was also the most eager to grasp at a new trend toward making its ballpark into an urban entertainment zone. It is worth comparing Comerica Park to Progressive Field in Cleveland, another city with a manufacturing economy that was gradually being transformed; Cleveland's ballpark, designed by the same architect, was more focused on baseball itself, partly because the owners of the Cleveland Indians at the time the park was built, the Jacobs brothers, did not have Mike Ilitch's zeal for entertainment, but also because baseball itself had evolved more toward ancillary amusements in the six years between the Cleveland and Detroit ballparks.

In the end, however, it is hard to evaluate Comerica Park without coming back to Tiger Stadium. If Comerica were replacing a concrete doughnut it would be a welcome improvement and a happy presence; as an alternative to Tiger Stadium, however, it is something less. It stands as a reminder that Detroit, which as the end of the twentieth century approached was one of the three cities with a classic ballpark still in use, could have done what Boston would do with Fenway and Chicago would do with Wrigley, and upgraded Tiger Stadium to work for the twenty-first century. But Detroit chose differently.

The year after the opening of Comerica Park brought one of HOK Sport's greatest triumphs, PNC Park in Pittsburgh, which opened in 2001. Pittsburgh, unlike Detroit, had replaced its classic ballpark, Forbes Field, long ago in favor of the banal Three Rivers Stadium, and locals viewed the possibility of an alternative to Three Rivers not with the ambivalence with which Detroit greeted its new stadium plans but with the same pleasure that San Franciscans hailed the news of a replacement for Candlestick Park. In Pittsburgh, however, the happiness was not because baseball, as in San Francisco, was escaping from the suburbs. Three Rivers was located in the heart of the city; the problem was that everything about its architecture denied any connection either to urban life or to baseball.

PNC Park turned out to be exactly the opposite, a ballpark that brilliantly reverses its predecessor's indifference to the city. The ballpark is set on a riverfront site just across a short bridge from the central business district. The bridge, named for Pittsburgh's beloved right fielder Roberto Clemente and swarming with pedestrians before and after every game, gives the ballpark a tightly woven connection to its city's urban fabric that equals or exceeds that of AT&T Park in San Francisco. Almost every seat at PNC Park has a view of its city's skyline that is more intimate, and more powerful, than the vista of Cleveland's skyscrapers is from Progressive Field.

In addition, PNC Park was built with thirty-eight thousand seats, between five and ten thousand fewer than most ballparks built in the post–Camden Yards era, and it is the only recent park built with two rather than three decks. (There are still luxury skyboxes, but the structure was designed so that they could be hung from the second deck and tucked, almost invisibly, below it.) While the two-deck design expanded

the footprint of the ballpark somewhat, pushing more seats toward the outfield than there might otherwise have been, the trade-off was that it gave PNC a modesty of scale that ties it, more closely than any other twenty-first-century ballpark, to the baseball parks of an earlier era. The seats in the last row of the upper deck still have an excellent view of the field, and they are reached by stairs that are less steep than at many ballparks, as well as by a handsome open rotunda of ramps that epitomizes the way in which the design of the ballpark evokes the past without literally mimicking it.

Earl Santee, who was the principal in charge of design for HOK Sport, told the *Pittsburgh Post-Gazette* that the notion of a two-deck ballpark in which skyboxes were hung discreetly from the upper deck was "clearly a new idea in how the building was organized." Santee said that "from day one, intimacy was the first word that came from everyone's mouth. The only way to do that was to have a two-deck [design] and hide the suites."

PNC differed from many of HOK Sport's other traditionally styled ballparks in that its exterior was faced in Kasota stone, a yellowish lime-

Pittsburgh's PNC Park, beside the Three Sisters bridges. The bridge closest to the park is named after Roberto Clemente, a famous Pirates player. Many seats offer a view of the skyline.

A view of PNC Park's rotunda, looking onto the field

stone, rather than the red brick that had become so common. In Pittsburgh, a city with numerous stone buildings, including a recent theater designed by Michael Graves sheathed with the same Kasota stone, and with a plethora of steel bridges painted yellow, the switch of materials made sense. So, too, with the decisions to paint the seats in a deep blue rather than the green that had become ubiquitous in new ballparks, to color the steel girders blue and silver, and to design narrow, vertical light standards that recall the old lights at Forbes Field. In each case, the design breaks from what had become a common standard to reflect some element of Pittsburgh, either as it was or as it is.

As Joe Spear had tried to do in Cleveland, Santee and his colleagues immersed themselves in Pittsburgh. "We learned to live in the city. We went to Primanti Bros. [a Pittsburgh restaurant chain famous for its sandwiches], we went to the North Shore, we went everywhere, we just lived that life," Santee told the *Pittsburgh Post-Gazette* in a piece the paper published in 2016 entitled "What Makes PNC Park So Good?"

Pittsburgh was not immune to the political and financial issues that other cities faced. When an investor group led by Kevin McClatchy bought the Pirates in 1996, major league baseball made approval of the sale conditional on the city agreeing to build a new, baseball-only stadium. That led to calls for a new football stadium and convention center as well, during a time when Pittsburgh, if not as economically challenged as Detroit or Cleveland, was facing the same decline of its manufacturing industries and tax base. A proposal to raise the sales tax to finance

the projects was defeated by voters, at which point a coalition of county, state, and city officials, along with the team and Pittsburgh corporate leaders, patched together alternative financing and all three projects moved forward.

But Pittsburgh's story is more than a financial and political one. It is also a saga of urban design. PNC Park's success as a work of urban design was an outgrowth of a long-term effort, begun long before the ballpark was a reality, to rethink Pittsburgh's downtown, to connect it more to the riverfronts, and to encourage more pedestrian activity. As Paul Farmer, the former head of the American Planning Association and the deputy director of planning in Pittsburgh during the 1980s and 1990s, put it, visitors to PNC Park "are experiencing the work of urbanists over a decade and a half. PNC was the result of a concerted effort of baseball

The Kasota stone façade of PNC Park

enthusiasts and planning enthusiasts that began in the 1980s. Great cities take time to build."

It would be naïve to think that the planners' priorities drove the entire process in Pittsburgh, but urban design never seemed to be fully subordinated to the team's business needs, either. Somehow the city and the Pirates managed to remain unified in their desire to build a ballpark that would both be intimately connected to the city and be on the small side for major league baseball. In 2003 ESPN declared it the best stadium in major league baseball, and took note, at least implicitly, of the ballpark's relative modesty. "When building a stadium, most teams just look at the most recent new one and say that they want one just like it, only bigger and more expensive," wrote Jim Caple of ESPN. "Not Pittsburgh. The Pirates and the public built a stadium that is not only located in Pittsburgh but is part of Pittsburgh. Ray Kinsella was wrong. Baseball heaven isn't in Iowa. It's in Pittsburgh, along the banks of the Allegheny River."

Two baseball parks of decent but not exceptional quality followed PNC: Great American Ball Park in Cincinnati, which in 2003 replaced the banal Riverfront Stadium of 1970 and was also designed by HOK Sport, and Citizens Bank Park in Philadelphia, which opened in 2004 as a replacement for Veterans Stadium, a concrete doughnut not unlike Cincinnati's Riverfront, designed by HOK in association with EwingCole, a Philadelphia firm.

The Cincinnati ballpark, whose name is not a proclamation of self-importance but the result of a naming rights deal with an insurance company, occupies a downtown riverfront site next door to its predecessor, which the team continued to occupy even after the outfield portion of its seating was removed to allow construction to start on the adjacent site. (Cincinnati, like Pittsburgh, had moved baseball downtown in the 1970s; its classic early ballpark, Crosley Field, like Pittsburgh's Forbes Field, was located away from the heart of the city.)

Great American Ball Park has several design elements that attempt to give it character, of which its red seats, nearby rose garden in honor of Pete Rose, and the famous signoff words of Cincinnati's legendary broadcaster Joe Nuxall, "Rounding third and heading for home," inscribed atop the building, are the most appealing. Less successful is a feature

called the "Power Stacks," a play on old steamboats in the form of two huge smokestacks, a paddle wheel, and large illuminated images of baseballs, which, according to the Ballparks of Baseball website, "makes noise, shoots fireworks, creates mist and is a general source of entertainment" when a Cincinnati Reds player hits a home run.

As at Pittsburgh, the Cincinnati ballpark faces the river, but here the river frontage puts it at the edge of the city, not in the middle, and facing away from the downtown skyline. To compensate, the ballpark was designed with a break in the grandstand to allow views back toward the city from some seating areas, as well as to allow a sliver of a glimpse into the ballpark from some vantage points within the city. It is a well-meaning gesture, if one that has little real impact, and the gap in the grandstand gives an unwelcome discordancy to the overall design.

If Great American Ball Park is marked by a degree of tentativeness in the way it expresses its relationship to the city's downtown, at least Cincinnati's downtown is there to be related to. In Philadelphia, which opened its new ballpark the following year, the problem is that down-

Great American Ball Park in Cincinnati, with its distinctive red seats, faces the river rather than the downtown.

town is nowhere near the ballpark, which was constructed on a site in south Philadelphia convenient to both to public transportation and to expressways, but suburban in its wide access roads and acres of paved parking lots. The "Philadelphia Sports Complex" site was once home to Veterans Stadium and then became what is, in effect, a suburban mall of sports facilities, with the city's arena and its football field as the ballpark's neighbors. It is the Kansas City idea of separate facilities for different sports sharing huge parking lots, with the added advantage of public transit access. And as at Kansas City, whatever quality the architecture has is compromised by the absence of any serious degree of urban planning.

Citizens Bank Park is especially unfortunate since its design has many of the better qualities of post–Camden Yards ballparks. It is an urban ballpark without an urban site. There are attractive views to the Philadelphia skyline three and a half miles to the north, and here the use of red brick connects to the city's long tradition of red brick row houses. Sightlines are good, and there are welcome but never cloying references to the city's beloved early ballparks like Shibe Park/Connie Mack Stadium. Recent renovations have expanded the amount of spaces for fans to socialize and watch a game while eating and drinking, following a trend that has spread to most major league ballparks.

If Citizens Bank Park had been built closer to the center of Philadel-

Citizens Bank Park in Philadelphia—an urban ballpark in search of an urban setting

phia, its well-meaning architectural gestures would make more sense. When planning for a new ballpark began, John Street, the mayor of Philadelphia, pushed hard for a location closer to what Philadelphians call Center City, and a site at the corner of Broad and Spring Garden Streets, just a few blocks north of City Hall, was his first choice. It would have given Philadelphia a ballpark much more like those of Cleveland, Baltimore, Denver, and San Francisco, with a close-in view of the skyline and the potential to reinvigorate a section of Center City just north of City Hall that was in need of development. But despite what by then was becoming a lengthy track record of successful downtown ballparks in older cities, none of which have had serious problems with parking and stadium-related traffic congestion, the site was vetoed by a state senator with jurisdiction over the area, mainly due to his concerns that it would bring too much traffic, and by the Phillies, who initially considered the downtown location but ultimately decided that the site outside of Center City would be easier for their suburban fans.

The importance of siting was made clear in two other ballparks that were completed at around the same time: Petco Park in San Diego, which also opened in 2004, and Nationals Park in Washington, D.C., which opened four years later. Both cities made a choice that was the opposite of Philadelphia's, and constructed their new ballparks on central urban sites. The two locations were very different from each other—Petco Park is at the edge of the so-called Gaslamp Quarter of San Diego, an entertainment zone that is one of the few pedestrian neighborhoods downtown, and adjacent to the East Village, a newly developing residential neighborhood; Nationals Park is in the area known as Near Southeast, beside the Anacostia River south of the United States Capitol, a desolate part of town that was filled with warehouses, scrapyards, and vacant lots. *The Washington Post* called Near Southeast in the years before Nationals Park "an urban backwater where some streets were unpaved, hardly anyone lived and commerce was negligible."

The prime force behind Petco Park's urban design was Larry Lucchino, who became president of the San Diego Padres after leaving Baltimore. For Lucchino, Petco was the same kind of opportunity that Jacobs Field in Cleveland had been for Joe Spear, an opportunity to carry the lessons of Camden Yards forward and express them in a fresher way, unencumbered by historical detail and reconceived for the specifics of a new city.

Petco Park, nicely integrated into San Diego's rapidly developing East Village and Gaslamp Quarter

Lucchino brought back HOK Sport, but this time paired the longtime ballpark architects with Antoine Predock, a prominent architect based in Albuquerque who had never designed a ballpark but was known for his sophisticated interpretations of the vernacular architecture of the American Southwest. HOK brought stadium expertise; Predock was expected to bring a degree of design finesse that could raise the project to the level of a major work of architecture, and assure that it would "look and feel and taste and smell southern California," in Lucchino's words.

If the result is not quite an architectural masterwork, it did turn out to rank with PNC Park in Pittsburgh and AT&T Park in San Francisco as one of the most successful integrations of a new ballpark into an existing urban fabric that any city has pulled off, with expansive concourses, ramps and terraces lined in sandstone, and white-painted steel, open both to the sky and to views of the city. The sandstone was intended to

evoke southwestern mesas, and if it does not quite do that, it is handsome in itself, and gives Petco some degree of distinction. This is less a ballpark that offers any single iconic image than one that is made up of multiple forms and multiple materials, neatly assembled in a complex whole that fits gracefully into the city itself. An old warehouse, the Western Metal Supply Company, has been integrated into the ballpark in the manner of Union Station in Houston; the warehouse's top level contains a bar and viewing platform for the field. The seating bowl, which is broken into sections both to reduce the scale and to enhance views, is punctuated by towers. At the street level, Petco is exceptionally well woven into the streetscape, respecting the lines of the surrounding streets and never looking so big that it overwhelms, but just big enough to exert a kind of benign magnetic pull on the pedestrian. As in older parks set into the urban fabric, the light standards are often the first thing you

The exterior of Petco Park, designed by HOK with the aid of noted architect Antoine Predock

see from a distance, and they beckon you forward toward this modern structure.

It is not an easy building to read, in part because it does not have an easily identifiable form, but that is, in a sense, its strength: the design prioritizes urbanistic relationships over architectural image. If there is any problem with Petco, it is that the Gaslamp Quarter and the East Village neighborhoods are themselves blandly generic. Most of the other old buildings the area may have had of the quality of the Western warehouse are gone, replaced by dull and conventional hotels, restaurants, bars, and garages. Better this than suburban parking lots, of course, and at least these dull streets are often filled with people. One of the main gates leads to a long outdoor pedestrian street filled with food vendors and children's play areas that is kept open to the public on non-game days, a welcome blurring of the line between the ballpark and the city. (When there is a game, the area is restricted to ticket holders.) The surroundings also include several new condominiums, some of which, in a pleasing allusion to the illegal rooftop viewing platforms atop row houses opposite early ballparks, have terraces and decks looking into the ballpark. San Diego's light rail system stops beside Petco Park, and the city's convention center is just a couple of blocks away, assuring that while the presence of the ballpark may be responsible for surges in urban activity, it is not the only thing going on in this part of town.

When the Washington Nationals decided to build a ballpark in the Near Southeast, they did run the risk of being the only thing in their part of town. The old Washington Navy Yard was not far away, but when Mayor Anthony Williams in 2003 proposed using the area for a new home for the latest attempt to make major league baseball work in the nation's capital,* construction on the new headquarters for the U.S. Department of Transportation, which would open nearby in 2007, had not even begun. There were a few residents, mainly concentrated in a single housing project that the *Washington Post* called "decrepit." By most measures, the neighborhood was a near wasteland.

But it was an exceptionally convenient wasteland, with subway access, a riverfront, and only a short distance to the United States Capitol and

---

* The Nationals replaced the first Washington Senators team, which left in 1960 to become the Minnesota Twins, and the second, which became the Texas Rangers in 1972.

the rest of official Washington. It was, in a sense, an ideal neighborhood for a baseball park to rejuvenate, because it offered enough space for a structure with a large footprint without disrupting other things, and if the ballpark succeeded in stimulating growth, there were plenty of sites available on which to build. But it was still part of the District of Columbia, which happily precluded any possibility of using the land for a suburban-style stadium surrounded by acres of parking.

Williams, at least as much as the team management, was the driving force behind giving Nationals Park the urbanistic qualities that it has. Earl Santee of HOK Sport produced a design that made some modest attempts to acknowledge the architecture of Washington, mainly by making the exterior of the ballpark a mixture of glass, precast stone, and metal that looks a lot like the banal modern office buildings with which the District of Columbia is filled. Santee knew better, happily, than to try to give Nationals Park a Washington identity by designing it as a piece of monumental classicism; there are no classical pediments or Doric columns, although there are a few walls inside the structure of gray fieldstone, a material that is used in some older Washington buildings; the walls, while handsome in themselves, seem disconnected from

Nationals Park runs along South Capitol Street in southeast Washington, D.C., with the Capitol Building just visible in the distance.

Cranes loom beyond the perimeter of Nationals Park in Washington, D.C., as construction continues to boom in the developing neighborhood

the rest of the design. Nationals Park tightly hugs South Capitol Street and feels very much an urban building, which is all to the good, although unfortunately the designers passed up the opportunity to line the street façade with shops and restaurants. Two large parking garages flank the main gate on N Street, and since the ballpark was completed, a construction boom has filled in many of the neighboring sites with hotels, condominium apartments, and office buildings. Most of them are generic and dull, but they certainly prove the rightness of the mayor's gamble that the ballpark would stimulate growth. "Where there was once only a convenience store and a liquor shop alone on a block of rubble, there are now 52 restaurants, with seven more opening this year," said *The Washington Post,* which noted the arrival of a Whole Foods, the ultimate sign of gentrification, and a further indication that the neighborhood had quickly evolved into a mixed-use residential district, a kind of modern version of an old ballpark neighborhood like Corktown in Detroit.

Philip Kennicott of *The Washington Post* called the ballpark "a machine for baseball and for sucking the money out of the pockets of people who like baseball, and it makes no apologies about its purely functional design," and suggested that the old RFK stadium, one of the worst of the concrete doughnuts, "might be a better building—more visual interest, more presence on its prominent site, and a better mix of modern style with the city's vernacular gravitas—but it was a lousy experience. Today, we have a great experience but, alas, a lousy building."

Kennicott's observation, perhaps inadvertently, gets to the heart of what a ballpark is. Most of the best ballparks have not, in fact, been particularly memorable pieces of architecture by any formal standard: they are irregular, opportunistic structures, often altered and adjusted over the years to respond to changing market demands and changing urban conditions. Other than the handsome façades of ballparks like Shibe Park, Ebbets Field, and Forbes Field, they have generally not turned their best faces toward the street, and even those classic ballparks are better remembered for the world they made within, their magnificent juxtapositions of soft green playing fields and tough, lyrical steel and concrete structures. Ballpark architecture was never about the gravitas of form: if it is a machine, as Kennicott says, it is at its best a machine for creating a certain kind of experience, rooted in a particular place. Nationals Park is, in fact, an apt reflection of Washington as it is now—a city defined as much by sleek new buildings as by monumental or picturesque old ones.

Another ballpark opened in the first few years of the twenty-first century, in St. Louis, where in 2006 a new Busch Stadium replaced one of the few visually distinctive concrete doughnuts, the previous Busch Stadium built in 1966.* That Busch was located in downtown St. Louis adjacent to the site of the new ballpark, so there was no need for the city to play catch-up in terms of location. But the new Busch was very much designed—by HOK Sport, naturally—so that St. Louis might catch up with the retro trend in other ways. It is a structure of red brick with large entry arches, and while it is far more suited to baseball than its predeces-

---

* The 1966 Busch stadium is actually the second to bear the name of team owner August Busch of the Anheuser-Busch brewery. In 1953, the name of St. Louis's old Sportsman's Park was changed to Busch Stadium. The current Busch Stadium is sometimes referred to as Busch III. Even though it is part of a lineage of three Busch stadiums, continuing the name into the present day required a naming rights deal with the brewery, not the owner's assent.

sor, by 2006 most of its distinctive design elements other than its bright red seats had taken on the feel of post–Camden Yards cliché.

That said, the new Busch opens out to the city in a way that its fully enclosed predecessor could never do, with a vista from the seating bowl focused on the best element of the St. Louis skyline, the monumental Gateway Arch designed by Eero Saarinen. If the skyline views of Detroit and Cleveland are not all that easy to distinguish from each other, no one can mistake what you see from the seats of Busch Stadium: no other city has a freestanding arch more than five hundred feet high, and its elegant shape—which from the stadium seems like it is tracing the arc of a distant pop-up fly ball—punctuates the vista with power and grace.

The aspect of Busch Stadium that may have the greatest influence on ballpark design, however, is something that was added after the stadium opened. In 2014, the St. Louis Cardinals, working with a private real estate developer, opened the first phase of a complex on the site of the former Busch Stadium, adjacent to the new one; the team dubbed it St.

New Busch Stadium rises in St. Louis as its predecessor is demolished.

Louis Ballpark Village and advertised it as "the first ever sports
anchored entertainment district."
It contains restaurants, bars, a
museum of Cardinals history,
and various other attractions, and
has been so successful that plans
were announced for its expansion. If the Ballpark Village suggests the increasing connection
between cities and theme parks,
and confirms the extent to which
so many cities now seek to redefine themselves as places of leisure
and entertainment, it also har-
kens back to the St. Louis of yore,
to the days of Chris Von der Ahe,
the flamboyant tavern owner who
controlled the St. Louis Browns
in the late nineteenth century
and built the original Sportman's
Park as part baseball park, part
beer garden. Von der Ahe saw
baseball as a means of selling beer
and providing other ancillary
amusements. The baseball park
as entertainment zone is deeply
embedded in St. Louis's history.*

Then again, even Von der Ahe, for all his swagger, never extended his
concept of the ballpark to include full-time residency. That is what the St.
Louis Cardinals have planned for the next phase of the St. Louis Ballpark
Village, which will have a high-rise condominium tower. The development's website, an eager merger of real estate hype and team boosterism,
describes it as follows: "Luxury living like never before is coming to Ball-

* See Chapter 2 for a detailed discussion of Chris Von der Ahe and his impact on ballparks
and the game.

*Busch Stadium in
downtown St. Louis,
with its iconic arch*

park Village. Introducing One Cardinal Way. Where hometown history is all around and you can live the Cardinal Way every day. With alluring amenities, first-rate features and breathtaking views of Busch Stadium and the Gateway Arch, it's an opportunity you won't find anywhere else. Your chance to truly be a part of the Cardinals family is here. And the time to step up is now."

Ballpark Village, on the site of old Busch Stadium, which will expand to include condos and more

New York Retro, Miami Modern

HOVERING OVER THE RETRO TREND was the question, asked more often by architecture buffs than by baseball team owners, of exactly how much baseball really wanted to be seen as looking backward. Yes, the sport had an extraordinary history, richer and more deeply embedded in American lore than any other, but does that mean its new architecture should be treated mainly as an invitation to wallow in that history? After Camden Yards there were some attempts to do otherwise, such as at Jacobs Field in Cleveland, the Great American Ball Park in Cincinnati, and Petco Park in San Diego, but the design of most new ballparks was still heavily driven by a desire to evoke the past. Baseball's nostalgia was itself a form of marketing, of course, and as such it was inevitably combined with the very latest forms of commercialism, which meant that the retro architectural details of new ballparks were invariably accompanied by things that had nothing to do with classic ballparks like enormous electronic scoreboards and digital screens, lavish food courts and dining clubs, children's play areas, and bar areas to attract younger fans who had no interest in spending nine innings sitting in a seat, and preferred to drink while mingling and watching a bit of baseball on the side.

New York City, where baseball parks began in the mid-nineteenth century, where Ebbets Field rose and fell, and where Yankee Stadium was built as baseball's great monument, may have seen itself as more sophisticated than many other baseball markets, but it was not immune to any of the post–Camden Yards trends. Indeed, although New York came late to the retro party, it would come to epitomize the style. When it finally joined the caravan of cities building new ballparks, it erected not one but two retro ballparks, one for the Mets and one for the Yankees, each a different and distinct statement about history, nostalgia, commercialism, and team identity.

New York's two ballparks, the new Yankee Stadium and the Mets' Citi Field, were both completed in 2009, the only time in history that two major league ballparks have opened in the same city at the same time. They were both unusually expensive: Yankee Stadium and its ancillary facilities, such as a new parking garage and new public playing fields on the site of the old stadium, totaled $1.5 billion, roughly half of which was covered by some form of public subsidy. Citi Field was a relative bargain at $850 million, more than half of which also came, either directly or indirectly, from the taxpayers. As with so many other new ballparks, New York's are owned not by their teams but by the city, so as to be exempt from property taxes; the teams pay rent, against which they deduct many operating expenses, and their leases generally allow them to keep most or all of the income from tickets, concessions, and parking.

Both New York ballparks were the work of design teams at Populous, which is the new name that HOK Sport, the prolific stadium architects of Kansas City, gave itself when it broke away from its parent firm in St. Louis and became an independent entity in 2009. The unusual name was a "rebranding" effort intended to evoke the public, communal nature of the large stadiums that were the firm's specialty, and whether or not it did, the firm's dominance over baseball park design continued undiminished. At Populous, Ben Barnert was in charge of design for Citi Field, which was replacing the much-maligned concrete doughnut of Shea Stadium. Earl Santee took charge of the new version of Yankee Stadium, in some ways a more complex challenge since it was replacing arguably the world's most famous baseball park, but one that had been so drastically altered in the 1970s that it bore only a passing resemblance to the Yankee Stadium of lore.

Both new ballparks were constructed just beside their predecessors, which in the case of Yankee Stadium offered an opportunity to engage

more deeply with the Bronx neighborhood where the Yankees had been since 1923, and in the case of Citi Field compounded an error that began when Robert Moses, having failed to convince Walter O'Malley to build a new ballpark for the Dodgers in Flushing Meadows, got his wish when the Mets' original ballpark was put there in 1964. While the site of Citi Field is reachable by public transportation, it is ten miles from the heart of Manhattan, denying New Yorkers the chance to have the kind of easy, relaxed movement from downtown desk to ballpark seat that one imagines is a staple of summer urban life for residents of Cleveland, Pittsburgh, Baltimore, St. Louis, Denver, and Boston—even though in all of these cities many fans come by car from the suburbs. Yankee Stadium is no more conducive to the fantasy of a stroll from desk to ballpark, but its location offers both historical resonance and urban density. In Flushing Meadows, Citi Field, however accessible by subway, like Shea Stadium before it was, is a physical outlier, suburban in all but name.

That said, New York has never had a ballpark close to its central business district; when baseball was played at Madison Square in the mid-nineteenth century, that area was on the outskirts of developed

Old Yankee Stadium after its renovation in the 1970s, when most of its traditional elements were stripped away

Manhattan, and as the city grew, baseball moved farther out with it. New York real estate has always been far too expensive, and the city's development pressures too great, to allow for the luxury of a downtown ballpark. Ebbets Field, the Polo Grounds, and Yankee Stadium were deeply embedded in urban residential neighborhoods, and as a consequence very much part of the urban fabric, but they were not central. Then again, as John Pastier has pointed out in his elegy to Tiger Stadium,* Detroit's old stadium was an exception in being close to its city's center; most ballparks of the classic era, like the ones in New York, were priced out of their city's downtowns, and were located in dense urban neighborhoods a short to medium distance away from the center. True downtown baseball is a relatively recent phenomenon.

The great opportunity for New York to join other cities with new downtown ballparks would have been to have built either Yankee Stadium or the Mets ballpark over the railyards to the west of Pennsylvania Station, in midtown Manhattan, one of the sites that the Yankees explored before settling on the Bronx in 1923, that the Giants flirted briefly with before going to San Francisco,† and that both the Yankees and the Mets would consider again. The Mets looked at the railyards site, at least casually, in the mid-1990s, when they first began discussions with Mayor Rudolph Giuliani's administration about a replacement for Shea Stadium. At a press conference in which HOK Sport unveiled an early version of the new ballpark that looked surprisingly similar to what would be built a decade later—but with a retractable roof and the bizarre notion of a field that could be slid onto the parking lot for additional exposure to the sun—Fred Wilpon, the majority owner of the Mets, told *The New York Times* that he had considered the railyards site on the West Side of Manhattan but that he preferred the parking lot next to Shea for the simple reason that it would be easier. "It isn't a question of a downside on the West Side, but it was timing and what you think you can get done. I'm not degrading the West Side. Under certain circumstances, we'd have liked it," Wilpon said.

Giuliani negotiated generous deals with both the Mets and the Yankees for new ballparks in the 1990s, and the Yankees arguably came a

* See Chapter 10, pages 258–9.

† See Chapter 5, page 116.

good deal closer to going to the West Side railyards. George Steinbrenner, the imperious long-term owner of the team, had been unhappy about the location of Yankee Stadium for years, and made no secret of his view that the Bronx was both dangerous and inconvenient. He repeatedly threatened to move the team to New Jersey. Both Giuliani and Mario Cuomo, the governor in the early 1990s, felt that the West Side Manhattan location would at least forestall the catastrophe of losing the New York Yankees to another state, and Steinbrenner was known to view it favorably. In 1996 the Yankees released the results of a study, prepared by a team of consultants including the architects of HOK Sport, that argued in favor of the West Side railyards as the site of a new Yankee Stadium. The study looked at multiple sites, including Pelham Bay Park and Van Cortlandt Park in the Bronx, both of which it rejected. "The report said a 50,000-seat baseball-only park 'would provide a strong image' for the 'relocated franchise,'" according to *The New York Times,* which noted that the study also considered the possibility of "a two-sport stadium seating 70,000" that would have a retractable roof.

There would be no decision for several years. Steinbrenner, an unpopular owner of a popular team, seemed to take pleasure in playing cat-and-mouse with New York politicians over whether he would go to New Jersey, go to midtown Manhattan, or stay in the Bronx. For much of the 1990s, the midtown location appeared to have the edge: it seemed the only way to avoid what for New Yorkers would have been unthinkable, which was to let the city's most famous sports franchise escape to New Jersey, and what for Steinbrenner would have been uncomfortable, which was to renew his commitment to an outlying part of the city that he made no secret of his distaste for.

Neither team's stadium plan was finalized by the end of Giuliani's term, however, and his successor, Michael Bloomberg, was considerably less enamored of publicly funded stadiums. Bloomberg was also preoccupied with the challenges of rebuilding downtown New York after the terrorist attack that destroyed the World Trade Center shortly before his election in 2001, and when he took over at the beginning of 2002, he exercised an option to cancel the city's commitment to build the new stadiums. Soon afterward Bloomberg became more interested in a plan by his deputy mayor, Dan Doctoroff, to try to win the 2012 Olympics for New York, and Doctoroff and his chief of Olympics planning, Alexander Garvin, proposed that the West Side railyards site be used for an Olym-

pic stadium that would be the centerpiece of the city's bid. Bloomberg and Doctoroff convinced the New York Jets to agree that the Olympic stadium would become the football team's new permanent home after the Olympics, making the Jets the city's partner in building over the railyards. To win further support the plan called for the huge, roofed building to also serve as expansion space for the neighboring Javits Convention Center. This rendered the site, the rest of which the city wanted to develop with high-rise office and residential towers, unavailable for baseball.

While an Olympic stadium is far closer in size to a football stadium than a baseball park, making its conversion relatively easy, the notion was nevertheless ill conceived. A football stadium, with its huge seating capacity and usage only about ten times a season, is poorly suited to an urban location, and it was never clear how smoothly it would double as a convention center. The sheer scale of any football stadium, no matter how well designed, defies easy integration into the urban fabric, while a baseball park, with its smaller footprint and more frequent usage, is a more natural neighbor to office buildings, apartment towers, shops,

A scale model of the proposed Jets football stadium, on the West Side of Manhattan

and other urban amenities. And football stadiums are occupied mainly on Sundays, by crowds for whom tailgating in parking lots is part of the experience. The casual, even spontaneous, transition from work to a sporting event on a midweek evening, a major factor in the allure of downtown baseball, has no relevance to professional football.

The football stadium over the railyards engendered enormous opposition, based in part on the not unreasonable fear that putting an eighty-five-thousand-seat stadium on the West Side of midtown Manhattan would create intolerable congestion. The site, adjacent to the rapidly gentrifying Chelsea neighborhood that had become the epicenter of the New York art gallery scene, was culturally a world away from professional football, and it is probably fair to say that not many of its gallery owners and their patrons looked forward to sharing their neighborhood with the Jets. And then, in 2005, shortly before the International Olympic Committee was to make its decision regarding the 2012 Olympics, a state oversight board that had authority over the project because the railyards were controlled by the Metropolitan Transportation Authority, abruptly rejected the proposal, killing the stadium outright.

Plans for the Manhattan football stadium engendered huge opposition.

The decision, paradoxically, revived the notion of building two new baseball parks. Bloomberg and Doctoroff, desperate for an alternative way to keep New York's Olympics bid alive, decided that the second-best place for the Olympic stadium was in Flushing Meadows next to Shea Stadium, and offered to build a new stadium for the Mets if the team would agree to vacate it for the 2012 season and play at Yankee Stadium while their new ballpark was temporarily expanded to contain the eighty thousand seats that the Olympics required. When the Olympics were over, the stadium would be cut down in size and turned back into a baseball park, in the manner of Turner Field in Atlanta. The Mets, who were more than happy to remain at Flushing Meadows, quickly agreed to the idea, at which point Bloomberg had no choice but to offer similar public funds toward a new stadium for the Yankees.

The Olympics bid was unsuccessful—the 2012 Olympics went to London—but it became a classic example of the law of unintended consequences. First, it forced Bloomberg to abandon his position of opposition to public financing of stadiums for privately owned teams and hastily negotiate not one but two new ballparks, neither of which would end up on the midtown Manhattan site that had started off the whole process. While there was no certainty that a baseball park on the railyards site would engender the same degree of opposition that the larger football stadium had, the climate after the bitter controversy over the Jets was such that it made little sense to take the chance that baseball could win approval there.

Like an old married couple for whom squabbles seem a permanent state of affairs, the city government and New York's two baseball teams had been bickering and negotiating about stadiums for well over a decade, with little incentive to reach a conclusion. The Olympics bid changed the situation, and suddenly Bloomberg and Doctoroff were under pressure to move quickly. In the interest of expediency, any thoughts of reviving the notion of putting the Yankees on the railyards site—if they were ever serious—were quickly put aside. Staying in the Bronx, it turned out, was easier: the decision could be justified as a way of acknowledging both the team's history and the fact that the rising tide of urban life in New York, as in so many other cities, in the past decade had made the Bronx less problematic as a location than it had been in the days when Steinbrenner seemed to make a sport of disparaging it. By 2005, the cycle of crime and decay that had afflicted the Bronx in the 1970s and 1980s had abated, and the notion of a new Yankee Stadium next door to the original one was far easier for everyone, including the team's management, to accept.

A not dissimilar set of factors led to the decision of the Mets to remain at Flushing Meadows, even though one important fact was different: the team's majority owner, Fred Wilpon, unlike Steinbrenner, was never dissatisfied with his team's longtime location. At first, when the baseball/Olympics combination stadium was a possibility, staying at the old site was a given. But once the Olympics bid had evaporated and the team went back to building a conventional baseball park, Wilpon saw no reason to make what he considered an unnecessary relocation. He had waited a long time for a new ballpark, and now that it was within his grasp, his reasoning went, why complicate matters? He preferred to do the simplest thing, as the Yankees had. As he made clear to *The New York Times,* he had little inclination to take on the more consuming challenges of the West Side site, whatever its virtues might be.

And thus downtown baseball did not come to New York. Neither did any kind of adventuresome or innovative ballpark architecture, although both the new Yankee Stadium and Citi Field represent vast upgrades in design over their predecessors. It was hard not to improve on either of the old ballparks. Shea Stadium had never been much more than enormous, round, and banal. Yankee Stadium had once been a unique and monumental ballpark, but since it had been shorn of almost all of its classic design elements in the 1970s, it had little appeal beyond the remnant of an aura that, for visitors who had never seen the stadium in its original form, still lingered within its harsh concrete structure.

Both of New York's new ballparks looked backward, but to very different histories. The new Yankee Stadium is unapologetically grandiose: it is not so much a copy of the original Yankee Stadium as a stage set–like evocation of it, at once more monumental and less eccentric than the original. Populous produced a façade of limestone, granite, and cast stone with tall, narrow arches and the words YANKEE STADIUM engraved in gold lettering high over formal entry portals that look designed for the ceremonial arrival of the pope, or at least George Steinbrenner. The façade, Joe Mock of baseballparks.com wrote, has "a stateliness that is fit

New Yankee Stadium's
façade, announcing its
monumental aspirations

for the capitol building of a superpower." Inside is not a conventional concourse but a space called the Great Hall, an ode to Yankees history under a translucent roof.

Yankee Stadium's architecture has a veneer of almost comical self-importance, but beneath its pompous surface is a ballpark that is more smoothly integrated into its neighborhood than its predecessor was, has more comfortable seats and better if not perfect sightlines, and is in almost every way a better place in which to experience a ball game. In a gesture that comes off as affectionate more than pretentious, the classic frieze of the old Yankee Stadium has been reproduced, and it forms a whimsical counterpoint to the enormous digital screens and scoreboards that are part and parcel of every new ballpark. Another beloved element of the old Yankee Stadium, the glimpses into it from the elevated tracks of the Lexington Avenue subway, has been replicated through a break between the right field stands and the scoreboard, and you can see the trains sliding by, each one its own small exclamation of continuity. If you approach the stadium by driving along Jerome Avenue, you see a couple of the Bronx's finest Art Deco apartment houses across the street from the west façade, a surprising and welcome hint of the subtle counterpoint that once existed between a baseball park and its urban setting.

The site of the new Yankee Stadium is slightly to the north of the old stadium and a bit farther from the Harlem River, just enough to make it feel more deeply inserted into the city. The stadium is bigger and more imposing than anything around it, and now has an enormous parking garage beside it, but even so it seems to grow out of its surroundings in a way that its predecessor did not, and this somehow saves it from its own pomposity. The apartment houses on Jerome Avenue, the jumble of storefronts and bars under the elevated tracks on River Avenue, and the constant presence of street life were all there before, but they seem to impact the new Yankee Stadium more positively than they did the old one. The old Yankee Stadium seemed intended to rise above the city, a temple to the might of the Yankees as much as anything else. The architecture of the new one tries hard to do the same thing with its elaborate façade of historicizing grandeur, but that exterior is wrapped around a ballpark that is more successfully integrated into the urban fabric than its namesake was. The new Yankee Stadium at once soars over the city and burrows itself into it.

One positive result of the worshipful view of Yankee history that underlay the design for the new Yankee Stadium was the presumption that if the new stadium was truly to make fans feel as if they had walked into an idealized version of the 1923 original, just with better food and

The Great Hall at Yankee Stadium

more toilets, then it could not carry a different name. It could only be called Yankee Stadium, and in perhaps the only example of true restraint anywhere in the project, the Yankees never sought to convince a corporation to write the team a huge check to turn the stadium into an advertising vehicle. This had always been Yankee Stadium, and Yankee Stadium it would remain, its name the one thing that was not for sale.

The Mets, of course, had no such desire to evoke their previous ballpark. Shea Stadium was a name most New Yorkers would prefer to forget, which is how the Mets ballpark became Citi Field, the result of a naming rights deal with Citigroup, the parent company of Citibank. Citi Field looks back not to the history of the Mets, which is shorter and far less distinguished than that of the Yankees, but to that of the Brooklyn Dodgers and their beloved Ebbets Field. Largely at the insistence of Fred Wilpon, who grew up as a Dodger fan, the architects of Populous used

The cornice at new Yankee Stadium loosely replicates the original.

Ebbets Field as an inspiration for Citi Field, even to the point of creating an Ebbets-like entry rotunda behind home plate that is named for Jackie Robinson, who never wore a Mets uniform. It is as if the Mets decided to treat the New York City history of the National League as abandoned property, which in a sense it is. But wrapping a pastiche of the Dodgers' former field in Brooklyn around the façade of another team's twenty-first-century ballpark in Queens is nothing if not disingenuous, a claim to a history that belongs, more properly, to the team that plays at Dodger Stadium in Los Angeles—itself now a venerable historic stadium, older than Ebbets Field was when it was demolished.

The façade of Citi Field, apart from its faux-Ebbets elements, is an easygoing, casual mix of red brick and dark gray steel elements, which give it a pleasing balance between retro and industrial. Like Citizens Bank Park in Philadelphia, this is an urban ballpark without an urban setting. Every element of it, and not just the portion that mimics Ebbets Field, is designed to look at home in the city. The problem is that there is no city around it. A long office wing for the Mets is set behind right field, parallel to 126th Street, which would be a nice piece of urban design if it had an urban setting. Most of the ballpark faces parking lots, with expressways beyond.

While Citi Field has nearly fifteen thousand fewer seats than Shea Stadium, as with most new ballparks its overall footprint is just as large, if not larger, than that of the higher-capacity ballparks of the previous generation. As at Yankee Stadium, almost everything inside the ballpark is larger and more comfortable than in its predecessor, including a new version of Shea Stadium's one eccentricity, the large red apple in center field that rose when a Met hit a home run. The Citi Field version is four times as big.

Citi Field has a welcome casualness that stands in clear contrast to the haughtiness of the stadium in the Bronx. It is clear and easy to navigate, with far more expansive concourses and amenities than Shea had—like most of the ballparks of the post–Camden Yards generation, it is designed to encourage fans to wander, and the concourses are open to views of the field. If its generous dimensions had any problem, it was not in the public areas but on the playing field. Citi Field was very much a pitcher's park, with large outfield dimensions. In 2012, after three seasons characterized by an exceptionally low number of home runs, the right

center field wall was moved in from 415 feet to 390 feet, and in 2015 it was pulled in another ten feet.

Less relevant to the game, but perhaps more important to the overall identity of the ballpark, was another change that came just a year after Citi Field opened: in 2010, in an implicit acknowledgment that the original ballpark design seemed more respectful of the history of the Dodgers than that of the Mets, a Mets Hall of Fame was added adjacent to the Jackie Robinson Rotunda. Fred Wilpon admitted to Jeffrey Toobin of *The New Yorker* that he had gotten carried away in allowing his nostalgia for the team of his childhood to loom so large at Citi Field that it overshadowed the legacy of the team for which the ballpark had been built. "All the Dodger stuff—that was an error of judgment on my part," Wilpon told Toobin.

The New York Mets' Citi Field from above, with its rotunda based on Ebbets Field in the lower right

Only a year separated the opening of Yankee Stadium and Citi Field from the next ballpark to be finished, Target Field in Minneapolis, but Target, designed by Earl Santee and Bruce Miller of Populous, seemed

fresher than either of the New York ballparks, if only because, like Petco Park and Progressive Field, it was clean, straightforward, and modern in an understated way. It was also neatly integrated into downtown Minneapolis, marking the final step in the Minnesota Twins' gradual march toward urbanism from their first home in Metropolitan Stadium in suburban Bloomington, which epitomized the suburban ballpark set amid acres of parking, to their second home, the widely disliked Hubert Humphrey Metrodome, which brought them to downtown Minneapolis but at the cost of sharing uncomfortable indoor quarters with the Minnesota Vikings football team.

The Twins began to plan for a baseball-only park in 1994, and the sixteen years it took before Target Field was completed were filled with arguments over the pros and cons of multiple sites, disputes between rival municipalities, fights over public financing, and difficulties over reaching agreement on the value of the privately owned downtown location that, once it was finally selected as the preferred site, was condemned by eminent domain. In 2001, at roughly the midpoint of the sixteen-year campaign to build a new ballpark, there was even a brief time when it appeared that the team might disappear in a proposed "contraction" of major league baseball. It was saved by the Minnesota courts, which declared that baseball's antitrust exemption made the team a "community asset," and that it could not simply go out of business.

Citi Field's façade, again taking its cue from Ebbets

The well-loved Target Field in Minneapolis—its relatively low seating capacity, of under forty thousand, offers an intimate game-day experience.

In comparison to the nearly endless political and economic squabbles that preceded Target Field, any issues over its design were relatively minor, and mainly involved whether or not the ballpark would have a retractable roof. (It does not, mainly due to cost, as well as the absence of enough room on the site to allow the option of a one-piece sliding roof, as in Seattle.) Perhaps because so much energy was dissipated in the long battles over where the ballpark would be, how the land would be obtained, and how the project would be financed, the design was almost an afterthought, but to its benefit: this is a ballpark without frills but also without pretension. Target seats 38,649, putting it in the category of PNC Park in Pittsburgh and Fenway Park as one of major league baseball's smaller venues. If more than fifty thousand seats almost always makes a ballpark feel too large, under forty thousand almost always assures that it will feel pleasingly comfortable, no matter how it is configured. If Target does not manage quite the intimacy of the two-decked PNC Park it is nevertheless one of the most inviting of the new parks, with an exterior, like PNC, of Kasota stone, and a position in the warehouse district at the edge of downtown that is convenient both for urban dwellers arriving on foot or by public transit, and for suburbanites coming by car. And most of the seating is focused toward views of the skyscrapers of downtown Minneapolis. After years of looking up to see nothing but the white fabric roof of the Metrodome, Twins fans had to be relieved to see their city's skyline. Target Field is amiable, which in the history of baseball parks may be the highest compliment.

Two years later would come a far more ambitious effort to build a truly modern ballpark, one whose architecture has not the faintest whiff of retro about it: Marlins Park in Miami, a swooping, elliptical, bright white stucco, steel, and glass structure that, from a distance, looks more like an airline terminal or a convention center than a ballpark. Only one aspect of Marlins Park, its retractable roof, looks back even slightly, since the fashion for roofs that open and close had appeared to ebb by the time Marlins Park was completed, twenty-three years after the SkyDome in Toronto and more than a decade since the most recent one, at Miller Park in Milwaukee. If the frequently cold weather in Minneapolis was deemed insufficient to make a roof a necessity for the Minnesota Twins, the extreme heat and humidity as well as frequent thunderstorms suffered by fans of the Marlins led to a different decision, driven by the realization that the Miami climate during much of the baseball season is at least as uncomfortable as that of Phoenix, which brought retractable roofs to American ballparks in 1998.

The architect of Marlins Park was Earl Santee of Populous, who showed yet again how the architecture firm that has designed almost every major league ballpark since Camden Yards has made a practice of taking cues from its clients rather than promoting any single mode of design. In some ways Marlins Park seems like a rejection of everything that Populous has designed in New York, Pittsburgh, San Francisco, and many other cities in which retro design ruled the day, and it does not even have that much in common with the firm's somewhat more modern ballparks like Petco and Target. Yet Marlins Park was not a disavowal of Populous's recent work but rather an embrace of the wishes of a very different client, a client who would have the same determined impact on design that Eli Jacobs had two decades earlier when he insisted that the firm give the Baltimore Orioles a traditional-looking ballpark at Camden Yards in downtown Baltimore.

That client was Jeffrey Loria, like Eli Jacobs a New York–based owner with a longstanding interest in architecture. Loria, however, could claim at least a tangential professional connection to architecture: he had made his money as an art dealer, and he liked to think of himself as an arts patron as well as a baseball owner. Loria had long been involved in professional baseball, although with mixed results. He had been the owner of the unsuccessful Montreal Expos when the team, along with the Minnesota Twins, was threatened with elimination by major league baseball, which had hoped to close down both unprofitable franchises. While the Twins fought, and won, a legal action against major league baseball to survive, Loria made no effort to keep his hapless team in Montreal. Instead he participated in a complicated three-way trade in which he sold the Expos to the baseball commissioner's office, which in turn resold the team to investors in Washington, D.C., who turned the Expos into the Nationals, while Loria landed on his feet as the new owner of the Florida Marlins, whose previous owner, John Henry, became the controlling partner in the Boston Red Sox.

Loria was not a popular owner in Montreal, and after the three-way deal he was widely viewed as having unnecessarily given up the city's baseball franchise. In Florida he did little to win any more admiration, especially when he sold off many of the franchise's star players immediately after the team won the World Series in 2003. Loria installed his stepson, David Samson, who had run the Expos, as president of the Marlins, who then played in the enormous, seventy-five-thousand-seat Sun Life Stadium, built as Joe Robbie Stadium in 1987 for the Miami Dolphins, the football team that continued to use it. Despite elaborate renovations before the Marlins began play in 1993, the stadium remained notably unsuitable for baseball, and paid attendance was often no more than two thousand per game, a tiny number that looked smaller still within the vastness of the football stadium. It was clear that if the Marlins were to have a long-term future in south Florida, a new, baseball-only venue was needed.

It would take a long time, and multiple threats by Loria to move the team to another city, before a deal would be done to build a new ballpark on the site of the old Orange Bowl in the Little Havana neighborhood of the city. As in Minneapolis, the other city that had been plagued by poor attendance, there was intense political feeling on all sides: the team management argued that the unpleasantness of Sun Life Stadium was a major factor in the lack of public interest in the team and that only a new, publicly financed ballpark would make baseball popular enough to be profitable in Miami; many Miamians saw a new ballpark less as a civic good than a form of corporate welfare to help a wealthy and unpopular team owner enhance his profits. In the spring of 2009, the ballpark deal was complete, with the city of Miami and Miami-Dade County committed to issuing bonds to cover roughly 80 percent of the cost of the $634 million project, in exchange for which the team would "rebrand" itself and change its name from the Florida Marlins to the Miami Marlins. Later that year, the long-term burden the ballpark financing would put on taxpayers became a major issue in the Miami mayoral election. When city commissioner Joe Sanchez, an active supporter whose campaign was assisted by the Marlins (and even included appearances by the team mascot) was soundly defeated by Tomás Regalado, an outspoken stadium opponent, it was a clear signal that the deal the city and county had made was deeply unpopular with the voters. And if there was any doubt, the voters cleared it up fifteen months later, when they recalled the county mayor, Carlos Alvarez, and the county manager, who had negotiated the deal with the Marlins.

But a deal is a deal, and the project went ahead. While Loria and his management team were probably no more concerned with the long-term relationship of their team to its home city than they had been in Mon-

Miami's Marlins Park, on the site of the former Orange Bowl, boasts the first retractable roof since Miller Park in 2001.

treal, when it came to the ballpark itself, Loria turned out to be one of baseball's most knowing and sophisticated architectural clients. Marlins Park, like so many publicly funded sports facilities, may not have been the best financial deal for local taxpayers, but it did turn out to be a memorable work of architecture.

Loria told Beth Dunlop of the *Miami Herald* that he wanted something "different and experimental" and said, "I thought it was time for baseball to be innovative." He wanted to go beyond the somewhat anodyne corporate modernism of both Petco and Nationals, and Earl Santee delivered what is arguably the most inventive ballpark design since Camden Yards, which opened almost twenty years to the day before Marlins Park. This is not a ballpark that "fits in," because there is no way that a structure of this enormous size would blend smoothly into the low-rise cityscape of the Little Havana neighborhood, no matter what it looks like. It is inevitably an alien object, but its rounded form and light color make it the most benign alien object imaginable. Like a huge ship docked beside a modest seaside village, Marlins Park succeeds not because it matches what is around it, but because it seems to have floated in from

another universe entirely. A conventional building half as large would seem intrusive; but Marlins Park is like a huge marshmallow, big and gentle and porous. With its swoops and curves and expanses of glass it is a gentle cartoon of modern architecture, a structure that has more in common with the mid-century modern fantasies of Wallace K. Harrison or Eero Saarinen than with any other baseball park ever designed.

Marlins Park breaks most of the rules of good urbanism: it has little to do with the architecture around it, it hardly relates to the street, and it is heavily oriented toward automobile access, even to the point of having four garages around its perimeter like architectural sentries guarding its gates. Its success is certainly different from that of ballparks that are

A mosaic tiled walkway up to Marlins Park, in tropical colors

smoothly integrated into their urban surroundings, like Pittsburgh and Denver. In Miami, Marlins Park and Little Havana coexist rather than connect. Because the site once housed the Orange Bowl, it has a history of large-scale interruption of the urban fabric, a history that Marlins Park continues with a new architectural expression.

The sense that this is a different kind of ballpark extends within, mostly for the good. Jeffrey Loria's imprint is most visible in the unusual amount, and the high quality, of public art on display, most famously the "home run sculpture" by Red Grooms commissioned for center field, which, if not one of the artist's greatest achievements, is certainly a step above the Mets' home run apple.* More impressive, if less visible, are a ceramic

A tile mural by artist Joan Miró, one among many artworks at Marlins Park

* Loria sold the team for $1.2 billion in 2017 to a consortium led by Bruce Sherman and including Derek Jeter, who became the team's new chief executive and its public face. The new management, which so far has been unable to improve the team's dismal attendance record, is moving the Red Grooms to a new location outside the ballpark and converting the space it now occupies beyond center field into an area that can be sold as an event space for fans. Jeter has made no secret of his dislike of the art piece.

piece by Joan Miró and murals by Kenny Scharf, Larry Rivers, and Niki de Saint Phalle. There is even a wall painting by Roy Lichtenstein.

Loria also was responsible for the bright color palette inside the ballpark, which has blue seats and concourse sections in red, blue, yellow, and green, inspired by Miró, he has said. Huge glass panels over center field offer expansive views toward the downtown Miami skyline, which get better when the panels, which are designed to slide on tracks, are opened, an event that generally occurs in conjunction with the opening of the roof, something that happens infrequently given Miami's heat and humidity. And that, in the end, is the great shortcoming of Marlins Park: for all the ambition of its architecture, when the roof is closed it is still an indoor ballpark, with all of the shortcomings of that genre. It is full of modern white sleekness on the outside and bright tropical color on the inside, and it tries hard to express an idea of Miami as a city of modernist exuberance. Thanks to the wall of glass behind center field, it never feels totally enclosed. The city is always visible, out there somewhere. But the sky rarely is, to the detriment of baseball.

The view of the field through the aquarium behind the plate at Marlins Park

12

The Ballpark as Theme Park

IT IS A LONG WAY from Marlins Park to Wrigley Field, but both ballparks are, in their way, embedded in the city. True, the sleek white spaceship of Marlins Park is visually distinct from Little Havana more than the rambling structure of Wrigley stands apart from Wrigleyville, the neighborhood on the North Side of Chicago whose very name underscores the intimate tie between Wrigley and its surroundings. In Chicago, the ballpark and the neighborhood grew up together, and for a long time they shared a messy, raffish quality that was a big part of their allure. The nature of the connection between the raucous, beloved ballpark on the North Side of Chicago and the blocks around it has begun to change, however, and not because Wrigley Field is in trouble, or has deteriorated. Quite the opposite: Wrigley is as cherished as ever, and it has been thoroughly, and for the most part respectfully, renovated by the Ricketts family, who purchased the Chicago Cubs in 2009, and have overseen renovations, including the addition of digital screens to accompany the ballpark's famous hand-operated scoreboard, most of which are discreet enough not to significantly compromise the ballpark's historic qualities. Some of the best changes are invisible, like the new underground clubhouses for the Cubs and visiting teams, an excellent solution to the problem of Wrigley's woefully inadequate old facilities, which could no longer be passed off as quaint.

More conspicuous is the way that the ballpark's gleaming freshness is now spilling over to properties all around it. The Cubs organization has purchased many of the houses along Waveland and Sheffield Avenues with their famous rooftop seats, rogue properties that are now, for all intents and purposes, part of a larger corporate empire. A new Wrigleyville is taking shape all around the ballpark. A sleek glass six-story office building for the team's headquarters has been built adjacent to the ballpark, and a new hotel, named the Zachary in honor of Zachary Taylor Davis, Wrigley Field's architect, has gone up across Clark Street. The site between the office building and the ballpark has been cleared to make way for the Park at Wrigley, an open public plaza, as well as a children's play area of the sort that is now common in new ballparks. The neighboring structures now also include condominium apartments and a ten-screen cinema.

There is nothing wrong with any of these things in themselves, and they make Wrigleyville a fresher, cleaner place. But the hotel, however affectionate its name, looks as if it could be anywhere, and so does most of the rest of the Wrigley redevelopment. Once, Wrigley Field and its surroundings were unusual, if more than a little funky, a quality that has all but disappeared from this quarter. As the *Chicago Tribune* titled an opinion piece lamenting the upgraded neighborhood, "Welcome to the Boring, Tedious Confines of the New Wrigleyville." The writer, Chris-

Hotel Zachary, named in honor of architect Zachary Taylor Davis, who designed Wrigley Field, stands amid the remade neighborhood around the ballpark.

topher Borrelli, said that Wrigleyville had exchanged "a specific kind of tackiness" for "an assemblage of hard edges and smooth surfaces, offices, condos and storefronts, ice cream shops and sports bars and thoughtful hotels, arranged into gray and beige blocks, impersonal and dull alongside the remaining rowhouses . . . a neighborhood where all the restaurants are 'concepts' and all the culture is 'content.'" Wrigleyville was becoming, Borrelli said, "Stepfordville USA."

Wrigleyville in fact has a long way to go before it is indistinguishable from a suburban mall, and the ballpark remains unique, a place to watch baseball like no other. But as larger buildings go up around it Wrigley Field does not hold sway over its neighborhood in quite the same way it did, and its magnetic pull is reduced. Its aura once pervaded the neighborhood, even during the off-season, but now it sometimes feels like it is the old anchor to a new entertainment and shopping district that is growing up around it, as the Cubs organization, like almost all major league baseball teams, seeks more and more ways in which to make income. Profiting from the real estate outside the ballpark gates is an easy way to do it.

The Boston Red Sox, who possess in Fenway Park the only other classic ballpark still in use, would not respond to economic pressures in quite the same way as the Cubs. After spending much of the 1990s considering abandoning Fenway Park and building a new ballpark elsewhere in Boston—and even announcing plans for a new Fenway Park in 1999—a different ownership under John Henry reversed course in 2005 and announced its intention to keep the Red Sox at Fenway indefinitely. They then set out to restore and improve the ballpark under the guidance of Larry Lucchino, who served as the team's chief executive from 2001 to 2015, and Janet Marie Smith, who had worked with Lucchino on the design and construction of Camden Yards. The Baltimore colleagues, reunited in Boston, made numerous, understated changes to expand the income potential of Fenway, most famously adding seats atop the "Green Monster" left field wall, but they took care to do nothing to alter the basic nature of the Boston ballpark. They opened things up just enough so that Fenway does not feel as cramped and enclosed as it once did, but they did not make it feel fundamentally different. Their overriding goal, to use the lexicon of the twenty-first century, was to tie the branding of the Red Sox all the more closely to the team's historic ballpark and present Fenway's funkiness as a virtue, not a liability.

Even if Lucchino and Smith had wanted to, however, they could not expand Fenway either downward or outward as the Cubs had done with Wrigley. Fenway's site in Boston's Back Bay area is on landfill where the water table makes major underground construction difficult if not impossible, and there is little adjacent land available for the kind of neighborhood development that has been occurring around Wrigley. The section of Jersey Street in front of the ballpark (known for years as Yawkey Way in honor of the longtime former owner of the team) was turned into a pedestrian mall on game days in the manner of Eutaw Street outside Camden Yards, but otherwise, the ballpark's relationship to its surroundings remains mostly as it has been. Boston swirls on around its ballpark, as it has for more than a hundred years, and for all the upgrades, neither Fenway nor its neighborhood has been scrubbed too clean.

· · ·

New seating atop the "Green Monster" in Fenway Park

The situation is very different around SunTrust Park in Atlanta, which opened in 2017, a quarter century after Camden Yards. It is clean, very clean, and that is the whole idea. The Atlanta Braves, unlike every other team in major league baseball that has chosen a new location for a ballpark in the twenty-first century, moved away from their city's downtown rather than toward it, a decision that was made to allow the management of the team to build from scratch what the Chicago Cubs are trying to construct incrementally, which is an entire neighborhood under the team's control. St. Louis, with its Ballpark Village adjacent to Busch Stadium, is doing something similar; Arlington, Texas, is building Texas Live, a real estate development with restaurants, a hotel, and entertainment venues to supplement both the new Globe Life Field for the Texas Rangers and the nearby AT&T Stadium, home of the Dallas Cowboys: an artificial downtown for baseball and football fans both. The notion in Atlanta, as in Chicago, St. Louis, and Arlington, is to enable teams not just to earn income from restaurants and bars and retail shops outside the ballpark gates, but to manage as much of the environment around the ballpark as they possibly can, to determine what uses team management wants to see there and what kinds of buildings will contain them.

It is in the nature of cities, of course, that this is impossible—real urban places are untidy mixes of different uses and different buildings and different kinds of people, sharing the common space of the urban street, and because cities are absolutely and irrevocably public, a certain degree of disarray comes along with them. In a well-functioning city, there is order, but there is not rigid control, and public places in the form of streets and sidewalks define the nature of the place as much as any private property that sits beside them. They can be boisterous, even chaotic, and part of the urban idea is that a moderate amount of disorder is a fair trade-off for the virtue of having a truly public place. But the terms of the public realm have been changing in cities for a long time, not just around ballparks but in so many downtowns, where privately owned plazas, malls, and other places open to the public in a limited way have taken over many of the functions of public space. What the Atlanta Braves—and, to a more limited extent, the St. Louis Cardinals, the Chicago Cubs, and the Texas Rangers—are doing is extending the privately owned space of the stadium into a larger sphere.

The Atlanta Braves played for nineteen seasons at Turner Field, just

south of downtown Atlanta, a location that, to be fair, does not offer the best argument for urban baseball. Close to two freeways and not as well served by public transportation as many urban ballparks, it has none of the pleasures of a dense urban setting. Even though the center of Atlanta's downtown is just a couple of miles away, the old ballpark felt isolated. The Braves organization, frustrated by the limits of Turner Field's site, tried to interest the city of Atlanta in investing in improvements to Turner and in allowing the team to acquire adjacent land where it could create a development along the lines of St. Louis's Ballpark Village. When neither option was forthcoming, the team made the decision in 2013 to leave the city and travel to Cobb County, roughly fifteen miles to the northwest, where it could build not only a new ballpark, but an entire complex of shops, restaurants, bars, condos, hotels, and offices—what would amount to an entire neighborhood with the ballpark at its heart, and one that the Braves organization could control: Ballpark Village on steroids.

Whatever else can be said about SunTrust Park and the Battery at

The Battery at SunTrust Park in Atlanta—St. Louis's Ballpark Village on steroids

Atlanta, as the new development around it is called, it is nothing like the suburban ballparks of the 1950s and '60s. Atlanta's new ballpark has more in common with developments like Easton Town Center, outside of Columbus, Ohio, or CityPlace in West Palm Beach, Florida, all-new complexes of stores and restaurants and hotels that combine the elements of a shopping mall with the form of a traditional town or city. There are places like that all over the United States now. But the Battery is the first of them to have a major league ballpark as its centerpiece and reason for being.

Paradoxically, the Braves can claim to be in a more urban environment in Cobb County than they were in Atlanta, if only because the new ballpark flows naturally into pedestrian-oriented streets filled with places to eat, drink, and be entertained, and because a few lucky people—including those who buy condominiums in the building called, yes, Home—will be able to walk just a block to the ballpark. But it might better be called urbanoid than urban. The Battery is designed, the architects, Wakefield Beasley of Atlanta, state, so that "from the moment visitors enter the project until they reach the new home of the Atlanta Braves, they will be immersed in a comprehensive entertainment experience unlike any other in the Southeast."*

Indeed, the Battery, like other such places, is an "entertainment experience" more than a true urban neighborhood, a generic place built out of the same standardized, corporate taste that critics have feared has begun to erase the authenticity of Wrigleyville. It is clean and well-kept, a kind of theme park masquerading as a city. The Battery offers a privately owned, sanitized version of urbanism that you drive to and park your car in (or have it parked by a valet) before you stroll past the shops and restaurants and into the ballpark. It is a bubble, and like all such bubbles, it has a superficial appeal, but it is disingenuous to claim that it represents something truly urban: it is just too clean and neat for that. SunTrust is a mallpark as much as it is a ballpark.

---

* Wakefield Beasley were in charge of designing the Battery and coordinating with Populous, the architects of SunTrust Park. The New York City firm Beyer Blinder Belle was hired to design the plaza at the center of the Battery, a kind of grassy town square that sits between the ballpark, the hotel, and a reflective glass office building that serves as a regional headquarters for Comcast.

And the accessibility problems of Turner Field have only been exac-erbated by the Braves' move, since public transportation is even less available in Cobb County than at the old ballpark downtown, in part because the voters of Cobb County, which is predominantly white, chose to exclude themselves from Atlanta's regional MARTA transit system. Atlanta has been growing through sprawl for a long time, and many of its larger corporate headquarters are far from downtown. The Braves' new location serves middle- and upper-middle-class suburban fans who had been frustrated by driving through Atlanta's famously difficult traffic to reach Turner Field; at the same time it makes the trip to a baseball game more difficult for lower-income fans, many of whom are non-white, live closer to the center of the city, and rely on public transportation.

SunTrust Park was designed by both Joe Spear and Earl Santee of Populous, partners who usually work on separate projects but here joined forces. Financial concerns as well as time pressures led to the decision to design the park without a retractable roof, which is just as well, since a roof structure would have made SunTrust Park too big to fit comfort-

SunTrust Park in Atlanta, though without a roof, features a high, wide canopy over the upper deck.

ably into the neighborhood that has been manufactured to go around it. Without a roof, its scale works well with the buildings Wakefield Beasley has designed to go alongside it. The ballpark is big enough to feel like the neighborhood's anchor, but not so big as to risk being a deadweight in the Battery's heart during the six months of the off-season.

The architecture itself is similar to many of Populous's other ballparks that have predominantly red brick exteriors and exposed steel and concrete structural elements. It is neither assertively modern nor traditional, which is to say that its style leans toward retro, but in an understated way. It is a well-mannered ballpark that is designed to be comfortable, and to accommodate the faux-urban neighborhood around it. The most notable architectural feature is a high, wide canopy over the upper deck, a concession to the decision not to include a retractable roof intended to shield upper-deck seats from the sun. As at every new ballpark, the concourses are wide and the food and drink options numerous, with plenty of areas for standees to mingle and other areas that groups can rent as event spaces. The taller neighboring buildings of the Battery can be glimpsed from within the ballpark, and occupants can look back into the park as well, making SunTrust feel well connected to its own new neighborhood, if not to the larger skyline of Atlanta.

As at almost every ballpark now, new or old, there is a section that celebrates the team's history—in this case going all the way back to the team's origins as the Boston Braves, and including a remarkable sculpture that uses baseball bats to spell out the number 755, Hank Aaron's number of career home runs. Lest there be any doubt about the sacredness of this number to the team, the address of the Braves executive offices at Sun-Trust Park is 755 Battery Avenue. Battery Avenue goes through the center of the new development, but it extends for just a couple of blocks past the ballpark, and leads nowhere else except back to the freeway. That raises the question framed by Jason Henderson, a professor of geography at San Francisco State University who has studied Atlanta's growth patterns: "If the Braves win a World Series, where are they having the parade?"

If the Atlanta Braves abandoned the real city in favor of an ersatz one that the team and its partners could build and largely control, and the coming Globe Life Field suggests that the Texas Rangers are equally committed to the pseudo-urban notion of an entertainment zone as a way of expanding the reach of the team beyond the gates of the ballpark, the new ballpark that the Oakland Athletics are planning holds the promise of being a somewhat different model. The Athletics now play in one of baseball's least satisfying facilities, the Oakland-Alameda County Coliseum, adjacent to a freeway some distance from downtown and the only major league baseball stadium still in use that was constructed for both football and baseball.* The team has tried for years to build a new ballpark on sites within Oakland as well as in the region of San Jose, and a few years ago hired Snohetta, a creative, New York– and Oslo-based architecture firm, as its architect, breaking with major league's default position of ballpark designs by Populous.

The Snohetta project never went ahead owing to objections to its planned location on the grounds of a community college near downtown. The Athletics then switched both sites and architects. Instead of retreating to the suburbs, John Fisher, the team's owner, chose a challenging, gritty urban site, the Howard Terminal on the Oakland waterfront near Jack London Square, and an architect who had never designed a major league ballpark, the Bjarke Ingels Group, a New York– and Copenhagen-based firm known for the bold shapes of its buildings. It was a choice as striking as that of Snohetta.

BIG's design, which was made public toward the end of 2018, was for a sharply angular ballpark with adjacent high-rise housing that looked like the firm's Via 57 project in New York City. (The towers were later simplified, and the ballpark made rounder.) The project also has a gondola to connect the site with the nearest mass-transit station, ten blocks away—a distance that is probably the major shortcoming of this otherwise promising site, and one that a gondola, however dramatic, will do little to mitigate. The Howard Terminal project follows the current trend of extending a team's sphere of influence out beyond the ballpark gates and of trying to create a new neighborhood in which the ballpark can sit. Indeed, the team wants to control far more than the 55-acre Howard Terminal site; it has asked for development rights to the old 111-acre Oakland Coliseum site as well, where BIG has proposed to replace the Coliseum with a mix of manufacturing and office facilities around a sports park.

* See Chapter 7, pages 172, 180.

BIG's design for the new Oakland A's ballpark would have a High Line–style park atop its structure, and be in the middle of a new urban neighborhood of BIG's making.

For all that the Oakland project represents a vast expansion of a team's real estate ambitions—an expansion that the team claims is necessary if it is to privately finance the new ballpark—Howard Terminal is not a suburban theme park pretending to be an urban neighborhood but a project that seems to celebrate rather than reject urban density, and to be designed to be compatible with the industrial nature of its surroundings, however much it may also be an act of gentrification, cleansing the area's grittiness. The 34,000-seat ballpark itself would be as different from Populous's retro design in Atlanta as the Howard Terminal site is from the Atlanta suburbs. If built as designed, it would be the most frankly modern ballpark since Marlins Park in Miami.

Like much of BIG's work, the design of the Oakland ballpark seems more of a pure geometric shape than a response to the neighborhood around it. The most memorable element is BIG's plan to top the ballpark with a landscaped, accessible green roof, making it, in effect, a kind of High Line park in the sky. The "elevated park," as the team calls it, would slope down to meet the ground behind the outfield. The sketches released by the Athletics suggest a bold if still undeveloped idea, and the team's long history of unrealized schemes makes it far from certain that it will be built as designed. Still, the team has not hesitated to promote it largely as an urban amenity, "nestled carefully into its urban surroundings," in the words of a press release. "This design will allow us to blur the boundaries of a traditional ballpark and integrate it into the surrounding neighborhood," said Dave Kaval, the team's president, leaving unsaid that the neighborhood the ballpark would be integrated into was almost wholly a creation of BIG, the architects, and not a part of the city that exists now.

The city has always been part of the idea of baseball, if only because, as Peter Rutkoff has put it, "baseball's parklike theater provided a sunshiny, pastoral contrast to the darker reality of city life." The ballpark is more than just a place of escape from the city, however. It has always been our *rus in urbe,* but with a quality altogether different from that of the early parks and rural cemeteries that arose at the same time,* since the ballpark was the one place where the dialectic between city and country could be experienced within a single intense and lively piece of architecture, the one place where the energy of the city and the easy, relaxed pace of the country were not mutually exclusive, but mutually dependent. You went to the ballpark to escape the city and to experience it at the same time. That is why ballparks with roofs, even retractable ones, never seem quite right: the equilibrium between nature and the man-made is thrown off, tilted in favor of the man-made. For all that the city matters to the ballpark, so does the presence of nature. In the best ballparks, the rural and the urban, the natural and the man-made, are in harmonic balance.

The history of the baseball park inscribes an arc of a century and a half that begins with deep engagement with the city, moves away toward the suburbs, and then seeks to return and reconnect with the city. As such, it mirrors the attitudes Americans of each era have had toward their cities, which they first accepted as a necessity, then fled from when the automobile allowed them to do so, and then began to return to when baseball's popularity and its cultural resonance connected with a resurgence of interest in cities. That long arc is defined by places like South End Grounds, Shibe Park, and Ebbets Field in its first phases, by the likes of

---

* See Chapter 1 for a full discussion of the connection between early baseball parks, public parks, and cemeteries in the nineteenth century.

A later view of Wrigley
Field, in 1980

Candlestick Park and Shea Stadium in its second, and by Camden Yards and its many and varied progeny in its third phase, during which baseball has tried, with varying degrees of success, to return to its roots and re-establish its connection to urbanism. The sport whose playing field symbolizes the connection and the interdependency between the rural and the urban is also a metaphor for how we have chosen to deal with our cities, the extent to which we have seen them as a natural habitat versus the extent to which we have seen them as something to escape from, or, more recently, as something to try to return to.

But there are more than three phases to this saga, it turns out. There are really four, since baseball's complex relationship to the city is only now beginning to play out in a new way—a new way that may also indicate a change in how we are coming to treat our cities. In the first three phases, baseball, or more properly baseball parks, took the city as it was.

Even though ballparks engaged with the city in the first phase, rejected it in the second, and re-engaged with it in the third—often with the goal of stimulating local development—at no point, even when ballparks were successful at reshaping neighborhoods around them, did they try to erase the fundamentally public quality of the city and remake it as a different kind of entity.

In the fourth phase, the latest chapter in baseball's evolving relationship to the city, that is exactly what the shapers of baseball parks have begun to try to do: to use the baseball park as the keystone of a larger real estate development that re-envisions the city as a privately controlled series of spaces that mimic the traditional public space of the city. No longer is the ballpark dropped into the complex stew of the city, to affect it gradually over time; now it is increasingly the centerpiece of a kind of recalibrated urban vision that has as many of the qualities of a theme park as of a traditional city.

This, and not the architecture of SunTrust Park itself, is why the new ballpark in Atlanta is the most significant development in ballpark design since Camden Yards. After Baltimore, as so-called retro ballparks became more and more common, there have been frequent suggestions that they represent a less-than-authentic version of baseball, and that with their expensive seats, lavish dining clubs, and seemingly unending opportunities for the acquisition of expensive souvenir merchandise they were no longer representative of the diversity that has long been a critical part of baseball's fan base, but had become, instead, a way of withdrawing from the city into an upscale bubble. True enough, as Daniel Rosensweig, Sharon Zukin, Herbert Muschamp, and numerous other critics have pointed out; as Rosensweig put it, "excessive comfort, regularization, and privatization often has the effect of rendering these new urban spaces sterile, devoid of the facts of city life—such as diversity and unpredictability—informing their original appeal."

But even if Camden Yards or Progressive Field or Coors Field or Comerica Park are bubbles of entertainment and amusement that offer multiple forms of distraction from the stresses of the city, they are doing nothing that is not consistent with the history of the game, since the baseball park has long been far more than just a neutral venue for sport. Beginning with the way in which Chris Von der Ahe shaped a world of entertainment at the first Sportsman's Park in St. Louis in the 1880s, the ballpark has always been a place of multiple diversions. William Hulbert and his stuffy heirs may have tried, in the early years of the National League, to rid the ballpark, and the game, of its distracting amusements, but the fact is that the "parklike theater" has for most of its history also been a parklike amusement park, a parklike recreation center, and, most of all, a parklike bar and restaurant.

But still, all of these places, from the original Sportsman's Park with its beer garden in the outfield to the more recent Comerica Park with its Ferris wheel and other rides, were private zones that were created to offer a contrast to the disheveled, messy, and energetic city outside their gates. The real city always beckoned, just beside the ballpark. What makes Atlanta's Battery—and, to a lesser extent, St. Louis's Ballpark Village and Arlington's Texas Live district beside the new Globe Life Field—different from them is that it extends the entertainment zone outside the ballpark into a pseudo-urban neighborhood that has been created solely as a complement to the ballpark. It is a simulacrum of a city, which is very different from a real city created over time, with its mix of different kinds of buildings, different kinds of neighborhoods, and, most important, different kinds of people.

The ballpark has always been a privately owned form of public space, and it has worked, in part, because it sits within the larger sphere of the real city. The essential truth about great and even not-so-great cities is that they are deeply, profoundly, absolutely, and utterly public. Public means for everyone, and it also means, by implication at least, that they are accessible to all, and also that not every detail of them is controllable. In a real city we accept messiness as part of the deal—unevenness, disarray, complexity, a mixture of people and things, a certain amount of chaos, all go along with the extraordinary creative energy that emanates from real cities. Real cities, like organic objects, continually reinvent themselves. Real cities offer us the presence of true common ground. And real cities are all different from one another, at least somewhat; they offer us that elusive, difficult-to-define quality we might describe as a sense of authenticity.

What, in the end, does authenticity mean in baseball, the sport that has long traded on its history as much as its present? It should mean that each ballpark is a world unto itself, a place different from all the other places in which baseball is played: that all ballparks are not the same, and

that the game played within them is therefore different in subtle ways from ballpark to ballpark. And authenticity should mean connection not only to the past, but also to the present, not only to the *rus* but also to the *urbe*. The ballpark itself, as Bart Giamatti pointed out, is a simulacrum of a city, and whether it is the ornate façade of Shibe Park in 1909 or the sleek whiteness of Marlins Park in 2012, its beauty comes not only from the magnificent contrast between its man-made physical structure and the bright image of nature that the field represents, but also from the contrast between the whole of the ballpark, structure and field alike, and the real city outside. The simulacrum that the ballpark is does not need to be inside another simulacrum, in other words; the greatest joy it can bring us is when it is embedded in the real city, with all the energy, diversity, and dynamism a city can display at its best, and the exhilaration the baseball park offers becomes not only a celebration of sport, but of the whole of urban life.

Sportsman's Park on Grand Boulevard in St. Louis in the early 1950s: baseball in the American city

ACKNOWLEDGMENTS

It would not be entirely right to say that I grew up in a family of baseball fans. My mother was a passionate fan of the Brooklyn Dodgers, but when the Dodgers abandoned Brooklyn, she did not shift her allegiance to Los Angeles, and neither did she transfer it to another team in New York. She gave up on baseball altogether. Growing up in the New York suburbs in a family that would no longer tolerate even mention of the Dodgers, I followed the Yankees, although not with the unbridled passion of some of my friends. But this book may well have had its true origins at around that same time, on the day that my father managed to acquire a pair of tickets to a game at Yankee Stadium, just behind the dugout on the third-base line. I found myself with a front row seat at a world that was not only bigger and brighter and more majestic than I had ever imagined it to be, but greener, too. We had journeyed into the Bronx, and yet we were not in some urban jungle; we were facing a lawn more brilliantly perfect than that of even the grandest house in our suburban neighborhood. I was in awe of the combination of urban grandeur and natural beauty. Were we in the city or had we escaped from it? In the ballpark we seemed to have ascended to some heavenly form of urban existence.

Some years later, I covered my high school baseball team for the local newspaper in the New Jersey town in which we lived. The team played on a field smack in the center of town, next to the high school but also across from the main intersection, which meant that unlike most high school ballfields, this one was overlooked by the local bank, the town hall, and the library. It was for all intents and purposes the town's central civic space, its main square, used for athletics. By then the interest in architecture that would shape my professional life was already clear, and I saw, at least subliminally, that there was something unusual and special in the idea that baseball was played in the symbolic heart of the town. It tied the idea of a place to watch sports with the idea of public space. And it showed me that a place for baseball could be an important part of the public realm, which is the true message of this book.

It was only after David Remnick, the editor of *The New Yorker,* asked me in 2009 to write an architecture column about the two ballparks that were opening that year in New York, Citi Field and the new Yankee Stadium, that I began to think that there was a book to be written on the relationship between the ballpark, public space, and the American city. There is no shortage of writing about baseball and baseball parks, but relatively little about the idea of the ballpark as both civic space and a work of architecture, and so I set out to do that here.

I am in debt to those who have addressed aspects of this subject already, most particularly John Pastier, whose rigorous analysis of the various iterations of Tiger Stadium is unsurpassed and whose writing and research on baseball parks have long combined a love of architecture with a deep understanding of baseball's particular needs. I should also mention the writing on ballparks of Philip Lowry in *Green Cathedrals,* Michael Gershman in *Diamonds,* and G. Edward White in *Creating the National Pastime,* all of which have been helpful.

But I should also cite other writers on baseball who have not focused particularly on ballparks but who nevertheless have had important things to say. That list begins, as it must, with Roger Angell, whose words on Shea Stadium are quoted in Chapter 7, but whose influence goes far beyond that wonderful paragraph to encompass all that baseball is and all that it means, written with that matter-of-fact grace that is his stock in trade. To his name I would add John Thorn, Martin Nolan, George Will, Daniel Okrent, Douglas Alden, Peter Rutkoff, and A. Bartlett Giamatti, whom I was privileged to know when I was a student at Yale and he was the master of Ezra Stiles College and neither of us expected that the arc of either of our careers would ever in some way come to encompass baseball. His did in an extraordinary way, and when we last saw each other in the summer of 1989, after he had become commissioner of baseball, the talk turned, understandably, to the wretchedness of most contemporary ballparks. I wish he had lived to see the completed Camden Yards, the design of which was the fulfillment of his hopes that baseball would regain some sense of its architectural self. Bart Giamatti's ode to the ballpark, *Take Time for Paradise,* is surely part of the inspiration for this book.

There have been many useful books on individual ballparks, including George Will's delightful *A Nice Little Place on the North Side: Wrigley Field at One Hundred,* but two stand out as masterworks: Jerald E. Podair's *City of Dreams: Dodger Stadium and the Birth of Modern Los Angeles* and Bruce Kuklick's *To Every Thing a Season: Shibe Park and Urban Philadelphia, 1909–1976.* I should also mention here an unusual publication, *City Baseball Magic,* written by Philip Bess and published in 1989, an invaluable source for all who are interested in the points of intersection between baseball and the American city.

Philip Bess, whose project for Armour Field in Chicago is discussed in detail in Chapter 8, was exceptionally generous with his time, and it was through him that I found Matt Dureiko, a talented young architect who had just completed the design of an urban ballpark for his master's thesis. Matt moved to New York after he received his degree, in part so that he could serve as a research assistant in the early stages of this book. Happily for Matt but unhappily for me he soon was so busy in his own career as an architect that he had to step aside from full engagement with this project. He was succeeded by the extraordinary Damon Hatheway, a classical scholar with a passionate interest in baseball and ballparks, whose superb and focused work was critical to the early sections of this book. When Damon moved on to pursue a graduate degree in classical studies, my former student Bill Shaffer, a polymath with a knowledge of everything from museum history to baseball, stepped in and helped me bring the research to a smooth conclusion.

I owe special thanks also to Melissa Goldstein, picture researcher extraordinaire, who jumped into this project with a wonderful mix of enthusiasm and rigor, and understood from the beginning that this was both a book about sports and a book about cities. The various pieces of this book could not have come together as they did without the heroic efforts of Todd Portnowitz at Knopf, assistant to my editor, Ann Close. Todd was unfazed by the demands of organizing hundreds of pages of text and close to two hundred images under deadline pressure, and I am grateful to him for his sound judgment and good cheer throughout.

I have had the privilege of working with Ann Close on two other books, and once again her warmth, her sharp insights, and her graceful, unflappable presence have made every step of this process a pleasure. One expects intellectual rigor in a great book editor, but in Ann it is combined with what I can only call joyful engagement, whatever the subject. I am very grateful to have worked with her again, as well as with Maggie Hinders, who designed the book, John Vorhees, who designed the jacket, and Holly Webber, the copy editor, who read the manuscript with care and discernment.

My longtime friend and agent, Amanda Urban of ICM Partners, has supported this project from the beginning, and I am grateful to her, as always, both for her critical insight and her warm enthusiasm, neither of which has flagged even for an instant over the long period of research and writing.

Many others have helped me in different ways. I owe thanks to Janet Marie Smith, who has kindly shared insights and recollections from her career, which was shaped by Oriole Park at Camden Yards, and to Larry Lucchino, her colleague in both Baltimore and Boston. Eli Jacobs, who as owner of the Baltimore Orioles played an equally critical role in the achievement of Camden Yards, has been generous not only in sharing his recollections of those years, but in talking about his passion for ballpark architecture in general. Early on in this project, Eli presented me with his personal scorecard of all the major league ballparks, rated as to architecture.

Fay Vincent, who followed Bart Giamatti as commissioner of baseball, has been helpful, and I am grateful also to Douglas Alden, John Thorn, Paul Farmer, Mark Lamster, Stephen Blank, Stephen Brodie, Peter Diamond, Rick Salomon, Roy Geronemus, Joel Towers, Len Kronman, Ken Lerer, David Leven, George Felleman, and Peter Rutkoff for stimulating conversations, emails, and general thoughts. The architects at Populous, the firm that grew out of HOK Sport, have been exceptionally generous in offering their time and recollections, as well as in providing assistance in organizing visits to many of the ballparks in their portfolio. My special thanks go to both Joe Spear and Earl Santee, design partners at the firm, and also to Gina Stingley, who arranged a memorable day at the firm's offices in Kansas City, and thanks also to Patrick Tangen and Lindsay Santee, as well as to Daniel Molina, who has given us access to the firm's broad photo archive. At BIG, design partner Kai-Uwe Bergmann briefed me on the Oakland ballpark and Daria Pahhota provided additional help. I am grateful to Ronnie Bolton, whose @OTBaseballPhoto Twitter account is a consistently rich source of great vintage photography.

When you are writing a book about ballparks, almost everyone, it seems, is interested, and more than a few friends offered to help with my research. I am grateful to every friend who shared stories with me or spent a day at a ballpark, but the most important of these by far has been Pam Flaherty, a cherished, longtime friend and impassioned baseball fan who was retiring from a distinguished career as an executive at Citibank at just the time I was beginning to work on this book. Pam deflected questions about what she would do next by joking that her only plan was to help me with this book, and whether she meant it seriously, that is pretty much what happened, and she has been a consistent presence from the beginning of this project to the end. She has read each chapter with care and insight, and as an urbanist as well as a baseball fan she has helped me keep the right balance between baseball and architecture. And she even made what may be the ultimate sacrifice for a devoted Yankee fan: in the name of research she agreed to make her first visit to the enemy territory of Fenway Park when she joined me in 2017 to view the recent renovations to Boston's great ballpark. I have long been grateful for the friendship my wife and I have with Pam and her husband, Peter, but never more than during the years of working on this book, which could not have taken its final form without her.

In addition to Pam Flaherty, two other valued friends—Patrick Corrigan, who proved himself a brilliant research assistant on my previous book, *Building Art: The Life and Work of Frank Gehry,* and Peter Rutkoff, historian, baseball connoisseur, and novelist—both read the manuscript in its final stages, and each contributed important suggestions that improved the text.

At Fenway Park, Jonathan Giulula showed me and Pam Flaherty the work that had been completed since the team made the wise decision to remain at Fenway. Other executives have been equally welcoming at other ballparks: at the Los Angeles Dodgers, Stan Kasten, chief executive officer, and Emily Walthouse; at the Seattle Mariners, Rebecca Hale; at the San Diego Padres, Kameron Durham; at the Chicago Cubs, Crane Kenney, vice president, and Julian Green; at the Philadelphia Phillies, Dave Buck; at the Pittsburgh Pirates, Chris Hunter; at the Atlanta Braves, Beth Marshall; at the Miami Marlins, Claude Delorme; and at the Tampa Bay Rays, Dave Haller and Garrett Johnson. Harold Kaufman of the New York Mets and his colleagues Zach Becker, Lorraine Hamilton, and Laura Verillo graciously gave photographer Michael Lionstar and me access to CitiField to shoot the jacket photograph on a very un-baseball-like winter's afternoon, and we are both grateful to them, as well as to Ken Lerer for his help here.

My sons Adam, Ben, and Alex have been baseball fans, and baseball players, for their entire lives, and my grandson Thibeaux Hirsh plays baseball now. We have had many visits to ballparks together over the years, and while the observations Ben made about PNC Park when he joined me there in 2018 as part of my research for this book may have been more sophisticated than the observations he had about Wrigley Field and Comiskey Park when we visited them together when his age was in the single digits, I cherish equally the memories of all of these trips, both recent and long ago. So, too, the memory of traveling to Petco Park with Alex, a knowing urbanist who had much insight about the relationship of Petco to San Diego; and of many happy times spent with Adam and Thibeaux not only at Dodger, Yankee, and Shea stadiums, but in many smaller baseball fields beyond the scope of this book.

My three daughters-in-law, Delphine Hirsh, Melissa Rothberg, and Carolyna De Laurentiis, and my grandchildren, Thibeaux and Josephine Hirsh, have as always provided a wonderful circle of support for the work that I do. And my wife, Susan Solomon, who has been a supportive and enthusiastic reader for forty years, continues to make sharp and insightful observations that keep me, and my writing, grounded. I am grateful to her for so much in my life: the countless things that she has done to help me with this book, I can truthfully say, constitute but a tiny fraction of the debt that I owe to her.

NOTES

PROLOGUE

xi   "where self-definition starts": A. Bartlett Giamatti, *Take Time for Paradise: Americans and Their Games* (New York: Bloomsbury, 2011), 81.

xi   "obligations and instruments": Ibid., 77.

CHAPTER 1: BROOKLYN BEGINNINGS

5   nearly one hundred of them: Mike Wallace, *Greater Gotham: A History of New York City from 1898 to 1919* (New York: Oxford University Press, 2018), 733.

5   playing rules in 1845: John Thorn, *Baseball in the Garden of Eden: The Secret History of the Early Game* (New York: Simon & Schuster, 2012), 69.

5   was the winner: Ibid., 83.

6   city-owned open space: Ibid., 66.

7   "a gang as frequent it": George Templeton Strong, Milton Halsey Thomas, and Allan Nevins, *The Diary of George Templeton Strong* (Ann Arbor, Mich.: UMI, 1993), Vol. 1, 236.

8   "city of base ball clubs": James L. Terry, *Long Before the Dodgers: Baseball in Brooklyn, 1855–1884* (Jefferson, N.C.: McFarland & Co., 2002), 5.

8   "competitiveness toward other places": Warren Goldstein, *Playing for Keeps: A History of Early Baseball* (Ithaca: Cornell University Press, 2014), 101.

8   "the first-class matches": Daniel Rosensweig, *Retro Ball Parks: Instant History, Baseball, and the New American City* (Knoxville: University of Tennessee Press, 2005), 63.

9   "culture of middle class Victorian men": Goldstein, *Playing for Keeps*, 31.

10   a cut of the proceeds: Michael Gershman, *Diamonds: The Evolution of the Ballpark* (Boston: Houghton Mifflin, 1995), 12.

11   by paying its players: Terry, *Long Before the Dodgers*, 19.

11   "demand for building lots": Gershman, *Diamonds*, 7.

12   stolen base had been invented: Philip J. Lowry, *Green Cathedrals: The Ultimate Celebration of All 273 Major League and Negro League Ballparks Past and Present* (Reading, Mass.: Addison-Wesley, 1993), 34–35.

13 after the team was formed: Thorn, *Baseball in the Garden of Eden*, 237.

14 air of a soccer goal: Lowry, *Green Cathedrals*, 37.

15 "claimed only by baseball": George Vecsey, *Baseball: A History of America's Favorite Game* (New York: Modern Library, 2008), 4.

19 "glare of brick walls": Henry Hope Reed and Sophia Duckworth, *Central Park: A History and a Guide* (New York: C. N. Potter, distributed by Crown, 1972), 14–15.

19 "much larger numbers": Frederick Law Olmsted and Theodora Kimball Hubbard, *Forty Years of Landscape Architecture: Central Park [by] Frederick Law Olmsted, Sr.* (Cambridge, Mass.: MIT Press, 1973).

20 "sensitive to natural beauties": Ibid.

CHAPTER 2: AMUSEMENT VERSUS VIRTUE

24 "Proximity to streetcar lines": Bruce Kuklick, *To Every Thing a Season: Shibe Park and Urban Philadelphia, 1909–1976* (Princeton, N.J.: Princeton University Press, 1991), 19.

24 "moguls to own ball clubs": Gershman, *Diamonds*, 19.

24 by streetcar companies: Bob McGee, *The Greatest Ballpark Ever: Ebbets Field and the Story of the Brooklyn Dodgers* (New Brunswick, N.J.; London: Rutgers University Press, 2005), 34.

26 "the trains to clear": Bill Felber, *A Game of Brawl: The Orioles, the Beaneaters, and the Battle for the 1897 Pennant* (Lincoln: University of Nebraska Press, 2007), 60.

26 had a slight incline: "South End Grounds," *Ballparks:* https://www.ballparks.com /baseball/national/sthend.htm.

27 "one field: center": Michael Benson, *Ballparks of North America: A Comprehensive Historical Encyclopedia of Baseball Grounds, Yards, and Stadiums, 1845 to 1988* (Jefferson, N.C.: McFarland, 2009), 39.

29 to purchase tickets: Ibid.

29 the ballpark itself: Bob Ruzzo, "South End Grounds (Boston)," *Society for American Baseball Research:* https://sabr.org/bioproj/park/south-end-grounds-boston.

29 "various sizes and shapes": John Pastier et al., *Ballparks: Yesterday and Today* (Edison, N.J.: Chartwell Books, 2007), 13.

30 not deliver what was promised: Ruzzo, "South End Grounds (Boston)."

30 "jousting as a manly endeavor": Gershman, *Diamonds*, 42.

31 "without a Grand Pavilion": *Boston Globe*, February 23, 1890, p. 22. Quoted in Ruzzo, "South End Grounds (Boston)."

32 "admission to the pavilion": Ruzzo, "South End Grounds (Boston)."

33 "blow off a bit of steam": Rosensweig, *Retro Ball Parks*, 76.

34 "Coney Island of the West": "Sportsman's Park," *Project Ballpark:* www.projectballpark .org/history/na/busch1.html.

34 Edward Achorn has said: Achorn, *The Summer of Beer and Whiskey: How Brewers, Barkeeps, Rowdies, Immigrants, and a Wild Pennant Fight Made Baseball America's Game* (New York: Public Affairs, 2014), 1.

34 "a dazzling show": Ibid.

34   "czar of professional baseball": Ibid., 20.

35   agreed-upon schedules: David Nemec, *The Beer and Whisky League: The Illustrated History of the American Association—Baseball's Renegade Major League* (Guilford, Conn.: Lyons Press, 2004), 15.

35   field for Sunday games: Ibid.

36   "Vim, Vigor, Virility": Rosensweig, *Retro Ball Parks,* 73.

36   "Spalding worked tirelessly": Ibid., 69.

36   "respect for the Sabbath": Ibid.

36   drunk on the field: Achorn, *Summer of Beer and Whiskey,* 10.

37   unwilling to discipline players: Ibid.

38   caps and shirts: Nemec, *Beer and Whisky League,* 97.

39   "attraction in its own right": Gershman, *Diamonds,* 30.

39   "a comfortable segregation": Rosensweig, *Retro Ball Parks,* 77.

39   "accommodations and conveniences": Pastier et al., *Ballparks,* 12.

40   southwest of the earlier park: Ibid., 13.

41   "the Beer and Whiskey Circuit": Achorn, *Summer of Beer and Whiskey,* 27.

41   "American Association game": Ibid., 32.

42   "rule the roost": Ibid.

42   eight National League teams: Ibid., 34.

42   limited income potential: Ibid., 36.

43   from that point forward: Nemec, *Beer and Whisky League,* 242.

43   the American Association: Ibid.

44   "dump at 108th Street": Ibid., 62.

45   "six months of malaria": Ibid.

46   a reported $25,478: Ibid., 109.

47   any major league ballpark: Lowry, *Green Cathedrals,* 150.

47   landed in the other park: Ruzzo, "South End Grounds (Boston)."

47   team and his ballpark: Rosensweig, *Retro Ball Parks,* 81.

47   court-ordered receivership: Ibid.

47   his American Association: Ibid.

CHAPTER 3: FROM WOOD TO STEEL AND STONE

52   left 1,900 people homeless: "The Great South End Grounds Fire of 1894," *New England Historical Society*: http://www.newenglandhistoricalsociety.com/great-south-end-grounds-fire-1894.

52   $80,000 to replace: Ruzzo, "South End Grounds (Boston)."

52   "cathedral-like grand stand": Terry Gottschall, "May 15, 1894: 'It Was a Hot Game, Sure Enough!'" *Society for American Baseball Research:* https://sabr.org/gamesproj/game/may-15-1894-it-was-hot-game-sure-enough.

56   "our beloved city": "Baker Bowl," *Society for American Baseball Research:* http://research.sabr.org/journals/baker-bowl.

56   "'hang their clothes'": Benson, *Ballparks of North America,* 300.

57   rather than affection: Lawrence S. Ritter, *Lost Ballparks: A Celebration of Baseball's Legendary Fields* (New York: Viking Studio Books, 1994), 10.

58   "save a \$1.50 ball": Larry Granillo, "Guest Post: When the Phillies Arrested an 11-Year Old 'Ball Thief,'" *The Sports Daily* (July 23, 2010): http://wezen-ball.com/2010-articles/guest-post-when-the-phillies-arrested-an-11-year-old-qball-thiefq.html.

59   called Rooters' Row: Gershman, *Diamonds*, 74.

59   Michael Gershman's words: Ibid., 70.

59   through the ballpark site: Ibid., 74.

59   crumbling bleachers: Ibid.

62   "manager Connie Mack": Pastier et al., *Ballparks*, 22.

62   "a lasting monument": Kuklick, *To Every Thing a Season*, 25.

63   an electric scoreboard: Ibid., 29.

63   construct his park: Pastier et al., *Ballparks*, 22.

63   outside of New York: Pastier et al., *Ballparks*, 22.

63   "magnates like Shibe": Kuklick, *To Every Thing a Season*, 29.

63   "a shrewd business move": Ibid.

64   "cheek-by-jowl": Ibid.

65   closing was announced: Ibid., 24.

66   "Dreyfuss's Folly": Gershman, *Diamonds*, 88.

66   thirty thousand at its opening: Benson, *Ballparks of North America*, 312.

66   engineer named Charles Leavitt: Pastier et al., *Ballparks*, 24.

67   all advertising billboards: Gershman, *Diamonds*, 88.

67   "none in his park": Ibid., 90.

67   "home runs out of": Ibid.

68   John Pastier observed: Pastier et al., *Ballparks*, 25.

68   pitcher Ed Walsh: Gershman, *Diamonds*, 92.

68   Chicago stockyards: Ibid.

69   concrete would have: Ibid., 94.

70   subway expansion: Bill Lamb, "Hilltop Park (New York)," *Society for American Baseball Research:* https://sabr.org/bioproj/park/393733.

71   the playing field: Ibid.

73   Brush Stadium: Benson, *Ballparks of North America*, 103.

73   "messenger will summon you": Gershman, *Diamonds*, 101.

73   was unusually deep: Ibid.

74   abandoned the project: "The Yankees of Kingsbridge Grounds," *The Second Division:* https://theseconddivision.wordpress.com/2014/04/12/yankees-kingsbridge-bronx.

CHAPTER 4: THE GOLDEN AGE

77   "accommodations of the patrons": Glenn Stout, *Fenway 1912: The Birth of a Ballpark, a Championship Season, and Fenway's Remarkable First Year* (Boston: Houghton Mifflin Harcourt, 2011), 14.

78   "jewel boxes": Gershman, *Diamonds,* 106–21.

79   center 420: Pastier et al., *Ballparks,* 28.

79   new field boxes: Benson, *Ballparks of North America,* 102.

80   "great innovators": Ritter, *Lost Ballparks,* 45.

80   the same again: Ibid., 46.

82   "the classic parks": Pastier et al., *Ballparks,* 28–30.

85   the Taylors did: Stout, *Fenway 1912,* 16.

85   due to expire: Ibid., 14–15.

85   valuable enterprise: Gershman, *Diamonds,* 107–8.

86   Stout has written: Stout, *Fenway 1912,* 16.

86   public auction: Ibid., 15.

86   ballpark's construction: Ibid., 21–22, 108.

86   "built to last": Ibid., 28.

87   an upper deck: Ibid., 31.

87   in the World Series: Ibid., illustration 9, 106.

88   $24 per seat: Ibid., 95.

89   "inconsequential places": "Fenway Park Quotes," *Baseball Almanac:* www.baseball
     -almanac.com/quotes/fenway_park_quotes.shtml.

89   "watch baseball": Nolan, *A Ballpark, Not a Stadium,* from *The Red Sox Reader,* edited
     by Dan Riley (Boston: Mariner Books, Houghton Mifflin, 1991), 3.

90   ballpark's plot: Stout, *Fenway 1912,* 29.

91   were never replaced: Pastier et al., *Ballparks,* 122.

92   "no public laments": Michael Ian Borer, *Faithful to Fenway: Believing in Boston, Baseball,
     and America's Most Beloved Ballpark* (New York: New York University Press, 2008), 44.

93   "Brooklyn": Dennis Evanosky and Eric J. Kos, *Lost Ballparks* (London: Pavilion
     Books, 2017), 47.

93   fans to travel: Benson, *Ballparks of North America,* 59–60.

93   old Washington Park: Ibid., 61.

94   "in its infancy": McGee, *The Greatest Ballpark Ever,* 41–42.

94   all of the pieces: Gershman, *Diamonds,* 110–11.

95   process of assembling: McGee, *The Greatest Ballpark Ever,* 44.

95   at Ebbets's desk: Ibid.

96   "at its worst": Ibid., 46–47.

96   "was even close": Ibid.

96   Bob McGee: Ibid., 50.

97   "their new park": Ibid.

97   "in this park": Ibid., 50–51.

98   Italian marble columns: Ibid., 48, 62.

98   public transportation: Ibid., 48.

99   "and for baseball": Ibid., 53–54.

99   lose to the Giants: Ibid., 54.

99   "an exhibition game": Ibid., 66.

100 "near riot": Ibid., 68.

100 included twelve turnstiles: Lowry, *Green Cathedrals,* 40.

100 was quickly abandoned: McGee, *The Greatest Ballpark Ever,* 69.

100 denote an error: Lowry, *Green Cathedrals,* 40–41.

101 "in Prospect Park": McGee, *The Greatest Ballpark Ever,* 76.

102 an Ebbets staple: Ibid., 126–27.

102 center field bleachers: Eric Enders, *Ballparks Then & Now* (San Diego: Thunder Bay Press, 2015), 37.

103 architect from Queens: McGee, *The Greatest Ballpark Ever,* 116.

104 "they have no money": Stuart Shea, *Wrigley Field: The Long Life and Contentious Times of the Friendly Confines* (Chicago: University of Chicago Press, 2014), 17.

104 have asked for: Ibid., 16–17.

104 "$125,000 if necessary": Ibid., 30.

104 "the existing parks": Ibid., 27.

105 national baseball league: Ibid., 30.

105 for his ballpark: Ibid., 33.

105 Shea has written: Ibid.

105 along Sheffield Avenue: Ibid., 41–42.

105 Shea has written: Ibid., 42.

107 league owners themselves: Ibid., 81–84.

107 the Chicago Whales: Ibid., 85.

107 the ballpark gates: Ibid., 89.

108 "from the ball park": Ibid., 90.

108 major league owners did: Ibid., 96–97.

108 a serious crisis: Ibid., 97.

109 "your time to business": Ibid., 108.

109 along with the plan: Ibid., 101–2.

109 name had changed: Ibid., 114.

109 fond of saying: George F. Will, *A Nice Little Place on the North Side: Wrigley Field at One Hundred* (New York: Crown Archetype, 2014), 46.

110 newspaper ads put it: Ibid., 51.

110 "into a home run": Ibid., 50–51.

111 "a delightful day": Ibid., 86–87.

111 "the ballpark": Ibid., 87.

111 "ugly baseball": Ibid.

112 Veeck would write: Ibid., 88.

CHAPTER 5: ASPIRING TO MONUMENTALITY

114 first tried to acquire: Harvey Frommer, *Remembering Yankee Stadium: An Oral and Narrative History of "The House That Ruth Built"* (Guilford: Lyons Press, 2016), 28.

114 937 defeats: Ibid.

114 say of his purchase: Ibid.

114 1920 and 1921: Ibid.

115 "Fulton Fish Market": Robert Weintraub, *The House That Ruth Built* (New York: Back Bay Books, Little, Brown, 2013), 37.

115 the two teams: Ibid., 38.

116 eager to sell it: Ibid., 39.

116 fans to reach: Ibid.

116 jeopardize national security: Ibid.

116 the Yankees' schedule: Ibid., 39–40.

116 little-used lumberyard: Ibid., 41.

117 "on Manhattan Island": Ibid., 40.

117 suburbanization of baseball: Ibid., Introduction.

118 the plans himself: Ibid., 44.

118 construction of Swayne Field in Toledo: Pastier, *Ballparks Yesterday and Today*, p. 24.

120 "those of aviators": Frommer, *Remembering Yankee Stadium*, 81.

124 single spade of earth: Weintraub, *The House That Ruth Built*, 48–50.

124 easy to reach: Ibid., 50.

124 $60,000 per year to $75,000: Ibid.

124 "Are you interested?": Ibid., 52.

125 yards of topsoil: Ibid., 53–54.

125 (distance of 368 feet): Frommer, *Remembering Yankee Stadium*, 31.

125 according to Weintraub: Weintraub, *The House That Ruth Built*, 56.

126 even 70,000: "Yanks' New Stadium to Be Opened Today," *New York Times* (April 23, 1923).

126 sources put at 58,000: Frommer, *Remembering Yankee Stadium*, 34.

126 not fully elastic: Ibid.

126 were turned away: Lowry, *Green Cathedrals*, 161.

126 "was swallowed up": Weintraub, *The House That Ruth Built*, 25.

126 "near the home plate": Ibid.

126 the paper proclaimed: "Yanks' New Stadium," *New York Times* (April 23, 1923).

126 "eleven years to do it": Ibid.

126 said before the game: Weintraub, *The House That Ruth Built*, 27.

127 "home run of the year": Ibid., 30.

127 *The New York Times* noted: Ibid., 32.

127 the *Evening Telegram*: Ibid., 22.

129 a civic auditorium: James A. Toman and Gregory G. Deegan, *Cleveland Stadium: The Last Chapter* (Cleveland: Cleveland Landmarks Press, 1997), 8.

131 Michael Gershman: Gershman, *Diamonds*, 96.

131 any direction at all: Ibid., 96–98.

132 "play the outfield here": Toman and Deegan, *Cleveland Stadium*, 82.

134 by a home run ball: Pastier et al., *Ballparks*, 40.

CHAPTER 6: LEAVING THE CITY

138 "suburbanization of baseball": Pastier et al., *Ballparks*, 44.

138 "Not on your life!": James Murray, "The Case for the Suffering Fan," *Sports Illustrated* (August 19, 1956): 34.

139 "balls hit skyward": "Spectator's Guide," *Sports Illustrated* (August 15, 1957): 47.

139   David G. Surdam: David G. Surdam, *The Postwar Yankees: Baseball's Golden Age Revisited* (Lincoln: University of Nebraska Press, 2013), 108–9.

139   "demands than football's": Pastier et al., *Ballparks,* 44.

142   layout favored baseball: Ibid., 105.

147   worst attendance in the National League: Podair, *City of Dreams.*

147   for public housing: Thornley, "Polo Grounds (New York)."

149   the day went on: Gershman, *Diamonds,* 180–82.

149   "the wrong place": Ibid., 180.

152   "patronize it regularly": Podair, *City of Dreams,* 4.

152   "our present stadium": Ibid., 5.

153   year in Boston: Ibid., 10–12.

156   Bel Geddes, encouraged: Tom Meany, "Baseball's Answer to TV," *Collier's* (September 27, 1952): 60–62.

156   Bel Geddes said: William M. Simons, ed., *The Cooperstown Symposium on Baseball and American Culture, 2015–2016* (Jefferson, N.C.: McFarland, 2017).

156   "middle class suburban fans": Ibid.

156   winter ice skating: Meany, "Baseball's Answer to TV," 60–62.

157   "on the rather novel theory": Ibid.

158   "He deplores the pop fly": Ibid.

159   "3,000 miles" away: Podair, *City of Dreams,* 17.

160   "how to get it": Ibid., 29–30.

164   the city's downtown: Ibid., 268.

165   "the public life": Charles W. Moore, "You Have to Pay for the Public Life," *Perspecta* 9–10 (1965).

168   "the world outside": Ibid.

168   "the new stadium": Ibid., 246–47.

169   "about the Dodgers": Ibid., 247–48.

170   "best ballparks ever": Pastier et al., *Ballparks,* 47.

CHAPTER 7: ERA OF CONCRETE DOUGHNUTS

176   Kempton wrote: Nicholas Dawidoff, ed., *Baseball: A Literary Anthology* (New York: Library of America, distributed by Penguin Putnam, 2002).

179   "than we liked": Roger Angell, *The Summer Game* (Lincoln: University of Nebraska Press, 2004), 336.

183   "subtleties are minimized": Lowry, *Green Cathedrals,* p. 20.

183   "St. Louis or Philly": "1960s–1980s: The Cookie Cutter Monsters," *This Great Game:* www.thisgreatgame.com/ballparks-eras-1960s-1980s.html.

187   arrived to play the Astros: Gershman, *Diamonds,* 194.

188   "where first base is": Ibid.

CHAPTER 8: CAMDEN YARDS: BASEBALL RETURNS

200 "neighborhoods of our youth?": Neil DeMause and Joanna Cagan, *Field of Schemes: How the Great Stadium Swindle Turns Public Money into Private Profit* (Lincoln: University of Nebraska Press, 2008), 124.

202 "the new ballpark": Philip Bess, Society for American Baseball Research, and Ballparks Committee. *City Baseball Magic: Plain Talk and Uncommon Sense About Cities and Baseball Parks* (St. Paul, Minn.: Knothole Press, 1999), 30.

204 "modern suburban stadiums": Ibid., 39.

204 "It was politically naïve": Phillip Bess, interview with the author, March 28, 2018.

207 Three Rivers Stadium: Larry Lucchino, interview with the author, April 18, 2018.

207 "baseball-only facilities": Ibid.

211 "She is the real heroine": Eli Jacobs interview with the author, June 19, 2017, and May 26, 2018.

211 "we made that year": Lucchino, interview with the author, April 18, 2018.

211 was absolutely unacceptable: Peter Richmond, *Ballpark: Camden Yards and the Building of an American Dream* (New York: Simon & Schuster, 1993), 154.

212 "was in the contract": Jacobs, interview with the author, May 26, 2018.

212 "like what we wanted": Lucchino, interview with the author, April 18, 2018.

212 " 'we can be proud of' ": Jacobs, interview with the author, May 26, 2018.

212 "skyline of Baltimore," Jacobs said: Ibid.

213 the majority view: Richmond, *Ballpark*, 155.

216 "But he could.": Richmond, *Ballpark*, 154.

216 which closed in 1970: Tim Kurkjian, "A Splendid Nest," *Sports Ilustrated* (April 13, 1992).

218 "years of anticipation": Gildea, "It's a Grand Opening for Camden Yards," *The Washington Post* (April 7, 1992).

218 "amenities of the 1990s": Kurkjian, "A Splendid Nest."

218 "pleasures of professional sports": Paul Goldberger, "A Radical Idea: Baseball As It Used to Be," *The New York Times* (November 19, 1989).

218 "they broke the mold": Gunts, "This Diamond Is a Cut Above," *Baltimore Sun* (March 22, 1992).

219 "opening in 1992": Will, *A Nice Little Place on the North Side*, 167.

219 fans of the Orioles: Jacobs, interview with the author, May 26, 2018.

220 of Lucchino's vision: Janet Marie Smith, "Back to the Future: Building a Ballpark, Not a Stadium," keynote address at Cooperstown Symposium on Baseball and American Culture, 2014.

CHAPTER 9: AFTER BALTIMORE: LOOKING BACK OR LOOKING FORWARD?

224 the same thing everywhere: Joe Spear, interview with the author, June 14, 2018.

224 "do something different": Ibid.

225 and Joanna Cagan: DeMause and Cagan, *Field of Schemes*, 14.

225   "to distant neighborhoods": Rosensweig, *Retro Ball Parks*, 30.

226   "all about Cleveland": Spear, interview with the author, June 14, 2018.

227   Rosensweig put it: Rosensweig, *Retro Ball Parks*, 30.

227   (*Chicago Tribune* would comment): Blair Kamin, "Jacobs Field of Dreams," *Chicago Tribune* (April 27, 1994).

229   "into the cityscape": Richard Justice, "New Stadium, New Day for Cleveland," *The Washington Post* (April 5, 1994).

230   "game's other showcases": Ibid.

230   "walk of Jacobs Field": Ibid.

230   "Oriole Park at Camden Yards": Kamin, "Jacobs Field of Dreams."

230   "stirs the memory": Ibid.

230   had in Chicago: Ibid.

231   embraced its new ballpark: "Indians' Record-Setting Selling Streak Over," *USA Today* (April 5, 2001).

231   told *The New York Times:* Paul Goldberger, "At Home in the City, Baseball's Newest Parks Succeed," *The New York Times* (April 17, 1994).

232   "in a postwar suburb": John Pastier, "Play Ball," *Landscape Architecture* 85 (June 1995): 72.

232   "to the Ponte Vecchio": David Dillon, "Texas Leaguer," *Landscape Architecture* 85 (June 1995): 82.

237   urban entertainment district: Jon Murray, "LoDo: A Renaissance Owed to Coors Field, Urban Pioneers and Smart Politics," *Denver Post* (June 4, 2017).

240   "massive airport hangar": "Chase Field," *Ballparks of Baseball*, https://www.ballparksofbaseball.com/ballparks/chase-field.

247   "with a proven place": John Williams, "Not All Convinced Dome Area Best for New Baseball Stadium," *Houston Chronicle* (June 10, 1996).

247   51 percent to 49 percent: John Williams, Todd Ackerman, and Eric Hanson, "County Stadium Referendum Passes by Narrow Margin," *Houston Chronicle* (November 6, 1996).

248   its current name: Chris Isidore, "Astros Strike Out Enron," *Sports Illustrated* (Feb 27, 2002).

CHAPTER 10: LESSONS FORGOTTEN, LESSONS LEARNED

254   the deal was off: Murray Chass, "Look What Wind Blew Back: Baseball's Giants," *The New York Times* (November 11, 1992).

258   wrote of Tiger Stadium: Michael Betzold, John Davids, Bill Dow, John Pastier, and Frank Rashid, *Tiger Stadium: Essays and Memories of Detroit's Historic Ballpark, 1912–2009* (Jefferson, N.C.: McFarland & Company, Inc., 2018), 86.

258   Pastier wrote: Pastier, ibid., 69.

259   a thirty-year lease: Rashid, ibid., 137.

259   Pastier wrote: Pastier, ibid., 109.

259   recently been modernized: Ibid.

260   "he's talking about": Rashid, ibid., 134.

260   Little Caesars Pizza: "Lots of Red Ink With His Pizza," *The New York Times* (July 27, 1993).

260   "an amusement park": Betzold et al., *Tiger Stadium,* 112.

261   "the wrecking ball": Rashid, ibid., 136.

262   "replacing it were black": Ibid.

264   major league baseball: Ibid., 146, note 152.

264   Rashid wrote: Ibid., 146.

265   "play baseball there, too": Tim Newcomb, "Ballpark Quirks: Comerica Park's Carnival Atmosphere with a View," *Sports Illustrated* (June 6, 2014): https://www.si.com/mlb /strike-zone/2014/06/06/ballpark-quirks-comerica-park-detroit-tigers.

267   "hide the suites": Patricia Lowry, "The New Jewel on the Allegheny Might Be the Best Ballpark," *Pittsburgh Post-Gazette* (April 15, 2001).

268   "What Makes PNC Park So Good?": Elizabeth Bloom, "What Makes PNC Park So Good?" *Pittsburgh Post-Gazette:* https://newsinteractive.post-gazette.com/pirates/2016 /pnc-park-at-15.

269   projects moved forward: Ibid.

270   "the Allegheny River": Jim Caple, "Pittsburgh's Gem Rates the Best," *ESPN:* www .espn.com/page2/s/ballparks/pncpark.html.

271   hits a home run: "Great American Ball Park," Ballparks of Baseball: www.ballparksof baseball.com/ballparks/great-american-ball-park.

273   their suburban fans: Tommy Rowan, "What If the Phillies Ballpark Had Been Built in Center City?" *The Philadelphia Inquirer* (March 2, 2017).

273   "commerce was negligible": Marc Fischer, "Nationals Park Brings Growth, Worries to Southeast Washington," *The Washington Post* (July 14, 2018).

274   in Lucchino's words: Lucchino, interview with the author, April 18, 2018.

276   called "decrepit": Fischer, "Nationals Park Brings Growth."

278   Corktown in Detroit: Ibid.

279   "a lousy building": Philip Kennicott, "This Diamond Isn't a Gem," *The Washington Post* (March 31, 2008).

281   "sports anchored entertainment district": St. Louis Ballpark Village, "One Cardinal Way," www.stlballparkvillage.com.

CHAPTER 11: NEW YORK RETRO, MIAMI MODERN

286   Wilpon said: Richard Sandomir, "Mets Unveil Model Stadium: Its Roof Moves, As Does Grass," *The New York Times* (April 24, 1998).

287   a retractable roof: Richard Sandomir, "Study Recommends the Yankees Move to a West Side Site," *The New York Times* (April 5, 1996).

292   "building of a superpower": Joe Mock, "Yankee Stadium: Ruthian Size, Price Tag and Sponsorships," Baseballparks.com: www.baseballparks.com/indepth/nyynew.

296   Wilpon told Toobin: Jeffrey Toobin, "Madoff's Curveball," *The New Yorker* (May 30, 2011).

302   "baseball to be innovative": Beth Dunlop, "Marlins Park a Contemporary Landmark of Grand Gestures and Artistic Detail," *Miami Herald* (April 1, 2012).

CHAPTER 12: THE BALLPARK AS THEME PARK

307   "the New Wrigleyville": Christopher Borrelli, "Welcome to the Boring, Tedious Confines of the New Wrigleyville," *Chicago Tribune* (August 3, 2018).

308   "Stepfordville USA": Ibid.

312   "in the Southeast": "The Battery Atlanta," *Wakefield Beasley:* http://www.wakefield beasley.com/work/the-battery-atlanta-at-suntrust-park-mixed-use.

314   "having the parade?": T. M. Brown, "The Braves' New Ballpark Is An Urban Planner's Nightmare," *Deadspin:* https://deadspin.com/the-braves-new-ballpark-is-an-urban -planners-nightmare-1797593063.

315   "reality of city life": Peter Rutkoff, "Two-Bass Hit: Baseball and New York, 1945– 1960," *Prospects* 20 (1995): 285–308.

316   "their original appeal": Rosensweig, *Retro Ball Parks,* 156.

BIBLIOGRAPHY

Achorn, Edward. *The Summer of Beer and Whiskey: How Brewers, Barkeeps, Rowdies, Immigrants, and a Wild Pennant Fight Made Baseball America's Game.* New York: Public Affairs, 2014.

Adair, Robert K. *The Physics of Baseball.* New York: Harper Collins, 2002.

Angell, Roger. *Once More Around the Park: A Baseball Reader.* Chicago: Ivan R. Dee, 1991.

———. *The Summer Game.* Lincoln: University of Nebraska Press, 2004.

Ballparks. "South End Grounds." www.ballparks.com.

Ballparks of Baseball. "Chase Field." www.ballparksofbaseball.com.

———. "Great American Ball Park." www.ballparksofbaseball.com.

Baseball Almanac. "Fenway Park Quotes." www.baseball-almanac.com.

Benson, Michael. *Ballparks of North America: A Comprehensive Historical Encyclopedia of Baseball Grounds, Yards, and Stadiums, 1845 to 1988.* Jefferson, N.C.: McFarland, 2009.

Bess, Philip, Society for American Baseball Research, and Ballparks Committee. *City Baseball Magic: Plain Talk and Uncommon Sense About Cities and Baseball Parks.* St. Paul, Minn.: Knothole Press, 1999.

Betzold, Michael, John Davids, Bill Dow, John Pastier, and Frank Rashid. *Tiger Stadium: Essays and Memories of Detroit's Historic Ballpark, 1912–2009.* Jefferson, N.C.: McFarland, 2018.

Bloom, Elizabeth. "What Makes PNC Park So Good?" https://www.post-gazette.com, 2016.

Borer, Michael Ian. *Faithful to Fenway: Believing in Boston, Baseball, and America's Most Beloved Ballpark.* New York: New York University Press, 2008.

Borrelli, Christopher. "Welcome to the Boring, Tedious Confines of the New Wrigleyville." *Chicago Tribune,* August 3, 2018.

Brown, T. M. "The Braves' New Ballpark Is an Urban Planner's Nightmare," August 10, 2017. https://www.deadspin.com.

Caple, Jim. "Pittsburgh's Gem Rates the Best." http:// www.espn.com.

Chass, Murray. "Look What Wind Blew Back: Baseball's Giants." *The New York Times,* November 11, 1992.

Cohen, Marvin. *Baseball the Beautiful: Decoding the Diamond.* New York: Links Books, 1974.

Curlee, Lynn. *Ballpark: The Story of America's Baseball Fields.* New York: Aladdin Paperbacks, 2008. Originally published by Atheneum, 2005.

Dawidoff, Nicholas, ed. *Baseball: A Literary Anthology.* New York: Library of America. Distributed by Penguin Putnam, 2002.

Delaney, Kevin J., and Rick Eckstein. *Public Dollars, Private Stadiums: The Battle over Building Sports Stadiums.* New Brunswick, N.J.: Rutgers University Press, 2003.

DeMause, Neil, and Joanna Cagan. *Field of Schemes: How the Great Stadium Swindle Turns Public Money into Private Profit.* Lincoln: University of Nebraska Press, 2008.

Dillon, David. "Texas Leaguer." *Landscape Architecture* 85, June 1995.

Dunlop, Beth. "Marlins Park: A Contemporary Landmark of Grand Gestures and Artistic Detail." *Miami Herald,* April 1, 2012.

Dureiko, Matthew J. *Stadium Urbanism: Stadia, Sport and the Image of the American City.* Student project in Master of Architecture program, Kent State University, 2014.

Enders, Eric. *Ballparks Then & Now.* San Diego: Thunder Bay Press, 2015.

Evanosky, Dennis, and Eric J. Kos. *Lost Ballparks.* London: Pavilion Books, 2017.

Felber, Bill. *A Game of Brawl: The Orioles, the Beaneaters, and the Battle for the 1897 Pennant.* Lincoln: University of Nebraska Press, 2007.

Fischer, Marc. "Nationals Park Brings Growth, Worries to Southeast Washington." *The Washington Post,* July 14, 2018.

Frommer, Harvey. *Remembering Yankee Stadium: An Oral and Narrative History of "The House That Ruth Built."* Guilford, Conn.: Lyons Press, 2016.

Gershman, Michael. *Diamonds: The Evolution of the Ballpark.* Boston: Houghton Mifflin, 1995.

Giamatti, A. Bartlett. *Take Time for Paradise: Americans and Their Games.* New York: Bloomsbury, 2011.

Gildea, William. "It's a Grand Opening for Camden Yards." *The Washington Post,* April 7, 1992.

Goldberger, Paul. "Home in the City, Baseball's Newest Parks Succeed." *The New York Times,* April 17, 1994.

———. "A Radical Idea: Baseball As It Used to Be." *The New York Times,* November 19, 1989.

Goldstein, Richard. *Superstars and Screwballs: 100 Years of Brooklyn Baseball.* New York: Dutton, 1991.

Goldstein, Warren. *Playing for Keeps: A History of Early Baseball.* Ithaca, N.Y.: Cornell University Press, 2014.

Goodwin, Doris Kearns. *Wait Till Next Year.* New York: Simon & Schuster, 1997.

Gordon, Peter H., Sydney Waller, and Paul Weinman, eds. *Diamonds Are Forever: Artists and Writers on Baseball.* San Francisco: Chronicle Books, 1987.

Gottschall, Terry. "May 15, 1894: 'It Was a Hot Game, Sure Enough!'" Society for American Baseball Research. https://sabr.org.

Granillo, Larry. "Guest Post: When the Phillies Arrested an 11-Year Old 'Ball Thief.'" *The Sports Daily,* July 23, 2010. http://wezen-ball.com.

Gunts, Edward. "This Diamond Is a Cut Above." *Baltimore Sun,* March 22, 1992.

Isidore, Chris. "Astros Strike Out Enron." *Sports Illustrated,* February 27, 2002.

Justice, Richard. "New Stadium, New Day for Cleveland." *The Washington Post,* April 5, 1994.

Kahn, Roger. *The Boys of Summer.* New York: Harper Perennial Modern Classics, 2006. Originally published by Harper & Row, 1972.

Kamin, Blair. "Jacobs Field of Dreams." *Chicago Tribune,* April 27, 1994.

Kennicott, Philip. "This Diamond Isn't a Gem." *The Washington Post,* March 31, 2008.

Kohan, Rafi. *The Arena: Inside the Tailgating, Ticket-Scalping, Mascot-Racing, Dubiously Funded and Possibly Haunted Monuments of American Sport.* New York: Liveright, 2017.

Kuklick, Bruce. *To Every Thing a Season: Shibe Park and Urban Philadelphia, 1909–1976.* Princeton: Princeton University Press, 1991.

Kurkjian, Tim. "A Splendid Nest." *Sports Illustrated,* April 13, 1992.

Lamb, Bill. "Hilltop Park (New York)." Society for American Baseball Research. https://sabr .org.

Leventhal, Josh. *Baseball: Yesterday and Today.* St. Paul, Minn.: Voyageur Press, 2006.

———. *Take Me Out to the Ballpark: An Illustrated Tour of Baseball Parks Past and Present.* New York: Black Dog and Leventhal, 2006

Lowry, Patricia. "The New Jewel on the Allegheny Might Be the Best Ballpark." *Pittsburgh Post-Gazette,* April 15, 2001.

Lowry, Philip J. *Green Cathedrals,* first edition. Cooperstown, N.Y.: Society of American Baseball Research, 1986.

———. *Green Cathedrals: The Ultimate Celebration of All 273 Major League and Negro League Ballparks Past and Present.* Reading, Mass.: Addison-Wesley, 1993.

Mandelbaum, Michael. *The Meaning of Sports: Why Americans Watch Baseball, Football and Basketball and What They See When They Do.* New York: Public Affairs, 2004.

McGee, Bob. *The Greatest Ballpark Ever: Ebbets Field and the Story of the Brooklyn Dodgers.* New Brunswick, N.J.; London: Rutgers University Press, 2005.

Mock, Joe. "Yankee Stadium Ruthian Size, Price Tag and Sponsorships." https://www.base ballparks.com.

Moore, Charles W. "You Have to Pay for the Public Life." *Perspecta* 9–10 (1965): 57–106.

Murray, James. "The Case for the Suffering Fan." *Sports Illustrated*, August 19, 1956.

Murray, Jon. "LoDo: A Renaissance Owed to Coors Field, Urban Pioneers and Smart Politics." *Denver Post,* June 4, 2017.

Nemec, David. *The Beer and Whisky League: The Illustrated History of the American Association—Baseball's Renegade Major League.* Guilford, Conn.: Lyons Press, 2004.

Newcomb, Tim. "Ballpark Quirks: Comerica Park's Carnival Atmosphere with a View." *Sports Illustrated,* June 6, 2014. www.si.com.

New England Historical Society. "The Great South End Grounds Fire of 1894." http://www .newenglandhistoricalsociety.com.

The New York Times. "Lots of Red Ink with His Pizza." July 27, 1993.

———. "Yanks' New Stadium to Be Opened Today." April 23, 1923.

Nolan. "A Ballpark, Not a Stadium." *The Red Sox Reader,* edited by Dan Riley. Boston: Mariner Books, Houghton Mifflin, 1991, p. 3.

Olmsted, Frederick Law, and Theodora Kimball Hubbard. *Forty Years of Landscape Architecture: Central Park [by] Frederick Law Olmsted, Sr.* Cambridge, Mass.: MIT Press, 1973.

Pahigian, Josh, and Kevin O'Connell. *The Ultimate Baseball Road Trip: A Fan's Guide to Major League Stadiums.* Guilford, Conn.: Lyons Press, 2004.

Pastier, John. "Play Ball." *Landscape Architecture*, June 1995.

Pastier, John, Marc Sandalow, Michael Heatley, Ian Westwell, and Jim Sutton. *Ballparks: Yesterday and Today.* Edison, N.J.: Chartwell Books, 2007.

Peterson, Robert. *Only the Ball Was White: A History of Legendary Black Players and All-Black Professional Teams.* New York: Random House, 1970.

Podair, Jerald E. *City of Dreams: Dodger Stadium and the Birth of Modern Los Angeles.* Princeton: Princeton University Press, 2017.

Rader, Benjamin G. *Baseball: A History of America's Game.* Urbana: University of Illinois Press, third edition, 2008.

Rashid, Frank, ed. "Losing Tiger Stadium, 1987–1997." In *Tiger Stadium: Essays and Memories of Detroit's Historic Ballpark, 1912–2009.*

Ray, James Lincoln. "Connie Mack Stadium (Philadelphia)." Society for American Baseball Research. https://sabr.org.

Reed, Henry Hope, and Sophia Duckworth. *Central Park: A History and a Guide.* New York: C. N. Potter, 1972.

Richmond, Peter. *Ballpark: Camden Yards and the Building of an American Dream.* New York: Simon & Schuster, 1993.

Ritter, Lawrence S. *The Glory of Their Times: The Story of the Early Days of Baseball Told By the Men Who Played It.* New York: Harper Perennial, 2010; originally published by Macmillan, 1966.

———. *Lost Ballparks: A Celebration of Baseball's Legendary Fields.* New York: Viking Studio Books, 1994.

Rosensweig, Daniel. *Retro Ball Parks: Instant History, Baseball, and the New American City.* Knoxville: University of Tennessee Press, 2005.

Rosentraub, Mark S. *Major League Losers: The Real Cost of Sports and Who's Paying for It.* New York: Basic Books, 1999.

Rowan, Tommy. "What If the Phillies Ballpark Had Been Built in Center City?" *The Philadelphia Inquirer,* March 2, 2017.

Rutkoff, Peter. *Shadow Ball: A Novel of Baseball and Chicago.* Jefferson, N.C.: McFarland, 2001.

———. "Two-Bass Hit: Baseball and New York, 1945–1960." *Prospects* 20 (1995): 285–328.

Ruzzo, Bob. "South End Grounds (Boston)." Society for American Baseball Research. https://sabr.org.

Sandomir, Richard. "Mets Unveil Model Stadium: Its Roof Moves, As Does Grass." *The New York Times,* April 24, 1998.

———. "Study Recommends the Yankees Move to a West Side Site." *The New York Times,* April 5, 1996.

The Second Division. "The Yankees of Kingsbridge Grounds." https://theseconddivision.wordpress.com.

Shea, Stuart. *Wrigley Field: The Long Life and Contentious Times of the Friendly Confines.* Chicago: University of Chicago Press, 2014.

Simons, William M., ed. *The Cooperstown Symposium on Baseball and American Culture, 2013–2014.* Jefferson, N.C.: McFarland, 2015.

———. *The Cooperstown Symposium on Baseball and American Culture, 2015–2016.* Jefferson N.C.: McFarland, 2017.

Society for American Baseball Research. "Baker Bowl." https://sabr.org.

"Spectator's Guide." *Sports Illustrated,* April 15, 1957.

"Sportsman's Park," Project Ballpark. www.projectballpark.org.

St. Louis Ballpark Village. "One Cardinal Way." https://www.stlballparkvillage.com.

Stout, Glenn. *Fenway 1912: The Birth of a Ballpark, a Championship Season, and Fenway's Remarkable First Year.* Boston: Houghton Mifflin Harcourt, 2011.

Strong, George Templeton, Milton Halsey Thomas, and Allan Nevins. *The Diary of George Templeton Strong*. Ann Arbor, Mich.: UMI, 1993.

Sullivan, Neil J. *The Diamond in the Bronx: Yankee Stadium and the Politics of New York*. New York: Oxford University Press, 2001.

Surdam, David G. *The Postwar Yankees: Baseball's Golden Age Revisited*. Lincoln: University of Nebraska Press, 2013.

Swanson, Harvey. *Ruthless Baseball*. Bloomington, Ind.: Author House, 2004.

Terry, James L. *Long Before the Dodgers: Baseball in Brooklyn, 1855–1884*. Jefferson, N.C.: McFarland, 2002.

This Great Game. "1960s–1980s: The Cookie Cutter Monsters." www.thisgreatgame.com.

Thorn, John. *Baseball in the Garden of Eden: The Secret History of the Early Game*. New York: Simon & Schuster, 2012.

Thornley, Stew. "Polo Grounds (New York)." Society for American Baseball Research. https://sabr.org.

Toman, James A., and Gregory G. Deegan. *Cleveland Stadium: The Last Chapter*. Cleveland: Cleveland Landmarks Press, 1997.

Toobin, Jeffrey. "Madoff's Curveball." *The New Yorker*, May 30, 2011.

Tygiel, Jules. *Baseball's Great Experiment: Jackie Robinson and His Legacy*. New York: Oxford University Press, 1997.

USA Today. "Indians' Record-Setting Sellout Streak Over." April 5, 2001.

Valerio, Anthony, *BART: A Life of A. Bartlett Giamatti*. New York: Harcourt Brace Jovanovich, 1991.

Vecsey, George. *Baseball: A History of America's Favorite Game*. New York: Modern Library, 2008.

Veeck, Bill. *Veeck—As in Wreck*. Chicago: University of Chicago Press, 2001. Originally published by Putnam, 1962.

Wakefield Beasley & Associates. "The Battery Atlanta." www.wakefieldbeasley.com.

Wallace, Mike, and Edwin G. Burrows. *Greater Gotham: A History of New York City from 1898 to 1919*. New York: Oxford University Press, 2018.

Weintraub, Robert. *The House That Ruth Built*. New York: Back Bay Books, Little, Brown, 2013.

White, G. Edward. *Creating the National Pastime: Baseball Transforms Itself, 1903–1953*. Princeton: Princeton University Press, 1996.

Will, George F. *A Nice Little Place on the North Side: Wrigley Field at One Hundred*. New York: Crown Archetype, 2014.

Williams, John. "Not All Convinced Dome Area Best for New Baseball Stadium." *Houston Chronicle*, June 10, 1996.

Williams, John, Todd Ackerman, and Eric Hanson. "County Stadium Referendum Passes by Narrow Margin." *Houston Chronicle*, November 6, 1996.

INDEX

Page numbers of illustrations appear in *italics*.

ILLUSTRATION CREDITS

© 2009 WCBS Newsradio 880: 296

© 2010 Bergerson Photography: 298

Aerial Archives/Alamy Stock Photo: 249, 254, 274

AFP/Getty Images: 243

Al Fenn/The LIFE Picture Collection/Getty Images: 140

Al Messerschmidt via AP: 173 (top)

Allegheny Conference on Community Development, Detre Library & Archives, Heinz History Center: 173 (bottom)

American Photo Service, Manhattan Post Card Co.: 121

Anaheim Public Library: 180

Andrcy Kr/Deposit Photos: 271

AP Photo: 178

AP Photo/Don Brinn: 165

AP Photo/Ed Kolenovsky: 186

AP Photo/Jacob Harris: 153

© Armando Arorizo/ZUMAPRESS.com: 167

B. O'Kane/Alamy Stock Photo: 245

Bettmann/Getty Images: 100, 133, 148

BIG-Bjarke Ingels Group: 316

Bob Busser: 197, 202, 215, 241, 242, 248, 250, 264, 309

Brace Hemmelgarn/Minnesota Twins/Getty Images: 244

Brooklyn Daily Eagle Photographs—Brooklyn Public Library—Brooklyn Collection: 102

Canva Pty Ltd/Alamy Stock Photo: 318

Carnegie Library of Pittsburgh: 65

Chuck Franklin/Alamy Stock Photo: 220 (top)

City Kayak: 256

Collection of the New-York Historical Society: Speedway entrance (Harlem River driveway) looking northeast from above polo grounds towards High Bridge and Washington Bridge; photograph from July 19, 1914; William D. Hassler Photograph Collection, PR-083, id #66002- 1790, 75: High-angle view of Ebbets Field, Brooklyn, September 2, 1914. Photographed for the Success Postal Card Company. Identifier: nyhs_PR83_1920: 98

Courtesy of the Hotel Zachary: 307

Courtesy of Mechanix Illustrated: 161

Courtesy of Philip Bess: 203, 204

Courtesy Populous: 223, 281, 300

Dan Hardy for *The Houston Post,* June 13, 1965. Houston Metropolitan Research Center, Houston Public Library, RGD0006-1086: 185

© Dave DiCello Photography: 267

Deborah Ernest/Alamy Stock Photo: 263

Deposit Photos: 294

© Ed Massery: 269, 272

eddtoro35/Deposit Photos: 292

felixtm/Deposit Photos: 190

George Sheldon/Alamy Stock Photo: 221

© Jane Tyska/BANG/ZUMAPRESS.com: 172 (center)

Jeannette Hoss: 280

© Jeff Goldberg/Esto: 206, 213, 220 (top)

Jim West/Alamy Stock Photo: 238

© John J. Kim/TNS via ZUMA Wire: 112

© Josh Holmberg/Cal Sport Media/ ZUMAPRESS.com: 189

JTE Multimedia: 160

Julia Robertson/PhotoShelter: 172 (bottom)

Katherine Penn/Alamy Stock Photo: 297

Library of Congress: ii, iii, 7, 12, 13, 15, 36, 60, 61, 67, 68 (left), 70–72, 74, 88, 89, 94, 104, 110, 115, 119, 130, 141–142, 172 (top), 184, 285

Lorne Chapman/Alamy Stock Photo: 194

Mark Rucker/Transcendental Graphics, Getty Images: 26, 35, 44, 56, 78, 111

Matt Roth: 210

Michael Albans/NY Daily News Archive via Getty Images: 288

Missouri Historical Society, St. Louis: 321

MLB Photos via Getty Images: 173 (center)

National Baseball Hall of Fame and Museum, Cooperstown, N.Y.: 14, 27, 30, 31, 57–59, 63, 69, 92, 101, 123, 145

Noella Ballenger/Alamy Stock Photo: 191

Patti McConville/Alamy Stock Photo: 293

Paul Goldberger: 268, 277, 278, 303, 311

Peter Mintz/First Light/Alamy Stock Photo: 193

Ramin Talaie/Corbis via Getty Images: 289

© Rod Mar: 302, 304, 305

© Ryan Linton: 313

Scott Eells/Bloomberg via Getty Images: 209

SFMTA Photo Archive | sfmta.com/photo: 257

Sporting News/Getty Images: 128

St. Louis Cardinals: 282

Steve Hall of Hall + Merrick: 232, 233

© Timothy Hursley: 228, 229, 275

USC Libraries Special Collections: 162, 166

Yoon S. Byun/The Boston Globe via Getty Images: 208

A NOTE ABOUT THE AUTHOR

Paul Goldberger, a contributing editor at *Vanity Fair,* spent fifteen years as the architecture critic for *The New Yorker* and began his career at *The New York Times,* where he was awarded the Pulitzer Prize for distinguished criticism for his writing on architecture. He has also won the National Building Museum's Vincent Scully Prize. He is the author of many books, most recently *Why Architecture Matters, Building Up and Tearing Down: Reflections on the Age of Architecture, Up from Zero,* and *Building Art: The Life and Work of Frank Gehry.* He teaches at The New School and lectures widely around the country on architecture, design, historic preservation, and cities. He and his wife, Susan Solomon, live in New York City.

A NOTE ON THE TYPE

This book was set in Adobe Garamond. Designed for the Adobe Corporation by Robert Slimbach, the fonts are based on types first cut by Claude Garamond (c. 1480–1561). Garamond was a pupil of Geoffroy Tory and is believed to have followed the Venetian models, although he introduced a number of important differences, and it is to him that we owe the letter we now know as "old style." He gave to his letters a certain elegance and feeling of movement that won their creator an immediate reputation and the patronage of Francis I of France.

Composed by North Market Street Graphics, Lancaster, Pennsylvania
Printed and bound by LSC Communications, Crawfordsville, Indiana
Design by Maggie Hinders